BERTOLT BRECHT
COLLECTED PLAYS

Volume 2

BERTOLT

Bertolt Brecht: *Plays, Poetry, & Prose*

Edited by

Ralph Manheim and John Willett

Wolfgang Sauerlander, Associate Editor

BRECHT

COLLECTED PLAYS

VOLUME 2

A Man's a Man

Rise and Fall of the
City of Mahagonny

The Threepenny Opera

VINTAGE BOOKS, *A Division of Random House, New York*

VINTAGE BOOKS EDITION, July 1977
First Edition

Copyright © 1976, 1977 by Stefan S. Brecht

Library of Congress Cataloging in Publication Data
Brecht, Bertolt, 1898-1956.
    Collected plays.

    (His Plays, poetry, & prose)
    CONTENTS: v. 1. Baal. Drums in the night. In the
jungle of cities. The life of Edward II of England. The
wedding. The beggar, or the dead dog. He drives out a
devil. Lux in tenebris. The catch.—v. 2. A man's a
man. Rise and fall of the City of Mahagonny. The threepenny opera.

                                        —v. 5. Life of Galileo.
The trial of Lucullus. Mother Courage and her children.
[etc.]
    1. Manheim, Ralph, 1907-   ed. II. Willett, John, ed.
PT2603.R397A29   1971   832'.9'12   71-113718

Contents

Introduction

Berlin 1925-29:
The Implications of Success

When Brecht moved from Munich to Berlin in September 1924 he had already had four plays produced, though only one had yet been seen in the capital city. He had won the Kleist Prize two years earlier, had directed *Edward the Second* at the Munich Kammerspiele, and at twenty-six was regarded as one of the most unusual and promising talents in Germany. Like his almost exact contemporary Carl Zuckmayer he arrived with a year's contract to act as a junior "dramaturg" at the Deutsches Theater, a job which involved little if any routine work but gave him invaluable access to rehearsals (notably Max Reinhardt's), actors, directors, and fellow writers. According to Zuckmayer this appointment was due to Erich Engel, the theater's new artistic director, who had staged *In the Jungle* in Munich and was now about to direct its Berlin première, with Brecht's school friend Caspar Neher once again designing the sets. Bernhard Reich too, who had been Brecht's nominal superior at the Kammerspiele the previous year, decided to move to Berlin, and so did Lion Feuchtwanger, his Munich literary mentor.

Accordingly Brecht was able to start this new period of his life with a number of valued collaborators already around him. The five years which now followed were a time of stabilization in the checkered history of the Weimar Republic, an interlude between the confusions of 1923 (inflation, Ruhr occupation, Thuringian rising, Hitler's beer-cellar putsch) and the economic collapse of late 1929. Politically it can be termed the era of Stresemann (first as Chancellor, then as Foreign Secretary); and, short as it was, it was an interval of reconstruction, of American aid, of improved relations with Russia and the West, and of relatively liberal politics. It marked much of Brecht's thinking about the theater, and in *The Threepenny Opera* in 1928 saw his one outstanding success.

His first assault on Berlin three years earlier had ended in illness and failure, an experience which seems to have helped define his picture of that massive and hostile city, which he privately called "Mahagonny" or "cold Chicago." This time, however, he had brought rather heavier equipment. Besides a contract with the publisher Gustav Kiepenheuer, guaranteeing him a monthly advance of 1,000 marks, his baggage and intentions included some of the items which he listed in a note of July 1924. These ranged from a leather cap, a black rubber mackintosh, and raw silk khaki shirts, through the learning of such skills as driving, skiing, riding, and modern iambics, and the study of "economics/technology/anatomy/English/jiujitsu," to various theater plans of which *Jungle*, *Galgai*, *Fleischhacker*, and a "Mahagonny opera" were the most significant. *Jungle* he had promised to publish, and was now about to revise radically following the Berlin production. *Galgai*, subtitled *Man = Man*, was the great sprawling play on which he was currently hard at work, a new Kiplingesque development of the purely Bavarian *Galgei* scheme described in our notes, which had been in his mind since 1918. *Fleischhacker* was the project for a play based on Frank Norris's Chicago novel *The Pit* which occupied Brecht on and off throughout this period, led him to read Marx, and was to be announced for production by Erwin Piscator in his 1927–28 prospectus. As for the opera idea, it must already have related to the pseudo-American "Mahagonny Songs" which Brecht wrote around 1924; it was linked with the name of his first wife Marianne, who was a minor opera singer. Somewhere near the top of all this pile would have been his projected first book of poems—*Die Hauspostille*, or *Devotions for the Home*—which had already been announced by Kiepenheuer but laid aside in the theatrical flurry resulting from his prize.

Summing up his prospects as a free lance a year after leaving the Deutsches Theater, he reckoned that he had already accumulated the material to write the forty plays needed "to dominate the repertoire of a theater during a generation":

> My heroic landscape is the city, my viewpoint relativity, my given situation mankind's occupation of the great cities at the start of the third millennium, my subject our appetites (too great or too small), my exercise for the audience our society's great conflicts.

The impact of the city and its pressures is very evident in the poems which Brecht wrote at this time, and they, too, were to penetrate *Mahagonny* along with the more frivolous "Songs." This concept of cities as a form of jungle had already struck him in Munich when he was working on the *Galgei* scheme, and it seems to have been among the reasons leading him then to abandon this project in favor of *In the Jungle*. It was there that he had first projected a trilogy to be called *Asphalt Jungle*, of which the latter play was to be one element. This plan now resurfaced under the new overall name of *Mankind's Occupation of the Great Cities*, with *Fleischhacker* as the second play, and the somewhat later (but equally unfinished) *Fatzer* as the third. Linked with it was an almost biblical preoccupation with the Flood which would come and swallow such cities as it once did Sodom and Gomorrah. Brecht actually began writing a radio play on this theme, then updated and Americanized it as *Downfall of the Paradise City Miami*, which a hurricane was to destroy. Once again, the connection with *Mahagonny* is self-evident; indeed the very image of the arrow advancing on Pensacola (see p. 113) comes from the dossier of press cuttings on American hurricanes which his new assistant Elisabeth Hauptmann compiled for him in the autumn of 1926.

She had been sent to him by Kiepenheuer in late 1924 to help him get out the promised books. There were three of these due to be handed in by the end of 1925: first and foremost *Devotions for the Home*, then the revised *In the Jungle of Cities* and the completed *Galgai* play, now known as *A*

Man's a Man. Very soon, however, she became much more than a mere editorial assistant, and when the contract with Kiepenheuer fell through (because one of the firm's backers objected to the publication of the "Ballad of the Dead Soldier" from *Drums in the Night*) she stayed on as a full-time collaborator on virtually all Brecht's schemes till they both left Germany in 1933. This role was decided, according to her, by her suggesting how the elephant deal in *A Man's a Man* should be introduced ("Elephant? An elephant . . ." etc., on p. 31), and Brecht responded by having the script bound in red leather and presenting it to her at the end of the year. "It was a troublesome play," says a signed covering note,

> and even piecing together the manuscript from 20lb of paper was heavy work; it took me 2 days, ½ bottle of brandy, 4 bottles of soda water, 8–10 cigars and a lot of patience, and it was the only part I did on my own.

Another new collaborator on *A Man's a Man* was Emil Hesse Burri from Munich, a medical student whom Feuchtwanger had befriended, and the team so constituted remained closely linked. Thus Burri went on to work on the *Dan Drew* play which Brecht started at the end of 1925 on the basis of Bourke White's biography and Gustavus Myers's *History of the Great American Fortunes*, a book that greatly fascinated him. Hauptmann worked on the Baal revision *(Life Story of the Man Baal)* of 1926, wrote "The Model for Baal" under Brecht's name, contributed in still unknown measure to his short stories, and, as a former teacher of English, introduced him to Kipling in the original. Probably during 1925, she also supplied him with two English-language companions to the "Mahagonny Songs"—the "Alabama" and "Benares" songs, which will be found on pp. 89 and 309 respectively. Soon it became common to speak of the "Brecht Collective."

The climate of this collaboration was determined to a great extent by what was then going on in the Berlin theater; and Brecht had certainly chosen a good moment to arrive there. Shaw's *St. Joan* with Elisabeth Bergner, the Erich Engel production of *Coriolanus*, and Klabund's *Chalk Circle* (again with Bergner), all at the Deutsches Theater, were clearly of lifelong significance to him, while critics both then and later saw a connection between Reinhardt's Pirandello productions and the ambiguities of *A Man's a Man* and *The Baby Elephant* (whose subtitle is pure Pirandello). Shaw's *Major Barbara*, published in translation in 1926, is thought to have stimulated the team's curiosity about the Salvation Army, and certainly Shaw became linked with their new concept of "fun"—*Spass* in German—as an essential factor in art. This was something that Brecht found present in sporting events, with their bright lights, hard seats, and expertly critical audiences, rather than in the orthodox theater. In February 1926 one of his earliest theoretical essays appeared under the title "Emphasis on Sport" (*Brecht on Theatre*, p. 6), and around the same time he suggested that the ailing Berlin Volksbühne ought to sponsor an experimental stage, "a theatrical laboratory in which actors, writers and directors can work for their own fun, with no particular end in view." The collective used to go to boxing matches under the guidance of Burri, who had acted as second to the German middleweight champion Paul Samson-Körner; Brecht even began trying to write the champion's life, as well as some boxing stories. All this was permeated with the Anglo-American ideas, images and idioms typical of the time; the bowler hat became almost a symbol of the "Neue Sachlichkeit" or "New Matter-of-factness" of the mid-decade; while towering even above *Schweik*, *Potemkin*, Piscator's *Sturmflut* production and other key influences of 1926 was the figure of Charlie Chaplin, whose *The Gold Rush* was released that year. As yet ideology hardly entered into it, for Brecht at that time cited no political justification for his opinions but put them forward, often quite aggressively, as assertions on behalf of "the younger generation."

None the less the very notion of collectivity, of impersonality, is a social one, and it became quite as basic to Brecht's outlook as did his concern with plebeian art forms and the new technology. Practically speaking it modified his view of individual authorship, so that while he came more and more to take credit for the collective's work (with one significant exception) he was indifferent about his own contribution to that of his friends: to Feuchtwanger's Warren Hastings play,

for instance, or to Reich's Deutsches Theater production of
Camille (whose last act he rewrote). At the same time this
growing contempt for "originality" led him into trouble with
critics who objected to his unacknowledged borrowings from
other writers: Herwarth Walden, for one, who spotted the
Rimbaud quotations in *In the Jungle* on its production in
October 1924, and most notably Alfred Kerr when the *Threepenny Opera* songs were published four and a half years later
(see "A Statement," p. 323). It was an attitude which tied in
with the whole theme of *A Man's a Man* as Brecht first conceived it: the notion of personality as something adjustable,
relative, which could be molded like rubber. Originally the
molding was to be done by life itself ("he is lived" says the
diary note on *Galgai* cited on p. 248); then, in the new
Kiplingesque version, by three soldiers who make a fourth
man to save their own skins. To this concept, too, belonged
the slighting references to the notable "Personality" or "Char-
akterkopf," an untranslatable word for a man with an interesting face. But as the collective revised and re-revised that
play for production in 1926, further implications began to
emerge. As the new Interlude speech had it, Galy Gay was
simply "dismantled like a car": taken to pieces and reassembled
by what Brecht termed in an interview "three engineers of the
feelings." And in this light, and perhaps also in the light of
Soviet ideas about the "new man," he suddenly appeared as
a socially significant prototype, a "collective being" who, as
Brecht's broadcast introduction now argued (p. 236), "is
bound to win."

2

Such were the still-bubbling ingredients when Brecht, having
finished his stint at the Deutsches Theater, began in 1926 to
present the results of his own and his collaborators' work. In
February the "Junge Bühne" staged a Sunday performance of
Life Story of the Man Baal, which Brecht helped to direct,
followed in the spring by Burri's play *Tim O'Mara* (or *Amer-*

ican Youth) and their friend Marieluise Fleisser's *Fegefeuer in Ingolstadt*. But these were single performances only, and what mattered more was the double première of *A Man's a Man* at Düsseldorf and Darmstadt on September 25. At the former city the director was Josef Münch and the Galy Gay Ewald Balser, a ranting actor later a star of the Vienna Burgtheater. At Darmstadt, however, the theater was run by Ernst Legal, the eventual *Intendant* of the East Berlin State Opera, who himself played Galy Gay, bringing in Jakob Geis, an old Munich supporter of Brecht's, as director. With Neher as his designer, Geis now seems to have established the style for subsequent Brecht productions. His intention was, so he wrote in the theater magazine *Die Szene*,

> to show the play's underlying sense by making the surface meaning as clear as possible. In other words, no implications, secrets, ambiguities, half-light; but facts, brilliant illumination, light into every corner, absence of feeling, no humor with a catch in the throat. The theater considered as craft rather than art; avoidance of private affairs. These should make a secondary appearance, emerge as self-evident.

Several of the Berlin critics made the long trip to Darmstadt—evidence of the unusual interest taken in the young author's work—but their verdict on the play was mixed. *The Baby Elephant*, which in the 1924–25 version had been an integral part of it, was not performed. It appeared as an appendix to the published text not long after, but there is no evidence of its having been staged, whether "in the foyer" or anywhere else, until after World War II.

At the beginning of 1927 Brecht's new publisher Ullstein at last brought out *Devotions for the Home*, followed by the two promised plays. Then on March 23 *A Man's a Man* was broadcast by Berlin Radio, with Legal again as Galy Gay and Helene Weigel playing Begbick. This was the subject of two highly enthusiastic review articles in the radio paper *Der deutsche Rundfunk*, which termed it "the most novel and powerful play of our time." Shortly afterwards Brecht met the critic, a twenty-seven-year-old avant-garde composer called Kurt Weill who had recently written operas with Iwan Goll and Georg Kaiser, playwrights whom Brecht respected. Right away, by Weill's own account (p. 283), they began discussing the operatic medium, the notion of a "paradise city" and the name "Mahagonny" already given to the group of songs in the *Devotions*. A plan for a full-scale opera resulted, but before they could get down to it Weill was asked by the Deutsche Kammermusik committee to write a small "scenic oratorio" for their summer festival at Baden-Baden. The two men decided to use this as a "stylistic exercise" for the opera. Staged in a boxing ring with projections by Neher and with Weill's young wife Lotte Lenya playing Jenny, the resulting work consisted of the "Mahagonny Songs," both German and English, followed by a new finale. They called it a "Songspiel" on the analogy of the term "Singspiel," "Song" at that time being an ostentatiously Anglo-Saxon, jazz-flavored word.

As a theatrical piece this *Little Mahagonny*, as it came to be called, was far ahead of its time; indeed nobody chose to stage it again until the late 1950s. But as an exercise it undoubtedly worked, introducing Brecht not only to a form of "alternative theater" that was to become important to him later, but also to an inspired collaborator who could make use of his own limited, if surprisingly effective musical ideas. Throughout the rest of the year he and Weill worked together on the text of the full opera, with the help of Hauptmann and Neher, welding some fourteen of his poems into a loose structure derived partly from the *Flood* plan and partly from his private Mahagonny myth. Early in 1928 the script was ready for Weill to start making it into a unique "epic opera," a sequence of self-contained musical forms.

If Brecht was an exceptionally musical writer, Weill for his part was a highly intelligent and literate musician, who throughout the period covered by this volume was a weekly critic for *Der deutsche Rundfunk*, writing the equivalent (in wordage) of ten full-length books in the five years. Though the two men were never intimates, a program note to the *Little Mahagonny*, unsigned but written in Brecht's typical style, stated that

Weill's recent works show him to be moving in the same direction as those artists in every field who foresee the collapse of "society" art. *Mahagonny* is a short epic play which draws conclusions from the irresistible decline of our existing social classes. It is already addressing an audience which goes to the theater naively and for fun.

Both men supported Piscator's attempt to found his own "political theater" (unequivocally communist-dominated) after breaking with the Volksbühne in spring of 1927, Brecht becoming a member of his "dramaturgical collective" and working particularly on their epic adaptation of *Schweik*; while Weill wrote the music for Leo Lania's (another member of the collective) *Konjunktur*, a play about the oil business. It was, however, the Volksbühne, and not the Piscatorbühne, which staged the first Berlin production of *A Man's a Man*. This took place on January 5, 1928, about three weeks before the opening of the Piscator *Schweik*, and was directed by Engel with Heinrich George as an impressive Galy Gay and Weigel again as Begbick; the sets were once more by Neher. To Brecht's chief critical supporter Herbert Ihering, who had already seen the Darmstadt version, the revised play seemed to emphasize the notion of man as a kind of machine, and he greeted Brecht as the first writer who could take the machine age for granted, viewing him as a central figure who linked the comedy of Chaplin and Buster Keaton at once with the theatrical ideas of Piscator and with the musical experiments being pursued by such men as Klemperer, Hindemith and Weill. "All that has hitherto been running along parallel or divergent courses is now joining up. . . . The age of isolation is over."

In the Berlin theater this was the start of a phenomenal year. As Piscator's historic first season began heading for bankruptcy (so that his planned Brecht productions never came to anything), a new management loomed up, headed by a young actor called Ernst-Josef Aufricht. Having been given 100,000 marks by his father with which to open his own Berlin theater, Aufricht had already rented the Theater am Schiffbauerdamm and booked Engel to direct the opening production, if possible for his own twenty-eighth birthday on August 31. The problem now was to find a play. Wedekind, Karl Kraus (whose young friend Heinrich Fischer became Aufricht's deputy), Toller, Feuchtwanger, Kaiser, even Sudermann were considered or actually approached, but to no effect. Then in March or April Fischer saw Brecht accidentally in a café, introduced him to Aufricht, and asked if he had anything that would answer their needs. Brecht's own work in progress—presumably *Fleischhacker*—would not do; it was already promised—presumably to Piscator—and Aufricht appears to have been bored by his account of it. But Brecht also mentioned a translation of John Gay's *The Beggar's Opera* which Elisabeth Hauptmann had begun making the previous November. This eighteenth-century satire had been an immense success in Nigel Playfair's revival at the Lyric, Hammersmith some five years earlier, and to the two entrepreneurs the idea "smelt of theater." They read as much of the script as had so far been written, under the provisional title *Gesindel*, or *Scum*, and decided that this was the play with which to open.

Just how much Brecht had had to do with the script at this stage is uncertain, but he now took the lead and proposed that Weill should write modern settings for the songs. Aufricht, by his own account, went privately to hear two of Weill's Kaiser operas, was appalled by their atonality, and told his musical director Theo Mackeben to get hold of the traditional Pepusch arrangements in case Weill came up with something impossibly rebarbative. In mid-May the whole team were packed off to Le Lavandou in the south of France to complete the work: the Brechts, the Weills, Hauptmann, Engel. Here and subsequently on the Ammersee in Bavaria Brecht seems to have written some brand-new scenes (the stable wedding for instance, which bears no relation to Gay's original), and started adding his own songs, four of them piratically derived from a German version of Villon. On the first of August rehearsals started, with a duplicated script which, as our notes show, still contained a good deal of the original play, as well as songs by Gay himself and Rudyard Kipling which later disappeared. A succession of accidents and catastrophes then followed. Carola Neher, who was to play Polly, arrived a fortnight late from her husband Klabund's deathbed, and abandoned her part; Roma Bahn was recruited and learned it in four days. Feuchtwanger suggested the new title; Karl Kraus added the second verse to the "Jealousy Duet." Helene Weigel, cast as

Mrs. Coaxer the brothel madame, developed appendicitis, and the part was cut. The cabaret singer Rosa Valetti objected to the "Song of Sexual Obsession" which she had to sing as Mrs. Peachum, so this too went; Käte Kühl as Lucy could not manage the florid solo which Weill had written for scene 8, so it had to be eliminated and later the scene itself was cut. Lotte Lenya was accidentally left off the printed program; the play was found to be three-quarters of an hour too long, leading to massive cuts in Peachum's part and the dropping of the "Solomon Song"; the finale was only written during the rehearsals; and late on "The Ballad of Mack the Knife" was added as an inspired afterthought.

All accounts agree that the production's prospects seemed extremely bad, only Weill's music and Caspar Neher's sets remaining unaffected by the mounting chaos. Even the costumes were simply those available, so Brecht was to say later (p. 340), while the Victorian setting was decided less by the needs of the story than by the shortage of time. The dress rehearsal must have been disastrous, the reactions of the first-night audience a confirmation of this, lasting right into the second scene, even after the singing of "Pirate Jenny" in the stable. But with the "Cannon Song" the applause suddenly burst loose. Quite unexpectedly, inspiredly, improvisedly, management and collaborators found themselves with the greatest German hit of the 1920s on their hands.

3

It struck Berlin at a moment when Piscator had temporarily disappeared as an active force in the Left theater and the various collective groups which succeeded him had not yet got off the ground. For Brecht and Weill there was now the composition of *Mahagonny* to be resumed—something that was only completed in November 1929—as well as a small *Berlin Requiem* which Weill had agreed to write for Radio Frankfurt on texts by Brecht, and which they sketched out in November and December 1928. Both men probably also had some involvement in the production of Feuchtwanger's second "Anglo-Saxon Play" *Die Petroleuminseln* at the Staatstheater in the former month, for which Weill wrote the music and Neher once more provided sets. But the immediate effect of *The Threepenny Opera*'s success was to establish the Theater am Schiffbauerdamm as the leading left-wing theater of the moment in Berlin. Retrospectively Brecht came to speak of it as "his" theater, and indeed to a great extent he seems to have dominated its entire opening season. For with *The Threepenny Opera* temporarily transferred to another theater (and Carola Neher at some point assuming her original role as Polly), he took over the direction of Marieluise Fleisser's antimilitarist Bavarian farce *Die Pioniere von Ingolstadt*, a sequel to the play which he had recommended to the Junge Bühne three years earlier. This opened on March 31, 1929, and featured an unknown actor whom Brecht had advised Aufricht to engage on a three-year contract—Peter Lorre—along with Kurt Gerron and Lenya from his own play. The farce itself was too outspoken for the tastes of the police and the military, and had to be bowdlerized, but it none the less ran for two months and broke even; Aufricht later judged it the best of all the productions which he sponsored. Then *The Threepenny Opera* returned for the rest of the season, and the problem of the next play had to be faced.

Outwardly the position was as it had been a year earlier. Another success was needed, once again for August 31; Engel and Neher had been booked, a number of actors were already under contract, including Lorre, Gerron, and Carola Neher, and Aufricht evidently assumed that the miracle could be worked again. As before it was Hauptmann who had done the spadework, apparently as light relief from a serious Salvation Army play on which the collective had been working; so Brecht now submitted the first two-thirds of a Chicago Salvationist comedy which she called *Happy End*. Exactly as before he himself would provide the songs and Weill would set them; exactly as before the collaborators went to the South of France to finish the job. Brecht, however, thereafter seems (on the evidence of the typescripts) to have done much less to alter Hauptmann's structure and dialogue than in the case of the *Beggar's Opera* translation; he also supplied fewer, if qualitatively comparable songs. Partly this was because his links with the musicians of the Deutsche Kammermusik had led him to a fascinating new theatrical form, the so-called Lehrstück or didactic play, on which he had begun collaborating with Hindemith and Weill, and which will largely dominate our next volume. But partly also it was because his view of his political obligations had changed.

In July, when Brecht attended the Baden-Baden festival for the first two of the new Lehrstücke, Engel wrote begging him to rewrite *Happy End* after the end of Act Two. This evidently was not done, though it was Brecht who introduced a new character in the shape of the Lady in Gray. He had, it seems, by then decided that the play was not good enough for him to accept responsibility for it and should instead be attributed to a mythical Dorothy Lane. Weill insisted that he should at least put his name to the songs. However, when Engel finally walked out in view of the lack of a completed Act Three, Brecht took the direction over. In his memoirs Aufricht makes much of certain "strange figures" who began appearing with last-minute advice, notably the Bulgarian director Slatan Dudow and Reich, who was now resident in the USSR. Whatever the reason, the play's ending seems to have remained in semi-improvised confusion, till on the first night Weigel as Lady in Gray aggressively, but rather lamely, reiterated the words of Macheath at the end of *The Threepenny Opera*: "What's a jemmy compared with a share certificate?" and so on, followed by the chorus "Hosanna Rockefeller" which has since disappeared from the play. The audience responded by silence throughout most of Act Three, followed by an uproar of protest at the end. No comment was severer than that of Alfred Kemeny, or "Durus," the critic of the Communist Party daily, *Die Rote Fahne*, who found everything about the production phony except the acting, accused Brecht of "cheap rhymes and utterly threadbare sentimentalities," and saw the conclusion as mere cashing in, redeemed only by Weigel's earnestness. The production was taken off after a few days, and "at my theater," wrote Aufricht, "a Brecht intermission followed."

This was also the effective end of the creative period covered in this volume, for although *Mahagonny* was still not
ready for performance Brecht does not seem to have taken
much further interest in it. Thus the production notes discussed on pp. 288 ff. were written by Weill and Neher at the
end of the year, apparently without Brecht's participation;
while when he did publish the text later that year he wrote
notes of his own (p. 279) which diverge from Weill's view
and appear to deplore the work's operatic nature. Later, towards Christmas 1931 when Aufricht, with money from an
extremely curious-sounding financier friend of Trude Hester-
berg's (who wanted to play Begbick), organized a production
at the Theater am Kurfürstendamm, Brecht proved so quarrel-
some at rehearsals that Aufricht decided to stage the didactic,
explicitly Communist *The Mother* in order to get him out of
the way. From this experience, it seems, dates the split with
Weill, and thereafter Brecht virtually ignored the work, which
for instance is not mentioned once in the *Arbeitsjournal* that
covers the last seventeen years of his life. As for *Happy End*,
it was virtually expunged from the record, for it has never
been published at all in German and has always been treated
as Elisabeth Hauptmann's play, if not that of the nonexistent
Dorothy Lane. In an interview in the 1970s Hauptmann de-
fended the decision to omit it from Brecht's collected works
on the grounds that "after all it was only a bit of fun" ("ein
Spass"), a light relief for the collective from their involvement
in the new didactic plays. Moreover, it was of course soon to
be cannibalized to help make *St. Joan of the Stockyards*, which
once again figured under Brecht's name. But the decision must
be seen as misleading given the rôle the work played in
Brecht's fortunes at the time; it is questionable in view of
Hauptmann's considerable responsibility for works like *The
Threepenny Opera* (which was one of those on which she got
a royalty) and *Der Jasager* (of which she wrote the lion's
share); and it certainly suggests that Brecht's spirit of collectivity had its limits. "To you," Zuckmayer recalls telling
him about this time, "a collective is a group of intelligent
people all contributing to what one of them wants, i.e. you."

Wise after the event, distracted before it, he did not want *Happy End*.

But however Brecht himself might be altering at this time, *The Threepenny Opera* was a play which he had no wish to discard. Obviously it was a very much better and solider work than its successor, though the latter's rehabilitation in the 1960s (which has led it to be performed under Brecht's name in both England and the U.S.) shows the silliness of its text to be not quite the liability it once seemed. The essential difference, however, lay in the former work's enormous success, which kept it running in different parts of Germany until the Nazis took over and in other countries longer still. This did not immediately tempt Brecht to tinker with the text of the play (as he continued to do with *A Man's a Man*, which he now made less frivolous and more severely antimilitarist), but when Warner Bros. and Tobis, acting through producers called Nero-Film, contracted in May 1930 to make a film of it, he started looking at it with changed—and changing—eyes. Although sound film was still very much in its infancy, the prospects seemed good: G. W. Pabst was to be the director, Lania (of Piscator's old collective) to write the script; Carola Neher would play Polly, Lenya Jenny; while Brecht and Weill were given a say respectively in the script and the music. Two parallel versions would be made, one German and one French. That summer, accordingly, Brecht wrote Lania the treatment called "Die Beule," "The Bruise," which in effect ignores all that had remained of the *Beggar's Opera* and uses the characters and the Victorian London setting to point a radically changed moral. Everything now is on a larger scale—the gang is 120 strong, Peachum heads a Begging Trust—and a higher social level, with peers, a general, and a magistrate at Macheath's wedding in the ducal manège. The gang and the beggars this time are engaged in a war whose symbol is the bruise inflicted by the former on a beggar called Sam. Peachum accordingly uses the beggars to disfigure the smartly repainted slum streets through which the Queen is to pass; he interviews Brown with seven lawyers behind him, and secures Macheath's arrest after a bucolic picnic and a chase in which a car full of policemen pursues a car full of whores. There is no escape and no second arrest. Under Polly's direction the gang has simply taken over the National Deposit Bank and converted itself into a group of solemn financiers. Both they and Mrs. Peachum now become uneasy about the dangers of unleashing the poor; while Brown has a terrible dream, in which thousands of poor people emerge from under one of the Thames bridges as a kind of flood, sweeping through the streets and public buildings. So the "mounted messengers" this time are the bankers who arrive to bail Macheath out; and rather than disappoint the crowds Peachum hands over Sam to be hanged instead. The social façades are maintained as Macheath joins the reunited bourgeoisie awaiting the arrival of their Queen.

This scheme, on which Dudow and Neher also collaborated, was plainly unwelcome to the producers, and the fact that Brecht only met the agreed August deadline by communicating it to Lania orally did not improve matters. Though Lania needed him to continue working, Nero chose to dismiss Brecht at this stage, and brought in the Communist film critic Béla Balázs to help complete the script. A lawsuit followed, which Brecht lost, and thereafter he had no words too bad for Pabst's film, which meanwhile went obstinately ahead, to be shown in Berlin on February 19, 1931. Though the long theoretical essay which he thereafter wrote on the "Threepenny Lawsuit," as he termed it, is an illuminating work, not least for its links with the ideas of his new friend Walter Benjamin, the modern reader should not allow it to put him off the film. For in fact not only did the latter capture aspects of the original (for instance Carola Neher's interpretation of Polly) that necessarily elude any modern production; it also incorporates a surprising proportion of Brecht's changes to the story. These, however, continued to itch Brecht, so that while leaving the play itself as it had been in the 1928 production (with all its last-minute decisions and improvisations) he was soon planning its further development in *The Threepenny Novel*, his one substantial work of fiction, which he was to hand in to its Dutch publisher some months after leaving Germany in 1933. Engel, when he came again to direct the play at the Theater am Schiffbauerdamm for the Berliner Ensemble in 1960, after Brecht's death, wondered at first if he could not incorporate some of the ideas from "The Bruise" and the novel, but soon decided that they were too divergent from the play. Brecht for his part wrote some topical versions of the songs (pp. 315 ff.) for other directors in the immediate postwar years, but never made them a permanent part of the text; indeed they hardly merit it. All the same, his discussions in connection with Giorgio Strehler's Milan production in the last year of his life (p. 337) show that he regarded *The Threepenny Opera* as no inviolable museum piece, for he envisaged a new framework and welcomed Strehler's updating of the story to the era of the Keystone Cops.

4

The persistent element of flippancy, of fun, in Brecht's work during these five years makes it an awkward problem for solemn-faced interpreters. This is particularly so with *A Man's a Man* and *The Threepenny Opera*, for *Happy End* can be conveniently written off as another's play, while *Mahagonny*, being an opera, tends to be treated as a special case. The trouble arises from the fact that even in the heyday of his involvement with the Berlin commercial and semicommercial theater—in other words, the period covered by the present volume— Brecht's attitude to society and the theater was changing; the great turning-point both in his own views and in the history of the Weimar Republic coming in 1929 when the works in question had all been written but he was still altering them and writing extensively about them. Commentators may resist the temptation to judge his plays of the 1920s in the light of his later Communist and anti-Nazi reputation, yet still be mis-led by the time lag between the writing of *The Threepenny Opera* and *Mahagonny* and the important theoretical con-clusions which he drew from them two or three years later. But how many can even do that? Professor Ernst Schumacher, for instance, in his standard East German work on the pre-

1933 plays, written admittedly before it became simple to see the differences between their first and subsequent versions, treated Galy Gay in *A Man's a Man* as "a victim of capitalism," "a living illustration of Lenin's analysis," and the play itself as "a piece of gruesome colonial reality," anticipating later events in Korea and Vietnam. Because this is argued on the basis primarily of the 1931 text, the strong farcical element which was built into the play from the first and never wholly eliminated is virtually ignored.

The Threepenny Opera is the main challenge to this kind of interpretation, since its repeated success in the commercial theaters of bourgeois society takes some explaining away. Like Piscator's productions a few months earlier, it appealed to the fashionable public—"one has to have seen it," noted the elegant and cosmopolitan Count Kessler after visiting it with a party including an ambassador and a director of the Dresdner Bank —and if it gave them a more cynical view of their own institutions it seems to have prompted neither them nor, perhaps, anyone else to change these for the better. Brecht himself was naturally reluctant to admit its ineffectuality, as his somewhat wishful replies to Giorgio Strehler indicate (p. 337); but Durus, the "hard man" of *Die Rote Fahne*, wrote earlier in 1928 that Brecht had barely begun to relate to the class struggle; and even Ihering, in welcoming his discovery of "a new form, open to every possibility, every kind of content," added: "This content, however, has still to come." What confuses later observers' judgment of the work is the intense dislike which the German reaction came to feel for it. But 1929 saw the beginning of that extreme polarization of German politics which brought the Nazis to power, and if several of the theaters now veered sharply leftward (dragging part of the cinema with them) their middlebrow audience, together with the bulk of the established authorities, became much less hesitant to assert their prejudices. This affected a good deal more than *The Threepenny Opera*, leading among much else to the booing of the *Mahagonny* première, the prosecution and subsequent emigration of Piscator, the collapse of all efforts to stage *St. Joan of the Stockyards*, and the boycotting by other radio stations of the *Berlin Requiem*. It was a great wave of irrational feeling, and in so far as it was directed against this particular play it struck that shrewd, if foreign-based observer Kurt Tucholsky as ridiculous, an ersatz political battle. The work itself represented no danger. "This writer can be compared to a man cooking soup on a burning house. He's not responsible for the fire."

None the less the works with Weill were revolutionary in a less obviously political but still deeply disturbing sense. For, they struck, almost instinctively, at the whole hierarchical order of the arts, with opera on its Wagnerian pinnacle at the top, and reshuffled highbrow and lowbrow elements to form a quite new kind of musical theater which would upset every accepted notion of what was socially and culturally proper. This was what the best critics immediately recognized, Ihering writing that the success of *The Threepenny Opera* could not be overestimated:

> A theater that is not smart, not geared to "society," has broken through to the audience.

Far more so the musicians; thus Klemperer is reported to have seen the 1928 production ten times, while Heinrich Strobel compared it with *The Soldier's Tale* as "showing the way," and Theodor Adorno called it the most important thing since Berg's *Wozzeck*. In many ways the change implied here has proved harder for later societies to assimilate than have the somewhat random gibes at business, religious hypocrisy, individual charity, romantic marriage, and the judicial system which make up the political content of the text. Particularly when seen in conjunction with Brecht's and Walter Benjamin's current thinking about the "apparatus" of the arts, it suggests a complete cultural and sociological reevaluation which would alter all the existing categories, starting with those of opera and operetta (for it was neither), as well as the corresponding techniques of acting, singing, and so forth. Today, though certainly poverty, slums, corrupt business practices, and biased justice continue to exist in our most prosperous societies, we no longer feel that *The Threepenny Opera* has anything all that acute to say about them. But the implications of the new form for singers, musicians, and above all for institutionalized opera are still far from fully digested. And because Brecht and his friends never themselves managed to capture the "apparatus" of which they spoke, this holds good for Communist as well as for capitalist society.

For the evolution of Brecht's theoretical ideas it was a most fertile period. *A Man's a Man* helped him in 1926 to begin formulating his concept of "epic theater"; its 1931 production that of gestic acting. *Mahagonny* in 1927 taught him the value of projections, then in 1930 stimulated a definition of the differences between epic and dramatic theater which remains one of his major statements. His subsequent notes on *The Threepenny Opera*, too, are still basic reading. But what would be interesting to know is just how much the collaboration with Weill had to do with this. For it was the incidental music to the 1928 production of *A Man's a Man* that stimulated Brecht to write his first, hitherto unpublished note on the "separation of the elements," which was to become one of his central ideas:

> three elements mingled here without mixing completely: set, story and music. The set worked as images rather than illusion, the story became less of an experience and gave room for meditation, the music came not "out of the air" but out of the wings and remained like a concert piece. writing, music and architecture played their part as independent arts in an intelligible performance.

There is moreover an essay by Weill "On the gestic nature of music" which was published in the magazine *Die Musik* in March 1929 and thus antedates Brecht's first exposition of the "gest" by more than a year. Certainly the settings which Weill had been writing for his words must have done much to make Brecht grasp this principle—the notion that text, music, and performance must all combine to convey an attitude, a point— and from now on he thought of his own writing as "gestic" and of all form as a means of putting such attitudes across. This was not so well achieved perhaps in the more orthodoxly operatic stretches of *Mahagonny*, and it may have been Weill's evident wish to go on from there rather than from *The Threepenny Opera* that prompted the break. Brecht's great good luck was that in Hanns Eisler he had by then found another composer who, if he never created a comparable form, none the less took the gestic principle even further.

It is difficult in all this to disentangle the political element from the artistic and the personal; many of Brecht's disputes were exacerbated, sometimes to a decisive extent, by insulting or infuriating behavior on his part (which no doubt was returned in kind). But his political evolution in this period was enormously important, and it took him from near-indifference at the time of his arrival in Berlin (note the absence of any political resolutions in his initial list) through a "sociological" stage when he was beginning to see Marxism as a useful key to the world's workings, to a committed position close to that of the German Communist Party by the end of 1929. The problem here is one of pace, and all the evidence is that he moved much more rapidly at the end of the period than when he was writing these plays, the breaking up of the Berlin May Day demonstration that year, the world economic crisis, and the mounting German unemployment (3.2 million in January 1930, 4.9 million in February 1931, 6 million in January 1932) being major factors. This did not mean that the process was not already under way. His first consciously "proletarian" poems, for instance, date from the early summer of 1926, shortly before the *A Man's a Man* première; in April 1927 he was on a committee for the freeing of the communist guerrilla leader Max Hölz; while Piscator's theater, for which he began working that autumn, was to some extent under party discipline. But when exactly was the moment of which he wrote years later:

> Right, I thought . . . I can open my heart to pity. I needed some kind of reinsurance, you see, in order to register pity; possibly I was afraid that pity without prospect could destroy a man without reason.

This was the point at which he became emotionally committed, and all the signs are that it was not before he had committed himself to the completion of *Happy End*.

If you look at the evolution of the texts, as outlined in our notes, you will see what a very piecemeal writer he was. These works were patched together from a variety of sources, then

taken apart and restitched, sometimes with loose threads left
dangling; their eventual length and shape was never all that
clearly determined. In the process some marvelous pieces would
be discarded; thus in *A Man's a Man* Bloody Five, whose early
invective goes even beyond Kipling in its British military
authenticity, gradually becomes emasculated, more sadly than
Brecht meant, as he declines through the 1926 and 1928 versions to end as the dummylike Sergeant Charles Fairchild of
our text. The brothel scene in *Mahagonny*, again, was far
tauter and stronger in the original script, despite the beauty
of the Crane Duet which Brecht added and retained for the
published version; while in *The Threepenny Opera* Peachum's
original speech at the end of Act Two, besides being satir-
ically much sharper than the "Semiramis" speech which replaced it, is positively needed in order to explain what is going
on at the start of the next act. But this process of revision and
re-revision was Brecht's way of working, and once he had got
a set of characters who intrigued him, together with a con-
genial "poetic conception" like Macheath's London, or Blody
5's Indian army camp, he would cheerfully refunction them
to convey his changing ideas both of society and of his
medium. That this has confused his interpreters (and, worse
still, readers and directors) is only a small part of the trouble.
For on the one hand it damaged the inner consistency of the
chosen plays. And on the other it distracted him from finishing
those other plays which (judging from the fragments) looked
as if they would have conveyed the same ideas a good deal
more tightly and forcefully: *Fleischhacker, Fatzer, The Bread-
shop*. If *The Threepenny Opera* was Brecht's greatest success,
Mankind's Occupation of the Great Cities was at the same time
our saddest loss.

A Man's a Man

*The Transformation of
the Docker Galy Gay in
the Army Camp of Kilkoa
in the year nineteen
hundred and twenty-five*

Comedy

Collaborators: E. Burri, S. Dudow, E. Hauptmann, C. Neher,

B. Reich

Translator: Gerhard Nellhaus

CHARACTERS

URIAH SHELLEY
JESSE MAHONEY } the four members
POLLY BAKER } of a machine-gun
JERAIAH JIP } detachment of the
British army in India

CHARLES FAIRCHILD, known as
   Bloody Five, a sergeant
GALY GAY, an Irish docker
GALY GAY'S WIFE

MR. WANG, bonze of a Tibetan
   pagoda
MAH SING, his sacristan
LEOCADIA BEGBICK, canteen owner
SOLDIERS

Kilkoa

Galy Gay and his wife.

GALY GAY (*sitting one morning in his chair, says to his wife*) Dear wife, today, I have decided, I shall buy a fish in keeping with our income. A fish isn't beyond the means of a docker who doesn't drink, smokes very little, and is virtually without vices. Do you think I should buy a big fish, or do you require a small one?

WIFE A small one.

GALY GAY And of what kind should the fish be which you require?

WIFE I have in mind a nice flounder. But do watch out for those fishwives. They're a lecherous lot, always out after men, and you have a soft nature, Galy Gay.

GALY GAY That's true, but I should think they'd leave an indigent docker alone.

WIFE You're like an elephant, who is the most sluggish animal in the animal kingdom, but runs like a freight train once he gets started. Besides, there are those soldiers, who are the worst people in the world, and I hear that thousands of them are pulling into the station. They're certain to be hanging around the market place, we'll be lucky if they don't break into houses and kill people. And it's dangerous for a man to go out alone, because they always go around in fours.

GALY GAY They wouldn't want to hurt a simple docker.

WIFE You never can tell.

GALY GAY So just put water on for the fish, because I'm hungry already and I ought to be back in ten minutes.

2

Street Outside the Pagoda of the Yellow God

Four soldiers stop outside the pagoda. Military marches are heard.

JESSE Detachment, halt! Kilkoa! This is Her Majesty's city of Kilkoa where the army is being mustered for a long-awaited war. We've come here with a hundred thousand other soldiers, and we're thirsting to establish order on the northern borders.

JIP That calls for beer. (*He collapses*)

POLLY Just as our Queen's mighty tanks must be filled with petrol if we are to see them rolling over the God-damned roads of this oversized Eldorado, so troops must be filled with beer.

JIP How much beer have we got left?

POLLY There are four of us. We still have fifteen bottles. That means getting hold of another twenty-five bottles.

JESSE That calls for money.

URIAH Some people have it in for soldiers, but there's more copper in a single one of these pagodas than a full strength regiment needs to march from Calcutta to London.

POLLY Our friend Uriah's suggestion in regard to a pagoda, which is no doubt rickety and covered with fly shit, but may well be bursting with copper, surely merits our sympathetic attention.

JIP All I know, Polly, is that I've got to have more to drink.

URIAH Calm down, sweetheart. This Asia has a hole for us to crawl through.

JIP   Uriah, Uriah! My mother used to say: Do what you like, my darling Jeraiah, but remember, pitch always sticks. Everything around here smells of pitch.

JESSE   The door is ajar. Watch it, Jeraiah! There's devilry afoot.

URIAH   Nobody's going through this open door.

JESSE   Right. What are the windows for?

URIAH   Take off your belts. We'll make a long line to fish for the alms boxes. That's it.
(*They attack the windows. Uriah smashes one, looks inside and begins to fish*)

POLLY   Catch something?

URIAH   No, but my helmet's fallen in.

JESSE   Hell, you can't go back to camp without a helmet.

URIAH   Oh boy, am I catching things! This is a terrible establishment! Just look! Snares. Man traps.

JESSE   Let's give up. This is no ordinary temple, it's a trap.

URIAH   A temple's a temple. I've got to get my helmet back.

JESSE   Can you reach it?

URIAH   No.

JESSE   Maybe I can raise this latch.

POLLY   But don't damage the temple.

JESSE   Ow! Ow!

URIAH   What's wrong?

JESSE   My hand's caught.

POLLY   Let's give up.

JESSE (*indignantly*)   Give up? What about my hand?

URIAH   My helmet's in there too.

POLLY   Then we'll have to go through the wall.

JESSE   Ow! Ow! (*He pulls his hand out. It is covered with blood*) They're going to pay for this hand. I won't give up now. Got a ladder? Let's go!

URIAH   Stop! First give me your paybooks. A soldier's paybook must never be damaged. A man can always be replaced, but a soldier's paybook is sacred, if anything is.
(*They hand over their paybooks*)

POLLY   Polly Baker.

JESSE   Jesse Mahoney.

JIP (*crawling up*)   Jeraiah Jip.

URIAH   Uriah Shelley. All of the Eighth Regiment machine-gun detachment. Headquarters: Kankerdan. No shooting, men. No visible damage to the temple. Forward!
(*Uriah, Jesse and Polly climb into the pagoda*)

JIP (*calls after them*)   I'll mount guard. That way at least I won't have gone in. (*The yellow face of Wang, the bonze, appears in a small window in the upper story*) Good day! Are you the honorable owner? Nice place you've got here.

URIAH (*inside*)   Hand me your knife, Jesse. To pry these alms boxes open.
(*Wang smiles. Jip smiles too*)

JIP (*to the bonze*)   It's just awful to be mixed up with such hippopotamuses. (*The face disappears*) Come on out. There's a man walking around upstairs.
(*Electric bells are heard at intervals inside*)

URIAH   Watch where you step. What's that you say, Jip?

JIP   A man upstairs.

URIAH   A man? Everybody out! Hey!

THE THREE (*inside, shouting and cursing*)   Get your foot out of the way.—Let go! Now I can't move my foot. My boot's gone too. Don't give up, Polly. Never!—Uriah, now my jacket.—What's a jacket? This temple needs to be wiped out. Now what?—Damn, my trousers are stuck. That's what comes of being in a hurry. That idiot Jip!

JIP   Find anything? Whiskey? Rum? Gin? Brandy? Ale?

JESSE   Uriah's ripped his trousers on a bamboo hook. And the boot on Polly's good foot is caught in a trap.

POLLY   And Jesse's tangled up in an electric wire.

JIP   Just what I expected. When you go into a house, why don't you use the door?
(*Jip goes in through the door. The three climb out above, pale, bleeding and ragged*)

POLLY   This calls for vengeance.

URIAH   This temple doesn't fight fair! It's disgusting.

POLLY   I want to see blood.

JIP (*from inside*)   Hey!

POLLY (*bloodthirstily advances on the roof, but his boot gets stuck*)   Now my other boot's gone.

URIAH   I'm going to shoot the place up.

(*The three climb down and aim the machine gun at the pagoda*)

POLLY Fire!

(*They fire*)

JIP (*inside*) Ow! What are you doing?

(*The three of them look up, horrified*)

POLLY Where are you?

JIP (*inside*) Here. You've gone and shot me through the finger.

JESSE What the devil are you doing in that rat trap, you fool?

JIP (*appears in the doorway*) I wanted to get the money. Here it is.

URIAH (*joyfully*) Trust the biggest drunk of us all to get it first go off. (*In a loud voice*) You march right out of this door.

JIP (*sticks his head out the door*) Where? What?

URIAH Out of this door!

JIP Ow, what's that?

POLLY What's the matter with him?

JIP Look!

URIAH Now what?

JIP My hair! Oh, my hair! I can't go forward and I can't go back! Oh, my hair! It's stuck on something, Uriah, look and see what's sticking to my hair! Oh, Uriah, get me out of here! I'm hanging by my hair!

(*Polly goes to Jip on his tiptoes and looks at his hair from above*)

POLLY His hair is caught in the door.

URIAH (*shouts*) Your knife, Jesse, so I can cut him loose. (*Uriah cuts him loose. Jip staggers forward*)

POLLY (*amused*) And now he's got a bald spot.

(*They examine Jip's head*)

JESSE A piece of scalp came off too.

URIAH (*looks at the two of them, then icily*) A bald spot will betray us.

JESSE (*with a piercing look*) A living "Wanted" sign! (*Uriah, Jesse and Polly confer*)

URIAH We'll go to camp and get a pair of scissors. Then we'll come back after dark and cut off all his hair. That way they won't see his bald spot. (*He gives back the paybooks*) Jesse Mahoney!

JESSE (*taking his book*)   Jesse Mahoney!

URIAH   Polly Baker!

POLLY (*taking his book*)   Polly Baker!

URIAH   Jeraiah Jip! (*Jip tries to stand up*) I'll keep yours. (*He points to a palanquin in the courtyard*) Sit in that leather box and wait till dark.

(*Jip crawls into the palanquin. The three others walk off dejectedly, shaking their heads. When they are gone, Wang, the bonze, appears in the pagoda door, takes some of the hair that is sticking to it, and examines it*)

3

Highway between Kilkoa and the Army Camp

Sergeant Fairchild steps out from behind a shed and nails a poster to the shed.

FAIRCHILD   It's been years since I, Bloody Five, known also as the Tiger of Kilkoa and the Human Typhoon, a sergeant in the British Army, saw anything so amazing. (*Points at the poster*) Pagoda of the Yellow God looted. The roof of the Pagoda of the Yellow God riddled with bullets. Evidence: four ounces of hair stuck to the pitch. Given that the roof is riddled with bullets, a machine-gun detachment must be behind it. Inasmuch as four ounces of hair were found at the scene of the crime, there must be a man with four ounces of hair missing. If a man with a bald spot should be found in one of the machine-gun detachments, that detachment committed the crime. It stands to reason. But who's this coming?

(*He steps behind the shed. The three approach and read*)

the poster with visible horror. Then they go on their way dejectedly. Fairchild comes out from behind the shed and blows a police whistle. They stop short)

FAIRCHILD   Have you seen a man with a bald spot?

POLLY   No.

FAIRCHILD   Aren't you a fine mess! Remove your helmets. Where's your fourth man?

URIAH   He's answering a call of nature, Sergeant.

FAIRCHILD   Then we'll just wait for him. Maybe he's seen a man with a bald spot. (*They wait*) That's a long call nature's giving him.

JESSE   Yes, Sergeant.

(*They continue to wait*)

POLLY   Perhaps he went a different way.

FAIRCHILD   Get this straight: You'd be better off if you had summarily shot each other in your mothers' wombs than if you turn up at my roll call this evening without your fourth man. (*Goes out*)

POLLY   Let's hope that's not our new sergeant. If that rattle-snake calls the roll tonight, we can line up against the wall right away.

URIAH   We'll just have to find a fourth man before roll call.

POLLY   Here comes a man now. Let's look him over on the sly. (*They hide behind the shed. Widow Begbick comes down the street. Galy Gay is following her, carrying her basket of cucumbers*)

BEGBICK   What are you complaining about? You're getting paid by the hour.

GALY GAY   That makes three hours.

BEGBICK   You'll get your money. This is a road that hardly anyone uses. A woman might have a hard time dealing with a man who wanted to embrace her.

GALY GAY   But, madam, as the owner of a canteen, always dealing with soldiers, who are the worst people on earth, you must know certain holds.

BEGBICK   Ah sir, you should never say such things to a lady. There are certain words that stir a woman's blood.

GALY GAY   I'm only a simple docker.

BEGBICK   They'll be calling the roll for the new men in a few minutes. As you can hear, they're beating the drum right now. There's not a soul on the road at this hour.

GALY GAY If it's really as late as all that, I'll have to turn around and hurry back to Kilkoa, because I still have to buy a fish.

BEGBICK Would you mind my asking you, Mr.—I hope I've got the name correctly—Galy Gay, whether the docker's profession demands exceptional strength?

GALY GAY I'd never have thought that unforeseen events would once again delay me for almost four hours from quickly buying a fish and returning home, but when I finally get moving, I'm like an express train.

BEGBICK Yes, there's quite a difference between buying a fish to feed your face and helping a lady carry her basket. But perhaps the lady might be able to show her gratitude in a manner that would give you more pleasure than eating fish.

GALY GAY Frankly, I should like to go and buy a fish.

BEGBICK How can you be such a materialist?

GALY GAY You know, I'm funny that way. Sometimes I know before I even get out of bed in the morning: today I want a fish. Or I want a curry. When that happens, the world can come to an end, but I just have to get a fish or a curry as the case may be.

BEGBICK I see. But isn't it too late? The shops are closed and the fish is sold out.

GALY GAY Let me explain. I'm a man of great imagination; I've had enough of a fish, for instance, before I even lay eyes on it. Other people set out to buy a fish, and first they buy that fish, second they take that fish home, third they cook that fish till it's done, fourth they eat that fish, and at night, even after they've finished digesting, they're still preoccupied with the same miserable fish, because such people lack imagination.

BEGBICK I see, you're thinking only of yourself. (*Pause*) Hm. If you think only of yourself, I suggest that you take your fish money and buy this cucumber, which I'll let you have as a favor. The cucumber is worth more, but you can keep the difference for carrying my basket.

GALY GAY But I don't require a cucumber.

BEGBICK   I'd never have expected you to humiliate me like this.

GALY GAY   It's only that the water for the fish has already been put on the stove.

BEGBICK   I see. Have it your way. Have it your way.

GALY GAY   But, believe me, I'd be only too glad to oblige you.

BEGBICK   Not another word. You're only putting your foot in deeper.

GALY GAY   I really wouldn't want to disappoint you. If you'll still let me have the cucumber, here's the money.

URIAH (*to Jesse and Polly*)   There's a man who can't say no.

GALY GAY   Careful, there are soldiers about.

BEGBICK   God knows what they're doing around here at this hour. It's almost time for roll call. Quick, give me my basket. There's no point in my wasting any more of my time chattering with you. But I should gladly welcome you in my beer wagon at the army camp, for I am the Widow Begbick, and my beer wagon is famous from Hyderabad to Rangoon. (*She takes her basket and leaves*)

URIAH   That's our man.

JESSE   A man who can't say no.

POLLY   And he even has red hair like our Jip.

(*The three step out*)

JESSE   Pleasant evening, isn't it?

GALY GAY   Yes, sir.

JESSE   It's a funny thing, sir, but something tells me you come from Kilkoa.

GALY GAY   Kilkoa? Why, yes. That's where my hut is, so to speak.

JESSE   I'm glad to hear it, Mr. . . .

GALY GAY   Galy Gay.

JESSE   You've got a hut there, haven't you?

GALY GAY   You must know me if you know that. Or perhaps you know my wife?

JESSE   You're called, why yes, you're called . . . just a moment . . . Galy Gay.

GALY GAY   Exactly. That's my name.

JESSE   I knew it right away. You see, that's the way I am. For instance, I bet you're married. But why are we standing around like this, Mr. Galy Gay? These are my friends, Polly and Uriah. Won't you smoke a pipe with us in our canteen? (*Pause. Galy Gay looks at them suspiciously*)

GALY GAY   Many thanks. Unfortunately, my wife is waiting for me in Kilkoa. Besides, I myself haven't got a pipe, which may strike you as silly.

JESSE   A cigar then. No, you can't refuse, it's such a pleasant evening.

GALY GAY   Yes, you're right, I really can't say no.

POLLY   And you shall have your cigar.

(*All four go out*)

4

The Widow Leocadia Begbick's Canteen

Soldiers singing the "Song of Widow Begbick's Rolling Bar."

SOLDIERS
In Widow Begbick's rolling bar
You can smoke, sleep, drink ten years or more.
That's what you do in her old car
From Cooch Behar to Singapore.
Oh, in India's sunny clime
The best of men get lost some time
In Widow Begbick's bar to booze and yell
With toddy, gum and hi hi hi,
Passing heaven by and skirting hell.
Keep your mouth shut, Tommy, keep your hat on, Tommy
From the soda mountain to the whisky dell.

In Widow Begbick's rolling bar
Whatever you want's for sale.
All India had seen her car
Before you gave up mother's milk for ale.

Oh, in India's sunny clime
The best of men get lost some time
In Widow Begbick's bar to booze and yell
With toddy, gum and hi hi hi,
Passing heaven by and skirting hell.
Keep your mouth shut, Tommy, keep your hat on, Tommy,
From the soda mountain to the whisky dell.

While battles roar in Punjab Vale,
We'll ride in Widow Begbick's car.
We'll smoke and drink our bloody ale
And show those niggers who we are!
Oh, in India's sunny clime
The best of men get lost some time
In Widow Begbick's bar to booze and yell
With toddy, gum and hi hi hi,
Passing heaven by and skirting hell.
Keep your mouth shut, Tommy, keep your hat on, Tommy,
From the soda mountain to the whisky dell.

BEGBICK (*enters*)   Good evening, gentlemen. I'm the Widow Begbick and this is my beer wagon. Hooked to the long troop trains, it rolls over every railway line in India. And because you can drink beer and travel and sleep all at the same time, it's called Widow Begbick's Beer Wagon. From Hyderabad to Rangoon everybody knows that this is a place of refuge for many a soldier whose feelings have been hurt.
(*In the doorway stand the three soldiers with Galy Gay. They push him behind them*)

URIAH   Is this the Eighth Regiment canteen?

POLLY   Are we addressing the owner of the canteen, the world-famous Widow Begbick? We are the machine-gun detachment of the Eighth Regiment.

BEGBICK   Only three of you? Where's your fourth man? (*They enter without answering, pick up two tables and carry them to the left where they build a kind of partition. The other soldiers look on in astonishment*)

JESSE   What kind of a man is the sergeant?

BEGBICK   Not nice.

POLLY   It's unpleasant to hear that the sergeant is not nice.

BEGBICK   He's known as Bloody Five, the Tiger of Kilkoa, the Human Typhoon. He has an uncanny sense of smell, he can smell out crimes.

(*Jesse, Polly and Uriah look at each other*)

URIAH   Oh!

BEGBICK (*to her guests*)   This is the famous MG-detachment who decided the battle of Hyderabad and are known as "The Scum."

SOLDIERS   And now they've been assigned to us. Their crimes are said to follow them like shadows. (*A soldier brings in a "Wanted" sign and nails it up*) And right behind them there's another of those signs.

(*The guests stand up and slowly leave the canteen. Uriah whistles*)

GALY GAY (*enters*)   I know these high-class places. Music with your dinner. Printed menus. There's a great big one at the Siam Hotel, gold on white. I bought one once. With the right connections you can get anything. One thing on it is Chicauqua Sauce. And that's only a side dish. Chicauqua Sauce!

JESSE (*pushing Galy Gay toward the partition*)   My dear sir, you are in a position to do three poor soldiers in trouble a little favor with no inconvenience to yourself.

POLLY   Our fourth man has been delayed saying good-bye to his wife, and if there aren't four of us at roll call, we'll be thrown into the black dungeons of Kilkoa.

URIAH   So you see, it would help us if you put on one of our uniforms. You'd only have to be present when they count off the new arrivals and answer to his name. A mere formality

JESSE   That's all.

POLLY   And of course a cigar more or less that you might wish to smoke at our expense wouldn't be worth mentioning.

GALY GAY   It's not that I wouldn't like to oblige you, but unfortunately I have to hurry home. I've bought a cucumber for dinner, so you see, I can't do exactly as I should like.

JESSE   Thank you. Frankly, it's just what I expected of you.

You can't do as you'd like. You'd like to go home but you can't. Thank you, sir. You justify the confidence we placed in you the moment we laid eyes on you. Your hand, sir!
(*He seizes Galy Gay's hand. Uriah motions him imperiously to go into the corner behind the tables. As soon as he is in the corner, all three rush him and undress him except for his shirt*)

URIAH   Permit us, for the purpose just mentioned, to clothe you in the honored garb of the glorious British Army. (*He rings. Begbick appears*) Widow Begbick, can a man speak freely around here? We need a complete uniform.
(*Begbick brings out a box and tosses it to Uriah. Uriah throws it to Polly*)

POLLY (*to Galy Gay*)   Here is the honored garb, we've bought it for you.

JESSE (*shows him the trousers*)   Put the garb on, brother Galy Gay.

POLLY (*to Begbick*)   You see, he lost his uniform.
(*The three of them dress Galy Gay*)

BEGBICK   Oh, I see. He lost his uniform.

POLLY   Yes, a Chinaman in the bath house spirited our friend Jip's uniform away.

BEGBICK   Oh, I see. In the bath house?

JESSE   To tell you the truth, Widow Begbick, we're playing a little joke.

BEGBICK   Oh, I see. A joke?

POLLY   Isn't it true, dear sir? Isn't the whole thing a joke?

GALY GAY   Yes, it's got something to do with—with a cigar, you might say. (*He laughs*)
(*The three laugh too*)

BEGBICK   How helpless a weak woman is against four such strong men! No one will ever say that Widow Begbick kept a man from changing his trousers.
(*She goes to the rear and writes on a slate: 1 pair of trousers, 1 tunic, 1 pair of puttees, etc.*)

GALY GAY   What's this all about?

JESSE   Oh, nothing at all.

GALY GAY   Isn't it risky if we're found out?

POLLY   Not in the least. And in your case, one time is no time.

GALY GAY   Yes, that's what they say: one time is no time.

BEGBICK   The uniform will be five shillings an hour.

POLLY   Bloodsucker! Three and not a penny more.

JESSE (*at the window*)   Rain clouds are coming up fast. If it rains now, the palanquin will get wet, and if the palanquin gets wet, they'll take it into the pagoda, and if it's taken into the pagoda, Jip will be discovered, and if Jip is discovered, it will be all up with us.

GALY GAY   Too small. I'll never get into it.

POLLY   That's right, he can't get into it.

GALY GAY   And the boots pinch dreadfully.

POLLY   Everything's too small. Useless! Two shillings.

URIAH   Quiet, Polly. Four shillings because everything is too small, and particularly because the boots pinch so. Don't they?

GALY GAY   Yes, indeed. They pinch particularly.

URIAH   You see, the gentleman isn't a tenderfoot like you, Polly.

BEGBICK (*comes up to Uriah, leads him to the rear and points at the "Wanted" sign*)   This poster has been all over camp for the last hour. It says that a court-martial offense has been committed in the city. The guilty parties have not been found. I'm letting you have the uniform for only five shillings to keep the whole company from being involved in this crime.

POLLY   Four shillings is pretty steep.

URIAH (*comes forward*)   Be still, Polly. Ten shillings.

BEGBICK   Generally speaking, anything that might besmirch the company's honor can be cleared up in Widow Begbick's Rolling Bar.

JESSE   By the way, Widow Begbick, do you think it's going to rain?

BEGBICK   To answer that one, I'd have to take a look at Sergeant Bloody Five. The whole army knows that when it rains he gets into a dreadful state of sensuality. It transforms him outside and in.

JESSE   That's just what I was getting at. It had better not rain while we're playing our joke.

BEGBICK   On the contrary! Once it starts to rain, Bloody Five, the most dangerous man in the British Army, becomes as harmless as a kitten. During his fits of sensuality, he's blind to everything that's going on around him.

A SOLDIER (*calls into the room*)   Everybody out for roll call. It's that pagoda business. It seems a man is missing. They're calling the roll and checking paybooks.

URIAH   His paybook!

GALY GAY (*kneels down and wraps up his old clothes*)   You see, I take good care of my things.

URIAH (*to Galy Gay*)   Here's your paybook. All you have to do is call out our comrade's name, very clearly and as loud as possible. Nothing to it.

POLLY   Our lost comrade's name is Jeraiah Jip. Jeraiah Jip!

GALY GAY   Jeraiah Jip!

URIAH (*to Galy Gay as they walk off*)   It's a pleasure to meet well-bred persons who know how to conduct themselves in any situation.

GALY GAY (*stops just inside the door*)   And what about my tip?

URIAH   A bottle of beer. Come on.

GALY GAY   Gentlemen, as a docker I am obliged to look after my own interests in any situation. I was figuring on two boxes of cigars and four or five bottles of beer.

JESSE   But we need you for that roll call.

GALY GAY   Exactly.

POLLY   All right. Two boxes of cigars and three or four bottles of beer.

GALY GAY   Three boxes and five bottles.

JESSE   What is this? You just said two boxes.

GALY GAY   If that's your attitude, it will be five boxes and eight bottles.

(*A bugle call*)

URIAH   Time to be going.

JESSE   Right. It's a deal if you come along right away.

GALY GAY   Right.

URIAH   And what's your name?

GALY GAY   Jip! Jeraiah Jip!

JESSE   If only it doesn't rain.

(*All four go out. Begbick begins to pull tarpaulins over her wagon*)

POLLY (*comes back; to Begbick*)   Widow Begbick, we've heard that the sergeant becomes very sensual when it rains. And now it's going to rain. See to it that he's blind to everything that goes on around him for the next few hours; if you don't, we shall be in danger of getting caught. (*Goes out*)

BEGBICK (*looking after them*)   That man's name isn't Jip. He's Galy Gay, the docker from Kilkoa, and at this very moment a man who isn't even a soldier is standing in the ranks under the eyes of Bloody Five. (*She takes a mirror and goes to the rear*) I'll stand here where Bloody Five is sure to see me, and lure him in.

(*Second bugle call. Fairchild enters. Begbick looks at him seductively in the mirror and sits down in a chair*)

FAIRCHILD   Don't look at me so devouringly, you white-washed Babylon! Things are bad enough already: Three days ago I took to my bed and started washing in cold water. Thursday my unbridled sensuality compelled me to declare a state of siege on myself. All this is most inconvenient, because only today I sniffed out a crime unparalleled in the annals of the British Army.

BEGBICK

Follow, O Bloody Five, your powerful nature
Unseen! For who will know?
And in the pit of my arm, in my hair
Discover who you are. In the crook of my knee forget
Your accidental name.
Pitiful discipline! Pathetic order!
I entreat you, Bloody Five, come
To me in this night of warm rain
Just as you fear to come: as a man.
As a contradiction. As doesn't-want-to-but-must.
Come now as a man! As nature made you
Without a steel helmet! Confused and wild and wrapped up
   in yourself

Defenseless against your passions
The helpless victim of your strength.
Come—as a man!

FAIRCHILD   Never. The downfall of mankind began when the first of these Zulus left a button undone. The Infantry Training Manual has its weaknesses, but it's the only thing a man can fall back on, because it builds character and takes over man's responsibility before God. We ought to dig a hole in the ground and put dynamite in it and blow up the whole planet. That would show them we mean business. It stands to reason! But can you, Bloody Five, live through this rainy night without the widow's flesh?

BEGBICK   So, when you come to me tonight, I want you to wear a black suit and a bowler hat.

A VOICE OF COMMAND   Machine-gunners out for roll call.

FAIRCHILD   Now I must sit by this door post so as to keep an eye on that scum they're counting off. (*Sits down*)

VOICES OF THE THREE SOLDIERS (*outside*)   Polly Baker.—Uriah Shelley.—Jesse Mahoney.

FAIRCHILD   Ha, and now there will be a brief pause.

GALY GAY'S VOICE (*outside*)   Jeraiah Jip!

BEGBICK   Right.

FAIRCHILD   They're up to something again. Insubordination outside and insubordination inside. (*He stands up and starts to leave*)

BEGBICK (*calls after him*)   Just let me tell you this, Sergeant. Before the black rains of Nepal have fallen three nights, you will take a more lenient view of human failings, for you are probably the most sex-ridden man under the sun. You will sit down at a table with insubordination and the men who desecrated the temple will look deep into your eyes, for your own crimes will be numberless as the sand of the sea.

FAIRCHILD   Ho, my dear, in that case, believe me, we will take action against that insubordinate little Bloody Five; we will set an example for all time. It stands to reason. (*Goes out*)

FAIRCHILD'S VOICE (*outside*) Eight men up to the navel in hot sand for not having regulation haircuts!
(*Enter Uriah, Jesse and Polly with Galy Gay. Galy Gay steps forward*)

URIAH   A pair of scissors, please, widow Begbick!

GALY GAY (*to the audience*)   A little favor between men can't do any harm. Live and let live, that's my motto. Now I'll down a glass of beer as if it were water and say to myself: I've done these gentlemen a good turn. The one thing that counts in the world is to take a chance and say "Jeraiah Jip" same as another man would say "Good evening"—and to be what people want you to be, because it's so easy.
(*Begbick comes back with a pair of scissors*)

URIAH   And now let's see about Jip!

JESSE   A bad storm is blowing up.
(*The three turn to Galy Gay*)

URIAH   Sorry, sir, we're in a hurry.

JESSE   You see, we have to crop a gentleman's hair. (*They turn to the door. Galy Gay runs after them*)

GALY GAY   Couldn't I help you with that, too?

URIAH   No. We don't need you any more, sir. (*To Begbick*) Five boxes of cheap cigars and eight bottles of stout for this man. (*On the way out*) Some people keep poking their noses into other people's business. Give them a finger and they take a whole hand.
(*The three hurry out*)

GALY GAY

Now I could go away, but
Should a man go away when he is sent away?
After he's gone, perhaps
He'll be needed again. And can a man go away
When he is needed? Unless it has to be
A man should not go away.
(*Galy Gay goes to the rear and sits down in a chair by the door. Begbick takes beer bottles and cigar boxes and places them in a circle on the ground in front of Galy Gay*)

BEGBICK   Haven't we met? (*Galy Gay shakes his head*) Aren't you the man who carried my basket of cucumbers for me? (*Galy Gay shakes his head*) Isn't your name Galy Gay?

GALY GAY   No.

(*Begbick goes out, shaking her head. It grows dark. Galy Gay falls asleep in his chair. Rain falls. Begbick is heard singing to soft music*)

BEGBICK

No matter how often you look at the river, lazily
Flowing along, never will you see the same water.
Never will what flows down, never a drop of it
Turn back to its source.

5

Interior of the Pagoda of the Yellow God

Wang, the bonze, and his sacristan.

SACRISTAN   It's raining.

WANG   Bring our leather palanquin in out of the rain! (*The sacristan goes out*) Now today's takings have been stolen. And it's raining in on my head through those bullet holes. (*The sacristan drags the palanquin in. Moaning from within*) What's that? (*He looks in*) I knew it would be a white man when I saw how filthy the palanquin was. Oh, he's wearing a uniform! And he has a bald spot, the thief! They've gone and cut his hair off. What shall we do with him? A soldier and therefore devoid of understanding. A soldier of the Queen, covered with vomited liquor, more helpless than a newborn chick, too drunk to know his own mother. We could make a present of him to the police. But what good would that do? When the money is gone, what good is justice? All he can do is grunt. (*Furiously*) Take him out, you hole-in-a-Swiss-cheese, and stuff him into the prayer box, but make sure his head is on top. About all we can do is make a god of him. (*The sacristan puts Jip into the prayer box*) Bring me some paper. We must hang out paper flags immediately. We must paint posters for all we're worth. No false economy. I mean to do this on a large scale with posters that people can't overlook. What good is a god that nobody talks about? (*Knocking at the door*) Who can be knocking at this late hour?

POLLY   Three soldiers.

WANG   They are his comrades. (*He admits the three*)

POLLY   We are looking for a gentleman, or more precisely a soldier, who is sleeping in a leather box that was outside this rich and distinguished temple.

WANG   May his awakening be pleasant!

POLLY   But you see, the box has disappeared.

WANG   I understand your impatience, which springs from uncertainty; for I myself am looking for some men, perhaps three in all, soldiers to be precise, and I cannot find them.

URIAH   That will be very difficult. I think you may as well give up. But we thought you might know something about that leather box.

WANG   Unfortunately not. The disagreeable part of it is that all you honorable soldiers wear the same clothes.

JESSE   Nothing disagreeable about that. At the present time there is a very sick man in the aforementioned leather box.

POLLY   Moreover, having lost a certain amount of hair as a result of his illness, he is in urgent need of help.

URIAH   Have you seen such a man?

WANG   Unfortunately not. However, I have found some hair. But a sergeant in your army took it away with him. He wished to return it to the honorable soldier.

(*Jip groans inside the prayer box*)

POLLY   What's that, sir?

WANG   That is my cow, sleeping.

URIAH   Your cow doesn't seem to sleep very well.

POLLY   This is the palanquin we stuffed Jip into. Do you mind if we examine it?

WANG   It will be best if I tell you the whole truth. This is a different palanquin.

POLLY   It's as full of vomit as a slop bucket on the third day of Christmas. Jesse, it's clear that Jip was here.

WANG   You see? He could not have been in it. Nobody would get into such a filthy palanquin.

(*Jip groans loudly*)

URIAH   We must have our fourth man. Even if we have to murder our own grandmother.

WANG   The man you are looking for is not here. But to make it clear to you that the man who in your opinion is here but of whose presence I have no knowledge is not your man, allow me to explain the whole situation with the help of a sketch. Permit your unworthy servant to draw four criminals with chalk. (*He draws on the door of the prayer box*)

One of them has a face, it is possible to tell who he is; the other three have no faces, they cannot be recognized. Now the man with the face has no money. Consequently he is not a thief. But those who have the money are without faces, consequently they cannot be known. That is, they cannot be known unless they are together. Once they are together, the three faceless men will grow faces, and stolen money will be found on them. You will never make me believe that a man who might be here is your man.

(*The three threaten him with their weapons, but at a sign from Wang the sacristan appears with Chinese worshipers*)

JESSE   We shall not disturb your night's rest any longer, sir. Besides, your tea doesn't agree with us. Your drawing, to be sure, is very clever. Come along!

WANG   It grieves me to see you go.

URIAH   Do you really believe that when our comrade wakes up, no matter where, wild horses will prevent him from coming back to us?

WANG   Wild horses may not, but perhaps a small portion of domestic horse. Who knows?

URIAH   Once he's got the beer out of his brain, he'll be back.
(*The three leave amid deep bows*)

JIP (*in the prayer box*)   Hey!
(*Wang draws the attention of the worshipers to his god*)

6

The Canteen

Late at night. Galy Gay is sitting in his chair, still asleep. The three soldiers appear in the window.

POLLY   He's still sitting there. Doesn't he make you think of an Irish mammoth?

URIAH   Maybe he didn't want to leave on account of the rain.

JESSE   Maybe so. But now we're going to need him again.

POLLY   Don't you think Jip is coming back?

JESSE   Uriah, I know that Jip is not coming back.

POLLY   I don't see how we can tell this docker the same story again.

JESSE   What do you think, Uriah?

URIAH   I think I'm going to doss down.

POLLY   But if this docker gets up now and goes out that door, our heads will be hanging by a hair.

JESSE   Definitely. But I'm turning in now too. You can't expect too much of a man.

POLLY   Maybe we had all better doss down. It's too depressing and it's really all the fault of the rain.
(*The three go out*)

7

Interior of the Pagoda of the Yellow God

Toward morning. Large posters on all sides. The sound of an old phonograph and of a drum. Religious ceremonies seem to be going on in the background.

WANG (*approaches the prayer box; to the sacristan*) Roll those balls of camel-dung more quickly, you stinkpot! (*Close to the prayer box*) Is the honorable soldier still asleep?

JIP (*inside*) Are we getting out soon, Jesse? This car is shaking abominably, and it's as cramped as a shithouse.

WANG Honorable soldier, you must not imagine that you are in a railway car. If anything is shaking, it is the beer in your honorable head.

JIP (*inside*) Nonsense! What's that voice on the phonograph? Can't it stop?

WANG Come out, honorable soldier, eat a piece of cow meat!

JIP (*inside*) Oh, Polly, can I really have a piece of meat? (*He pounds on the sides of the prayer box*)

WANG (*running to the rear*) Quiet, you wretches. The god demands five taels. Hear him knocking on the walls of the holy prayer box. A grace is being shown unto you. Collect the offerings, Mah Sing.

JIP (*inside*) Uriah, Uriah, where am I?

WANG Knock a little more, honorable soldier. On the other side now, honorable general, kick with both feet vehemently.

JIP (*inside*) Hey, what is this? Where am I? Where are you? Uriah, Jesse, Polly!

WANG Your humble servant wishes to know what food and strong drink the honorable soldier commands.

JIP (*inside*)   Hey, who's that? What is that voice that sounds like the voice of a fat rat?

WANG   The moderately fat rat, colonel, is your friend Wang from Tientsin.

JIP (*inside*)   What city am I in now?

WANG   A wretched city, exalted patron, a hole known as Kilkoa.

JIP (*inside*)   Let me out!

WANG (*to the rear*)   When you have rolled the camel-dung into balls, lay them out on a platter, beat the drum and light them. (*To Jip*) At once, honorable soldier, if only you promise not to run away.

JIP (*inside*)   Open up, you voice of a muskrat. Open up, do you hear!

WANG   Wait, wait, ye faithful! Stay where you are for just one moment. The god speaks to you in three thunderclaps. Count them carefully. Four, no five. Too bad. Five taels is all he asks you to sacrifice. (*Taps on the prayer box; in a friendly tone*) Honorable soldier, here's a beefsteak to put in your mouth.

JIP (*inside*)   Oh, now I feel it, my insides are corroded. I must have rinsed them in pure alcohol. Yes, perhaps I have had too much to drink, and now I shall have to eat just as much.

WANG   You may eat a whole cow, honorable soldier, and a beefsteak is ready now. But I fear you will run away, honorable soldier. Do you promise me that you will not run away?

JIP (*inside*)   First let me see the steak. (*Wang lets him out*) How did I get here?

WANG   Through the air, honorable general. You came through the air.

JIP   Where was I when you found me?

WANG   Deigning to rest in an old palanquin, Exalted One.

JIP   And where are my comrades? Where is the Eighth Regiment? Where is the machine-gun detachment? Where are those twelve troop trains and four elephant parks? Where is the whole British Army? Where have they all gone, you yellow, grinning spittoon?

WANG   They went off beyond the Punjab Mountains a month ago. But here is your beefsteak.

JIP   What? What about me? Where was I? What was I doing when they marched away?

WANG   Beer. Much beer. A thousand bottles. And making money too.

JIP   Didn't some men come asking for me?

WANG   Unfortunately not.

JIP   That's bad news.

WANG   But if they should come now, looking for a man in the uniform of a white soldier, should I bring them to you, honorable Minister of War?

JIP   There's no need of that.

WANG   If you don't wish to be disturbed, Johnny, just step into this box, Johnny, if anyone comes who offends your eye.

JIP   Where's that beefsteak? (*Sits down and eats*) It's much too little. What is that ghastly noise?

(*The drum sounds and the smoke of the camel-dung balls rises to the ceiling*)

WANG   That is the prayers of the faithful who are down on their knees back there.

JIP   It's from a tough part of the cow. Who are they praying to?

WANG   That is their secret.

JIP   (*eating more quickly*)   This is a good beefsteak, but it's wrong that I should be sitting here. Polly and Jesse must have waited for me. Maybe they're still waiting. It's as soft as butter. It's not right for me to be eating. I can hear Polly talking to Jesse: Jip is sure to come back. As soon as he sobers up, Jip will be back. Maybe Uriah won't burst himself waiting, because Uriah is no good, but Jesse and Polly will say: Jip will be back. No doubt about it, this is just the right kind of meal for me after all that liquor. If only Jesse didn't trust his old friend Jip so blindly. But I know he's saying: Jip won't let us down. Naturally that's hard for me to bear. It's all wrong that I should be sitting here, but the meat is good.

8

The Canteen

Early morning. Galy Gay is still asleep in his chair. The three are eating breakfast.

POLLY   Jip will be back.

JESSE   Jip won't let us down.

POLLY   As soon as he sobers up, Jip will be back.

URIAH   You never can tell. In any case we won't let this docker out of our hands as long as Jip's in the bush.

JESSE   He didn't go away.

POLLY   He must be frozen stiff. He's spent the whole night on this wooden chair.

URIAH   While we had a good night's sleep and are in fine shape again.

POLLY   I say that Jip will be back. That is clear to my sound, well-rested, military mind. When Jip wakes up, he will want his beer, and then Jip will be back.

(*Enter Wang. He goes to the bar and rings. Widow Begbick enters*)

BEGBICK   I don't serve native trouble makers. Nor yellow ones either.

WANG   It's for a white man: ten bottles of good light beer.

BEGBICK   Ten bottles of light beer for a white man? (*She gives him the ten bottles*)

WANG   Yes, for a white man. (*Wang goes out, bowing to all. Jesse, Polly and Uriah exchange looks*)

URIAH   Jip won't be back now. We'd better tank up on beer. Widow Begbick, from now on would you keep twenty beers and ten whiskeys available at all times?

(*Begbick pours beer and goes out. The three drink and observe the sleeping Galy Gay*)

POLLY   But how are we going to pull it off, Uriah? All we've got is Jip's paybook.

URIAH This will do. This is all it will take to make a new Jip. There's too much fuss about people. One man is no man. Anything less than two hundred men at a time isn't worth mentioning. Of course anybody can have a different opinion. What's an opinion? An easygoing man can easily adopt two or three different opinions.

JESSE People who talk about "personality" can kiss my ass.

POLLY But what will he say if we turn him into Private Jeraiah Jip?

URIAH His kind change of their own accord. Throw him into a pond, and in two days he'll grow webs between his fingers. That's because he has nothing to lose.

JESSE Never mind how he takes it; we need a fourth man. Wake him up.

POLLY (*wakes Galy Gay*) Dear sir; it's a good thing you didn't go away. Circumstances have arisen which prevented our friend Jeraiah Jip from reporting here on time.

URIAH You're Irish, aren't you?

GALY GAY I think so.

URIAH That is fortunate. I trust you're not over forty, Mr. Galy Gay?

GALY GAY Oh no!

URIAH Excellent. Have you flat feet?

GALY GAY Slightly.

URIAH That settles it. Your fortune is made. You can stay here for the time being.

GALY GAY Unfortunately, my wife is waiting for me. On account of a fish.

POLLY We understand your hesitations. They are honorable and worthy of an Irishman. But we like your looks.

JESSE And what's more, you look the part. There's a possibility of your becoming a soldier.

(*Galy Gay is silent*)

URIAH A soldier's life is extremely pleasant. Every week they give us a handful of money and all we have to do is hike around India gazing at the highways and pagodas. Kindly take a look at the comfortable leather sleeping bags that are issued to a soldier free of charge. Cast a glance at this rifle with the trademark of Everett & Co. Mostly we amuse ourselves fishing, with tackle bought for us by Mum, as we jokingly call the army, while several military bands take turns providing music. You spend the rest of the day smoking in your bungalow or looking lazily at the golden palace of one of those rajahs, whom you can also shoot if you happen to be in the mood. The ladies expect a good deal of a soldier, but never money, and that, you will agree, is one more advantage.

(*Galy Gay is silent*)

POLLY   In wartime a soldier's life is especially pleasant. Only in battle does a man attain his full stature. Are you aware that you are living in momentous times? Before every attack a soldier is given a large glass of whiskey free of charge, after which his courage knows no bounds, that's it, no bounds.

GALY GAY   I can see a soldier's life is very pleasant.

URIAH   Definitely. So now, of course, you'll keep your uniform with its attractive brass buttons, and from this day on you can insist on being addressed at all times as Mr., Mr. Jip.

GALY GAY   You can't wish to make a poor docker unhappy?

JESSE   Why not?

URIAH   You mean you're going away?

GALY GAY   Yes, I'm going now.

JESSE   Polly, go and get his clothes.

POLLY   (*with the clothes*)   Why don't you want to be Jip?
(*Fairchild appears at the window*)

GALY GAY   Because I'm Galy Gay. (*He goes to the door*)
(*The three look at one another*)

URIAH   Wait just a minute.

POLLY   Have you ever heard the saying: More haste less speed?

URIAH   We are not the kind of men who like to accept favors from strangers.

JESSE   Whatever your name may be, you must be rewarded for your kindness.

URIAH   It's about—all right, keep your hand on the doorknob—it's about a business deal.
(*Galy Gay stops short*)

JESSE   You'll never find a better in Kilkoa, am I right, Polly? You know what I mean? If we can lay our hands on . . .

URIAH   We feel honor-bound to offer you a share in this stupendous business deal.

GALY GAY   Deal? Did you say deal?

URIAH   Possibly. But you have no time.

GALY GAY   There's such a thing as having time and not having time.

POLLY   I say you'd have time. If you knew about this deal, you'd have time. Lord Kitchener had time to conquer Egypt.

GALY GAY   I should think so. Then it's a big deal?

POLLY   It might be for the Maharajah of Peshawar. But maybe it wouldn't look so big to a big man like you.

GALY GAY   What would I be expected to do in this deal?

JESSE   Not a thing.

POLLY   At the most you might have to sacrifice your mustache. It might attract unwanted attention.

GALY GAY   I see. (*He takes his things and starts for the door*)

POLLY   What an elephant!

GALY GAY   Elephant? An elephant! Say, that's a gold mine. You'll never end in the poorhouse if you've got an elephant. (*Excitedly takes a chair and sits down in the middle of the group*)

URIAH   Elephant! Of course we've got an elephant!

GALY GAY   And you've got this elephant on hand?

POLLY   Elephant! He seems to have a thing about elephants.

GALY GAY   So you've got an elephant on hand?

POLLY   Have you ever heard of a deal over an elephant that wasn't on hand?

GALY GAY   Well, in that case, Mr. Polly, cut me in on the deal.

URIAH   (*hesitantly*)   There's only one trouble: the Devil of Kilkoa.

GALY GAY   The Devil of Kilkoa? What's that?

POLLY   Shh! Not so loud. You're pronouncing the name of the Human Typhoon, Bloody Five, our sergeant.

GALY GAY   What does he do to get names like that?

POLLY   Oh, nothing. Now and then when a man gives a wrong

name at roll call, he wraps him up in six feet of canvas and throws him under the elephants.

GALY GAY   In that case, you need a man with a head on his shoulders.

URIAH   You've got that head, Mr. Galy Gay.

POLLY   That head has something in it!

GALY GAY   Not worth mentioning. But I do know a riddle that might be of interest to cultivated gentlemen like you.

JESSE   We are, indeed, expert at riddles.

GALY GAY   It goes like this: What is white, a mammal, and sees as well behind as in front?

JESSE   That's a hard one.

GALY GAY   You'll never guess this riddle. I couldn't guess it myself. A mammal. White. Sees as well behind as in front. A blind white horse.

URIAH   That's an amazing riddle.

POLLY   And you can keep all that in your head?

GALY GAY   Most of the time, because I'm not very good at writing. But I believe I'm the right man for almost any deal.

(*The three go to the bar. Galy Gay takes a box of his cigars and passes it around*)

URIAH   Light, please.

GALY GAY   (*while lighting their cigars*)   Gentlemen, permit me to prove that you haven't chosen a bad business partner. Do you happen to have some heavy objects handy?

JESSE   (*points to some weights and clubs lying along the wall near the door*)   Over there!

GALY GAY   (*taking the heaviest weight and lifting it*)   You see, I'm a member of the Kilkoa Wrestling Club.

URIAH   (*handing him a bottle of beer*)   We can tell that by your behavior.

GALY GAY   (*drinking*)   Yes, we wrestlers have our own way of behaving. There are certain rules. For instance, when a wrestler enters a room full of people, he hoists his shoulders, raises his arms to shoulder height, and stands by the door for a moment. Then he lets his arms dangle and saunters into the room. (*He drinks*) With me for a partner you can't go wrong.

FAIRCHILD (*enters*)   There's a woman outside looking for a man called Galy Gray.

GALY GAY   Galy Gay! The man she's looking for is called Galy Gay!
(*Fairchild looks at him for a moment and then goes to get Mrs. Galy Gay*)

GALY GAY (*to the three*)   Don't worry. She's a gentle soul. She comes from a province where almost all the people are friendly. You can count on me. Galy Gay has tasted blood.

FAIRCHILD   Come in, Mrs. Gray. There's a man here who knows your husband. (*He comes back with Galy Gay's wife*)

MRS. GALY GAY   Excuse a humble woman, gentlemen, and pardon the way I am dressed, I was in such a hurry. Ah, there you are, Galy Gay. But can it really be you in that uniform?

GALY GAY   No.

MRS. GALY GAY   I can't make you out. How did you get into that uniform? It's not at all becoming to you, anyone will tell you that. You're a strange man, Galy Gay.

URIAH   She isn't right in the head.

MRS. GALY GAY   It's no joke being married to a man who can't say no.

GALY GAY   I wonder who she's talking to.

URIAH   Sounds like insults to me.

FAIRCHILD   In my opinion, Mrs. Gray is perfectly clear in her mind. Please go on, Mrs. Gray. I'd rather hear your voice than any opera singer's.

MRS. GALY GAY   I don't know what you're up to this time with your big ideas, but you'll come to no good end. Come along now. Why don't you say something? Lost your voice?

GALY GAY   You appear to be talking to me. I tell you, you've mistaken me for someone else, and what you're saying about him is stupid and out of place.

MRS. GALY GAY   What's that? I'm mistaking you? Have you been drinking? Drink doesn't agree with him, you see.

GALY GAY   I'm no more your Galy Gay than I'm commander in chief of the army.

MRS. GALY GAY   I put the water on the fire at this time yesterday, but you never brought the fish.

GALY GAY   What's this about a fish? You talk like a madwoman. And in front of all these gentlemen!

FAIRCHILD   This is an extraordinary case. It brings such terrible thoughts to mind that cold shivers run down my spine. Does any of you know this woman? (*The three shake their heads*) And you?

GALY GAY   I've seen many things in my life, between Ireland and Kilkoa, but I have never laid eyes on this woman.

FAIRCHILD   Tell the woman your name.

GALY GAY   Jeraiah Jip.

MRS. GALY GAY   This is outrageous! Still, when I come to look at him, sergeant, I almost get the feeling that he is somehow a little different from my husband Galy Gay, the docker. A little different, though I can't put my finger on it.

FAIRCHILD   Never mind, we'll soon put our finger on it.
  (*He goes out with Mrs. Galy Gay*)

GALY GAY (*dances to the center of the stage, singing*)

Oh moon of Alabama,
It's time you said good-bye.
Our dear old good old mama
Wants new moons in the sky.

(*He goes up to Jesse beaming*) All over Ireland the Galy Gays have a reputation for hitting the nail on the head.

URIAH (*to Polly*)   Before the sun sets seven times, this man must be another man.

POLLY   Can it really be done, Uriah? Changing one man into another?

URIAH   Yes. One man is like another. A man's a man.

POLLY   But, Uriah, the army can move off any minute.

URIAH   Of course the army can move off any minute. But this canteen is still here, isn't it? Don't you realize that the artillery is still putting on horse races? Do you think God would ruin men like us by marching the army off today? He'd think twice before doing a thing like that.

POLLY   Listen.
(*Drums and trumpets give the signal for departure. The three line up and stand at attention*)
FAIRCHILD (*shouting backstage*)   The Army is leaving for the northern border. Move off at zero two ten hours!

Interlude

Spoken by the Widow Leocadia Begbick.

A man's a man, says Mr. Bertolt Brecht
And that is hardly more than you'd expect.
But Mr. Bertolt Brecht goes on to show
That you can change a man from top to toe.
You'll see a man remodeled like a car
Without incurring the slightest loss or scar.
You'll see this man by the friendly treatment bested.
Gently but firmly he will be requested
To run with the wolves, however devilish
And forget about his private fish.
And whatever they may choose to make of him
They have made no mistake in him.
He's capable, if we let him out of sight
Of turning into a butcher overnight.
Mr. Brecht hopes the ground on which you stand
Will sink beneath your feet like shifting sand
And that while watching Galy Gay you'll see
That life on earth from danger is not free.

9

The Canteen

The sounds of an army breaking camp. A loud voice is heard from backstage.

THE VOICE   The long-expected war has broken out. The Army is moving off to the northern border. The Queen commands her troops, with their elephants and cannon, to entrain, and the trains to head for the northern border. Your general therefore commands you to take your places in the trains before the moon has risen.
(*Widow Begbick sits behind the bar, smoking*)

BEGBICK
In Jehu the city that's always crowded and
Where no one stays, they have a song
About the flux of things. It
Starts like this:

(*Sings*)
Oh, cling not to the wave
Breaking against your foot. As long as your
Foot stands in the water
New waves on it will break.

(*She stands up, takes a stick and starts pushing back the canvas roof*)

I lived seven years in one place. I had a roof over
My head
And I was not alone.
But the man who fed me and hadn't his like
One day
Lay unrecognizable under the sheet of the dead.

And yet that evening too I ate my supper.
And soon I rented out the room in which we had
Embraced.
And the room fed me.
And now that it feeds me no longer
I am still eating.
And I said:

(*Sings*)
Oh, cling not to the wave
Breaking against your foot. As long as your
Foot stands in the water
New waves on it will break.

(*She sits down at the bar again. The three enter with several other soldiers*)

URIAH (*in the center*) Comrades, war has broken out. The days of disorder are over. Private preferences must be put aside. Galy Gay, the docker from Kilkoa, must therefore be transformed into the soldier Jeraiah Jip, and at the double. To this end we shall involve him in a business deal, as people do nowadays, and this will require us to build an artificial elephant. Polly, take this pole and that elephant's head hanging on the wall. And you, Jesse, take this bottle and pour whenever Galy Gay looks to see whether the elephant can make water. I'll spread this map over the two of you. (*They build an artificial elephant*) We'll make him a present of this elephant and bring him a buyer. And when he sells the elephant, we'll arrest him and say: How dare you sell an elephant that's Army property? At that point, surely, he'll prefer to be Jeraiah Jip, the soldier on his way to the northern border, rather than Galy Gay, the criminal, who stands a good chance of being shot.

A SOLDIER Do you really think he'll take this for an elephant?

JESSE Does it look as bad as all that?

URIAH Of course he'll take it for an elephant. He'd take this beer bottle for an elephant if somebody pointed at it and said: I'll buy this elephant.

SOLDIER Then what you need is a buyer.

URIAH (*calling out*) Widow Begbick! (*Begbick steps forward*) Will you play the buyer?

BEGBICK Yes, because if nobody helps me pack, my beer wagon will be left behind.

URIAH Just tell the man who's coming now that you'd like to buy this elephant, and we'll help you pack up your canteen. You buy, we pack.

BEGBICK Agreed. (*She goes back to her place*)

GALY GAY (*enters*) Is the elephant here?

URIAH Mr. Gay, the deal is in full swing. It concerns the supernumerary and unregistered Army elephant, Billy Humph. The deal consists in unobtrusively auctioning him off, to a private party, of course.

GALY GAY That's plain enough. But who's going to auction him off?

URIAH Someone who signs as owner.

GALY GAY But who's going to sign as owner?

URIAH Would you like to sign as owner, Mr. Gay?

GALY GAY It there a buyer?

URIAH Yes.

GALY GAY I mustn't be named of course.

URIAH Of course not. Would you care to smoke a cigar?

GALY GAY (*suspicious*) Why?

URIAH Just to keep you from worrying. You see, the elephant has a slight cold.

GALY GAY Where's the buyer?

BEGBICK (*comes forward*) Oh, Mr. Galy Gay, I'm looking for an elephant. Do you happen to have one?

GALY GAY For you I may have one, Widow Begbick.

BEGBICK But first take the walls down, the artillery will be here soon.

THE SOLDIERS Yes, Widow Begbick.

(*The soldiers take down one wall of the canteen. The elephant can be seen dimly*)

JESSE (*to Begbick*) I tell you, Widow Begbick, that taking the long view, what we are doing here is a historic event. What are we doing here? We are examining personality under a microscope, dissecting the individual. Drastic action. Technology steps in. At the lathe or the conveyor belt the great man and the little man are the same, look at their stature. Personality! The ancient Assyrians, Widow Begbick, conceived of the personality as a tree branching out. Like this, branching out. And then, Widow Begbick, it branches in again. What does Copernicus say? What turns? The earth turns. The earth, and therefore, man. Says Copernicus. Therefore, man is not in the center. Just take a look at him! *That* in the center? Ancient history. Man is nothing. Modern science has proved that everything is relative. What does that mean? Table, bench, water, shoe horn—all relative. You, Widow Begbick, and I—relative. Look me in the eye, Widow Begbick, this is a historic moment. Man is in the center, but only relatively. (*Both go out*)

Number 1

URIAH (*announcing*)   Number One: the Elephant Deal. The MG-detachment turns over an elephant to the man who doesn't wish to be named.

GALY GAY   Another swig of that cherry brandy, another puff on this Corona-Corona, and then the plunge into life!

URIAH (*introduces the elephant to Galy Gay*)   Billy Humph, champion of Bengal, elephant in the service of the Grand Army.

GALY GAY (*sees the elephant. Alarmed*)   Is this the Army elephant?

A SOLDIER   He's got a bad cold. You can see by the muffler.

GALY GAY (*rather worried, walks around the elephant*)   The muffler's not the worst of it.

BEGBICK   I'm the buyer. (*She points to the elephant*) Sell me this elephant.

GALY GAY   You really want to buy this elephant?

BEGBICK   Big or little, it's all the same to me. I've wanted to buy an elephant ever since I was a little girl.

GALY GAY   Is he really what you imagined?

BEGBICK   As a little girl I wanted an elephant as big as the Hindu Kush, but now this one will do.

GALY GAY   Well, Widow Begbick, if you really wish to buy this elephant, I am the owner.

A SOLDIER (*comes running from the rear*)   Psst . . . psst . . . Bloody Five is going around camp inspecting the troop trains.

THE SOLDIERS   The Human Typhoon!

BEGBICK   Stay here. Nobody's going to take this elephant away from me.
   (*Begbick and the soldiers hurry out*)

URIAH (*to Galy Gay*)   Take care of the elephant a minute.
   (*Hands him the rope*)

GALY GAY   But what about me, Mr. Uriah, where should I go?

URIAH   Stay right here. (*He runs out after the other soldiers*)
   (*Galy Gay holds the rope by the extreme end*)

GALY GAY (*alone*)   My mother used to say: Nobody knows anything for certain. But *you* don't know anything at all. This morning, Galy Gay, you went out to buy a small fish. Now you've got a big elephant, and nobody knows what will happen tomorrow. Why worry as long as you get your check?

URIAH (*looks in*)   So help me, he's not even looking at the elephant. He's keeping as far away from him as he can. (*Fairchild is seen passing by in the rear*) The Tiger of Kilkoa was only passing by.
   (*Uriah, Begbick and the other soldiers come back again*)

Number II

URIAH (*announcing*)   Now comes Number Two: the Elephant Auction. The man who doesn't wish to be named sells the elephant.

(*Galy Gay fetches a bell. Widow Begbick sets a wooden bucket upside-down in the center of the stage*)

A SOLDIER   Have you any further doubts about the elephant?

GALY GAY   As someone's buying him, I have no doubts.

URIAH   Sure enough, if someone's buying him, he must be all right.

GALY GAY   I can't say no to that. An elephant is an elephant, especially if someone's buying him. (*He stands on the bucket to auction off the elephant, who is standing beside him in the center of the group*) Let's start the auction! I hereby put up for auction Billy Humph, champion of Bengal. He was born, as true as he's standing here, in the southern Punjab. Seven rajahs attended his cradle. His mother was white. He is sixty-five years old. A mere youngster. Weight: fourteen hundred pounds. To him a forest to be cleared is like grass in the wind. Billy Humph, just as he is, will be worth a small fortune to his happy owner.

URIAH   And here comes Widow Begbick with the check.

BEGBICK   Does this elephant belong to you?

GALY GAY   Like my own foot.

A SOLDIER   Billy must be pretty old; he seems uncommonly stiff.

BEGBICK   In that case, you'll have to come down on the price a little.

GALY GAY   He originally cost two hundred rupees, and that's what he'll be worth to his dying day.

BEGBICK (*examining him*)   Two hundred rupees with that sagging belly?

GALY GAY   All the same I believe he's just the thing for a widow.

BEGBICK   Very well. But is he in good health? (*Billy Humph makes water*) That's enough for me. I can see he's a healthy elephant. Five hundred rupees.

GAILY GAY   Five hundred rupees. Going! Going! Gone! He's yours, Widow Begbick! As the present owner of this elephant, I hereby turn him over to you. Your check, if you please.

BEGBICK   Your name?

GALY GAY   Is not to be named.

BEGBICK   Kindly lend me a pencil, Mr. Uriah, so I can make out a check to this gentleman who doesn't wish to be named.

URIAH (*aside to the soldiers*)   When he takes the check, lay hands on him.

BEGBICK   Here is your check, man who doesn't wish to be named.

GALY GAY   And here, Widow Begbick, is your elephant.

A SOLDIER (*placing his hand on Galy Gay's shoulder*)   In the name of the British Army, what are you doing?

GALY GAY   Me? Nothing. (*He laughs foolishly*)

THE SOLDIER   What's that elephant you've got there?

GALY GAY   Which one do you mean?

THE SOLDIER   Mostly the one behind you. Don't try to worm out of this, you!

GALY GAY   I do not know the elephant.

SOLDIER   Go on!

A SOLDIER   We can testify that this gentleman said this elephant belonged to him.

BEGBICK   He said it belonged to him like his own foot.

GALY GAY (*starts to go*)   Sorry, but I've got to go home. My wife is waiting for me impatiently. (*He forces his way through the group*) I'll be back to discuss the matter with you. Good evening! (*To Billy who is following him*) Stay here, Billy. Don't be so obstinate. There's some sugar cane over there.

URIAH   Halt! Cover that criminal with your army revolvers. That's what he is, a criminal.

(*Polly inside Billy Humph laughs loudly. Uriah hits him*)

URIAH   Shut up, Polly!

(*The front canvas slips off, Polly becomes visible*)

POLLY   Damn!

(*Galy Gay, now utterly bewildered, looks at Polly. Then he looks from one to the other. The elephant runs away*)

BEGBICK   What is this? That's no elephant, it's nothing but men and canvas. It's a fraud! A phony elephant for my good money!

URIAH   Widow Begbick, we will bind the criminal immediately and throw him into the latrine.

(*The soldiers bind Galy Gay and put him into a pit, so that only his head is visible. The artillery is heard rolling by*)

BEGBICK   They're loading the artillery. When are you going to pack my canteen? It's not just that man of yours, my canteen has to be dismantled too.

(*All the soldiers begin packing up the canteen. Before they have finished, Uriah chases them away. Begbick comes for-*

ward with a basket of dirty canvas, kneels down beside a small hollow in the ground and washes the canvas. Galy Gay listens to her song)

BEGBICK

So I too had a name,
And everyone who heard that name in the city said: that's
      a good
Name.
But one night I drank four glasses of whisky.
And next morning written in chalk on my door I found a
Bad word.
After that the milkman took the milk away.
My name was ruined
(She shows the linen)
Like linen that was white and gets dirty
And can turn white again if you wash it
But hold it up to the light and you'll see it's not
The same linen.
Don't harp on your name. What's the point
When the person you're referring to is always another?
And why sound off so loud with your opinion? Forget it.
Which one was it anyway? Why remember
A thing any longer than that thing endures?

(Sings)
Oh, cling not to the wave
Breaking against your foot. As long as your
Foot stands in the water
New waves on it will break.

(She goes out. Uriah and the soldiers come in from the rear)

Number III

URIAH *(announcing)*   Now comes Number Three: the Trial
of the Man who didn't Wish to be Named. Form a circle

around the criminal, question him, and don't stop until you know the naked truth.

GALY GAY   May I please say something?

URIAH   You've said a lot tonight. Who knows the name of the man who put the elephant up for auction?

A SOLDIER   His name was Galy Gay.

URIAH   Who can testify to that?

THE SOLDIERS   We can testify to that.

URIAH   What does the accused have to say?

GALY GAY   It was a man who didn't wish to be named.
    (*The soldiers grumble*)

A SOLDIER   I heard him say he was Galy Gay.

URIAH   Isn't that you?

GALY GAY (*slyly*)   If I were Galy Gay, I might be the man you're looking for.

URIAH   Then you're not Galy Gay?

GALY GAY (*under his breath*)   No, I'm not.

URIAH   And I suppose you weren't even present when Billy Humph was auctioned off?

GALY GAY   No, I was not present.

URIAH   But you saw him being sold by a man named Galy Gay?

GALY GAY   Yes, I can testify to that.

URIAH   So now you admit you were present?

GALY GAY   I can testify to that.

URIAH   Hear that? Do you all see the moon? The moon has risen, and he's up to his neck in this crooked elephant deal. As for Billy Humph, wasn't there something slightly wrong with him?

JESSE   There certainly was.

A SOLDIER   The man said he was an elephant, but he wasn't. He was nothing but paper.

URIAH   In other words, he sold a fake elephant. Which of course carries the death penalty. What do you say to that?

GALY GAY   Another elephant might not have taken him for an elephant. It's very hard to keep all this straight, Your Honor.

URIAH   All this is indeed very complicated, but I think you will have to be shot anyway, because your behavior has been extremely suspicious. (*Galy Gay is silent*) Come to think of it, I've heard of a soldier by the name of Jip, who even answered to that name at several roll calls, but that didn't prevent him from trying to make people think his name was Galy Gay. Could you be this Jip?

GALY GAY No, certainly not.

URIAH So your name isn't Jip either? Then what is your name? No answer? Then you must be a man who doesn't wish to be named. Are you by any chance the man at the elephant auction who didn't wish to be named? What? Again no answer? Extremely suspicious, almost enough to convict you. What's more, the criminal who sold the elephant is said to have been a man with a mustache, and you have a mustache. Come on, men, let's deliberate on all this.
(*He goes rear with the soldiers. Two stay with Galy Gay*)

URIAH (*on his way out*) You see? Now he doesn't want to be Galy Gay any more.

GALY GAY (*after a pause*) Can you hear what they're saying?

A SOLDIER No.

GALY GAY Are they saying that I'm this Galy Gay?

SECOND SOLDIER They're saying it's not so sure any more.

GALY GAY Just remember that one man is no man.

SECOND SOLDIER Has anybody found out who this war's against?

FIRST SOLDIER If they need cotton, it's Tibet; if they need wool, it's Pamir.

JESSE (*coming back*) Isn't that Galy Gay sitting here tied?

FIRST SOLDIER Hey, you, answer him!

GALY GAY You must be mistaking me for someone else, Jesse. Take a good look.

JESSE Well, aren't you Galy Gay? (*Galy Gay shakes his head*) Leave us for a moment. I've got to speak to him, he's just been sentenced to death.
(*The two soldiers go to the rear*)

GALY GAY Has the time come? Oh, Jesse, help me, you're a great soldier.

JESSE How did all this happen?

GALY GAY Well, Jesse, you see, I really don't know. We

were smoking and drinking, and I talked my soul away.

JESSE   I heard them saying over there that the man who was going to be shot was named Galy Gay.

GALY GAY   That's impossible!

JESSE   Well, aren't you Galy Gay?

GALY GAY   Wipe the sweat off my face, Jesse.

JESSE (*does so*)   Look me straight in the eye. I'm Jesse, your friend. Aren't you Galy Gay from Kilkoa?

GALY GAY   No, you must be mistaken.

JESSE   There were four of us when we left Kankerdan. Were you with us then?

GALY GAY   Yes, in Kankerdan I was with you.

JESSE (*goes rear to the other soldiers*)   The moon hasn't risen yet and already he wants to be Jip.

URIAH   All the same, I think we'd better put a little more fear of death into him.

(*The artillery is heard rolling by*)

BEGBICK (*enters*)   The artillery, Uriah! Help me fold these tarpaulins. And the rest of you, keep taking things down. (*The soldiers go on dismantling the canteen and loading the pieces into the car. Only one wall is still standing. Uriah and Begbick fold the tarpaulins*)

BEGBICK

I've also spoken with many people, and I've listened
Closely and heard many opinions.
I've heard many people say of many things: that is absolutely
      certain!
But the next time they came by, they spoke otherwise.
And of this other thing they said: that is certain.
Then I said to myself: of all things certain
The most certain is doubt.

(*Uriah goes rear. Begbick carrying her laundry basket follows suit, passing Galy Gay on the way. She sings*)

Oh, cling not to the wave
Breaking against your foot. As long as your

Foot stands in the water
New waves on it will break.

GALY GAY   Widow Begbick, would you kindly get a pair of
scissors and cut off my mustache.
BEGBICK   What for?
GALY GAY   Never mind, I know what for.
(*Begbick cuts off his mustache, wraps it in a cloth and takes
it to the wagon. The soldiers come forward again*)

Number IV

URIAH (*announcing*)   Now comes Number Four: the Execution of Galy Gay at Kilkoa Camp.
BEGBICK (*comes up to him*)   Mr. Uriah, I've got something
for you. (*She whispers something in his ear and gives him
the cloth with the mustache*)
URIAH (*goes to the latrine pit where Galy Gay is*)   Accused,
have you anything more to say?
GALY GAY   Your Honor, I have heard that the criminal who
sold the elephant was a man with a mustache, and I haven't
got a mustache.
URIAH (*silently showing him the open cloth with the mustache.
The others laugh*)   And what is this? You've really con-
victed yourself this time, my man. Cutting off your mustache
proves you had a guilty conscience. Come now, man without a name, and hear the verdict of the court martial of
Kilkoa. You are sentenced to be shot by a five-man firing
squad.
(*The soldiers drag Galy Gay out of the latrine pit*)
GALY GAY (*screaming*)   That's impossible!
URIAH   Oh no, it's not. Now listen carefully, you. One, for
stealing an army elephant and selling it, which is theft; two,
for selling an elephant that wasn't an elephant, which is
fraud; and three, for having no name or paybook and possibly being a spy, which is high treason.
GALY GAY   Oh, Uriah, why are you doing this to me?

URIAH   Come along now, and bear up like a good soldier, the way you've been taught in the Army. Forward march! Come along and be shot.

GALY GAY   Don't be in such a rush. I'm not the man you're looking for. I don't even know him. My name is Jip, I swear it is. What's an elephant beside a man's life? I never saw the elephant, I was only holding a rope. Don't go away! Please! I'm an entirely different man. I'm not Galy Gay. I'm not, I'm not.

JESSE   Oh yes you are, you and nobody else. Under the three rubber trees of Kilkoa, Galy Gay will see his blood flow. Forward march, Galy Gay!

GALY GAY   Oh God! Wait! There's got to be an official record, listing the charges and showing that I didn't do it and that my name isn't Galy Gay. Every detail must be weighed. You can't rush things like this when you're going to slaughter somebody.

JESSE   Forward march!

GALY GAY   What do you mean forward march? I'm not the man you're looking for. All I wanted was to buy a fish. Are there any fish around here? What's that artillery rolling by? What's that battle music blaring away? No, I won't move. I'll hold on to the grass. I demand a stop to all this. And why isn't there a crowd if a man's going to be shot?

BEGBICK   If you're not ready by the time they load the elephants, you'll all be done for. (*She goes out*)
(*Galy Gay is led back and forth. He strides like the protagonist in a tragic drama*)

JESSE   Make way for the criminal whom the court martial has condemned to death.

SOLDIERS   Look, that man's going to be shot. Maybe it's too bad. He's not very old.—And he doesn't know how he got into all this.

URIAH   Halt! Would you like to relieve yourself one last time?

GALY GAY   Yes.

URIAH   Guard him closely.

GALY GAY   I've heard that when the elephants get here the

soldiers will have to leave, so I'll make it slow to give the elephants time to get here.

SOLDIERS Make it quick!

GALY GAY I can't. Is that the moon?

SOLDIERS Yes.—It's late.

GALY GAY Isn't this the Widow Begbick's bar where we always used to drink?

URIAH No, my boy. This is the rifle range and that's the "Johnny-keep-your-pants-dry" wall. Hey! Go line up over there! And load your rifles. Five of them, there should be.

SOLDIERS Hard to see in this light.

URIAH Yes, very hard.

GALY GAY See here, this won't do. You've got to be able to see when you shoot.

URIAH (*to Jesse*) Take that paper lantern and hold it beside him. (*He blindfolds Galy Gay. In a loud voice*) Load! (*Under his breath*) What are you doing, Polly? You're putting a live round in the chamber. Take it out.

POLLY Oh, sorry. I almost loaded for real. That could almost have been a real tragedy.

(*The elephants are heard passing backstage. The soldiers stand still for a moment as though transfixed*)

BEGBICK (*calling from backstage*) The elephants!

URIAH That makes no difference at all. He's got to be shot. I'm going to count to three. One!

GALY GAY That's enough, Uriah. Can't you hear the elephants? Do I have to keep standing here, Uriah? But why are you all so frightfully still?

URIAH Two!

GALY GAY (*laughing*) You're a funny one, Uriah. I can't see you because you've blindfolded me. But your voice sounds as if you were in bitter earnest.

URIAH And one makes . . .

GALY GAY Stop, don't say three, or you'll be sorry. If you shoot now, you're sure to hit me. Stop! Don't. Wait a minute. Listen to me! I confess! I confess that I don't know what's happened to me. Believe me, and don't laugh. I'm a man who doesn't know who he is. But this much I know,

I'm not Galy Gay. I'm not the man who's supposed to be shot. But who am I? You see, I've forgotten. Last night when it was raining, I still knew. It did rain last night, didn't it? I beg you, when you look over here or in the direction where this voice is coming from, please believe it's me. Speak to that point in space, call it Galy Gay, or something else, have pity, give me a piece of meat. Where it goes in, that's Galy Gay, and so is where it comes out. Grant this at least: wheresoever you find a man who's forgotten who he is, it's me. And I beg you, just this once, let him go.

(*Uriah has whispered something in Polly's ear; then Polly runs up behind Galy Gay and raises a big club over his head*)

URIAH   One time is no time! Three!

(*Galy Gay lets out a scream*)

URIAH   Fire!

(*Galy Gay falls in a faint*)

POLLY   Stop! He's fallen down of his own accord!

URIAH (*shouts*)   Fire! So he can hear that he's dead!

(*The soldiers fire into the air*)

URIAH   Let him lie there. And get ready to move off.

(*Galy Gay is left lying, all the others go out*)

Number IVa

Begbick and the three are sitting outside the packed wagon at a table with five chairs. To one side lies Galy Gay covered with a sack.

JESSE   Here comes the sergeant. Widow Begbick, can you prevent him from poking his nose into our business?

(*Fairchild is seen approaching in civilian clothes*)

BEGBICK   Yes, because the man that's coming is a civilian. (*To Fairchild who is standing in the doorway*) Come, sit down with us, Charles.

FAIRCHILD   There you are, you Gomorrah! (*Standing over Galy Gay*) What's this drunken carcass? (*Silence. He pounds on the table*) Attention!

URIAH (*from behind knocks Fairchild's bowler down over his head*)   Shut up, you civilian!

(*Laughter*)

FAIRCHILD   Go ahead, mutiny, you sons of a gun! Look at my clothes and laugh! Tear down my name, famous from Calcutta to Cooch Behar! Give me a drink, and then I'll shoot you.

URIAH   My dear Fairchild, give us a sample of your marksmanship.

FAIRCHILD   No.

BEGBICK   Not one woman out of six can resist sharpshooter's tricks.

POLLY   Go on, Fairchild.

BEGBICK   You really ought to. For me.

FAIRCHILD   Oh you Babylon! Here I place an egg. How many paces?

POLLY   Four.

FAIRCHILD (*takes ten paces, which Begbick counts aloud*)   And here I have an ordinary army revolver. (*He fires*)

JESSE (*goes over to the egg*)   The egg is intact.

POLLY   Completely.

URIAH   If anything, it's a bit bigger.

FAIRCHILD   That's strange. I thought I could hit it.

(*Loud laughter*)

FAIRCHILD   Give me a drink! (*He drinks*) As true as my name is Bloody Five, I'm going to squash you all like bedbugs.

URIAH   Say, how did you come by the name of Bloody Five?

JESSE (*seated again*)   Show us.

FAIRCHILD   Should I tell the story, Mrs. Begbick?

BEGBICK   Not one in seven won't adore a savage soldier steeped in gore.

FAIRCHILD   Right. This is the Chadze River. And here are five Hindus, standing with their hands tied behind their backs. I come along with an ordinary Army revolver, I wave it in their faces and say: This pistol has been misfiring. I'd better test it. Like this. And I fire—bang! down you go!—and then four more times. That's the whole story, gentlemen. (*He sits down*)

JESSE   So that's how you came by the great name that has made this widow your slave? From a human point of view, you know, one might regard your conduct as indecent and say: You're just a bloody swine!

BEGBICK   Are you a monster?

FAIRCHILD   I should be very sorry if you took it like that. Your opinion means a great deal to me.

BEGBICK   But do you accept it as final?

FAIRCHILD (*looking deeply into her eyes*)   Absolutely.

BEGBICK   In that case, my dear man, my opinion is that I've got to finish packing up my canteen and that I haven't any time for private affairs, because I can hear the lancers trotting past as they take their horses to the train.

(*The lancers are heard riding by*)

POLLY   Are you going to insist on your selfish desires, sir, even though the lancers are loading their horses and you have heard that for military reasons this canteen has to be packed up?

FAIRCHILD (*bellowing*)   Yes, I insist! Give me a drink!

POLLY   All right, but we'll make short shrift of you, my boy!

JESSE   Sir, not far from here a man in the field dress of the British Army is lying under a rough piece of canvas. He is resting after a hard day's work. Only twenty-four hours ago he was still a babe in arms—from a military point of view. He was afraid of his wife's voice. For want of guidance he was incapable of buying a fish. He was ready to forget his father's name for a cigar. Some men took him in hand, it so happened they knew of a place for him. Now, at the cost of painful trials, he has become a man who will take his place in the battles to come. You, meanwhile, have degenerated back into a civilian. At a time when the army is leaving for the northern frontier to fight for law and order, which calls for plenty of beer, you, you big dungheap, are knowingly preventing the owner of an army canteen from loading her beer wagon on the train.

POLLY   How are you going to check our names at the last roll call and enter all four in your sergeant's roster as army regulations prescribe?

URIAH   In the state you're in how can you face a company

that's thirsting to confront the untold multitudes of the enemy? Stand up.

(*Fairchild rises unsteadily*)

POLLY You call that standing up?

(*He gives Fairchild a kick in the behind. Fairchild falls down*)

URIAH To think that that was once known as the Human Typhoon! Throw that wreck in the bushes or he'll demoralize the company.

(*The three start dragging Fairchild to the rear*)

A SOLDIER (*rushes in and stops at the rear*) Is Sergeant Charles Fairchild here? He's to fall his company in at the freight station. General's orders.

FAIRCHILD Don't tell him it's me.

JESSE There's no such sergeant around here.

Number V

Begbick and the three contemplate Galy Gay who is still lying under the sack.

URIAH Widow Begbick, we're at the end of our reconstruction job. We believe that our man has now been rebuilt.

POLLY All he needs now is a human voice.

JESSE Have you got a human voice for a case like this, Widow Begbick?

BEGBICK Yes, and something for him to eat. Take this crate and write "Galy Gay" on it with a piece of charcoal, and put a cross after it. (*They do so*) Then form a funeral procession and bury him. But you'll have to do it all in nine minutes flat, because it's already one minute after two.

URIAH (*announcing*) Number Five: the ceremonial interment and funeral oration of Galy Gay, the last personality, perished in the year nineteen hundred and twenty-five. (*The soldiers enter, packing their knapsacks*) Pick up this crate and form a nice funeral procession. (*The soldiers line up rear with the crate*)

JESSE   And I'll step up to him and say: You deliver the funeral oration for Galy Gay. (*To Begbick*) He won't eat.

BEGBICK   A man like him eats even when he's nobody.

(*She takes her basket over to Galy Gay, lifts the sack off him, and feeds him*)

GALY GAY   More!

(*Gives him more; then she signals to Uriah, and the procession comes forward*)

GALY GAY   What's that they're carrying?

BEGBICK   A man who was shot at the last minute.

GALY GAY   What's his name?

BEGBICK   Wait a second. If I'm not mistaken, his name was Galy Gay.

GALY GAY   And what's going to happen to him now?

BEGBICK   To whom?

GALY GAY   To this Galy Gay.

BEGBICK   Now they're burying him.

GALY GAY   Was he a good man or a bad man?

BEGBICK   Oh, he was a dangerous man.

GALY GAY   Yes, after all they shot him. I was there.

(*The procession passes. Jesse stops and speaks to Galy Gay*)

JESSE   Isn't that you, Jip? Jip, you've got to stand up right away and deliver the funeral oration for this Galy Gay, because you knew him, perhaps better than any of us.

GALY GAY   Hullo there! Can you really see where I am? (*Jesse points to him*) Yes, that's right. And what am I doing now? (*He bends his arm*)

JESSE   You're bending your arm.

GALY GAY   Now I've bent my arm twice. And now?

JESSE   Now you're marching like a soldier.

GALY GAY   Do you all march like this?

JESSE   Exactly.

GALY GAY   And what will you say to me when you want something?

JESSE   "Jip."

GALY GAY   Say: "Jip, walk around."

JESSE   Jip, walk around. Walk around under the rubber trees and cook up a funeral oration for Galy Gay.

GALY GAY (*goes over to the crate*)   And is this the crate he's in?
(*He walks around the procession who are holding the crate high. He walks faster and faster and tries to run away. Begbick holds him back*)

BEGBICK   Looking for something? The army's only remedy for all diseases, even cholera, is castor oil. A soldier doesn't get diseases that castor oil won't cure. Do you need castor oil?

GALY GAY (*shakes his head*)
My mother on her calendar marked the day
When I came out, and the thing that cried was me.
This bundle of flesh, nails and hair
Is me, is me.

JESSE   Yes, Jeraiah Jip, Jeraiah Jip from Tipperary.

GALY GAY   A man who carried cucumbers for tips. An elephant cheated him, he had to sleep in a hurry on a wooden chair for lack of time, because the fish water was boiling in his hut. And the machine gun hadn't been cleaned yet, because they presented him with a cigar and five rifle barrels, one of which was missing. What *was* his name?

URIAH   Jip. Jeraiah Jip.
(*Train whistles are heard*)

SOLDIERS   There go the train whistles.—Each man for himself.
(*They drop the crate and run off*)

JESSE   The train leaves in six minutes. He'll have to come along as is.

URIAH   Listen, Polly, and you too, Jesse. Comrades! We are three survivors, hanging over the abyss by a hair, and as that hair is badly frayed, listen carefully to what I am going to say, here by the outer wall of Kilkoa at two o'clock in the morning. This man, whom we need, must have a little more time, because it's for all eternity that he's changing. Therefore I, Uriah Shelley, now draw my army revolver and threaten you with instant death if you make the slightest move.

POLLY   But if he looks into the crate, it's all up.
(*Galy Gay sits down beside the crate*)

GALY GAY
I cannot look, on pain of instant death
At the blanked-out face in a crate
Of a certain man, once known to me from the water's
    surface
Into which looked a man who, as I know, has just died.
Therefore I cannot open this crate.
Because this fear is in the both of me, for perhaps
I am the both, just born
Upon the changing surface of the earth
A severed, bat-like thing, dangling
Between rubber trees and hut, at night
A thing that wishes it were joyful.
One man is no man. Someone must call out to him.
Therefore
I would have liked to look into this chest
Because the heart clings to its parents.

Given a forest, would it be there
If no one passed through it? Or suppose a man
Goes where a forest was:
How do they recognize each other?
When in a marsh a man sees his footprints filling
With water, does the puddle tell him something?
What is your opinion?

By what sign does Galy Gay know that he himself
Is Galy Gay?
If his arm were chopped off
And he found it in a hole in the wall
Would Galy Gay's eye know Galy Gay's arm?
And would Galy Gay's foot cry out: that's the one?
Therefore I will not look into this chest.
Moreover, in my opinion, the difference
Between yes and no is not so great.
And if Galy Gay were not Galy Gay

He'd be the drinking son of a mother who'd
Be someone else's mother if she
Were not his, and still he'd drink.
And would have been begotten in March, not in September—
Unless it should chance to be not March but September of
    this year
Or the September of the year before
Which would amount to a difference of only twelve brief
    months
That made one man into another.
And I, the one I and the other I
Are needed and therefore useful.
And since I did not look at the elephant
I'll close my eyes to my own case as well.
I'll shed what is disliked in me, and then I'll be
Agreeable.

(*Moving trains are heard*)

GALY GAY   What are those trains? Where are they going?

BEGBICK   The army is heading into the fire-spitting guns of the battles that are planned in the north. Tonight a hundred thousand men will be marching in one direction, from south to north. When a man is caught up in such a stream, he looks about for two to march beside him, one to the right, one to the left. He looks about for a rifle and a kit bag and an identity disc around his neck, and a number on the identity disc, so that when he's found they'll know what unit he belonged to and give him a place in a mass grave. Have you got an identity disc?

GALY GAY   Yes.

BEGBICK   What does it say?

GALY GAY   Jeraiah Jip.

BEGBICK   Well, Jeraiah Jip, you'd better wash. You look like a shit heap. Get ready to go. The army is leaving for the northern border. The fire-spitting guns of the northern battles are waiting. The army is thirsting to establish order in the populous cities of the north.

GALY GAY (*washing*)   Who is the enemy?

BEGBICK   They haven't announced yet what country we are making war on. But it's beginning to look more and more like Tibet.

GALY GAY   Did you ever stop to think, Widow Begbick: One man is no man. Until somebody calls out to him.
(*The soldiers march in with knapsacks*)

SOLDIERS   All aboard!—Everybody accounted for?

URIAH   Just a second. Your funeral oration, Comrade Jip, your funeral oration!

GALY GAY (*goes to the coffin*)   Lift up this crate belonging to Widow Begbick, with the mysterious corpse inside. Lift it two feet high, lower it six feet into the earth of Kilkoa, and hear the funeral oration delivered by Jeraiah Jip of Tipperary—which is difficult because I'm not prepared. Be that as it may, here lies Galy Gay, a man who was shot. He went out in the morning to buy a small fish, by evening he had acquired a large elephant, and that same night he was shot. Dearly beloved: don't get the idea that he was a nobody in his lifetime. He even had a straw hut at the edge of the city, and various other things besides, that had best not be mentioned. The crime he committed didn't amount to much, he was a good man. Let people say what they please, it was only a slight oversight. I was just too drunk, gentlemen, but a man's a man, and so he had to be shot. And now the wind is quite a lot cooler, as it always is toward morning, and I think we'd better be leaving, this place isn't very comfortable anyway. (*He steps away from the coffin*) But why have you all got your packs on?

POLLY   Because we've been ordered to entrain this morning, for the northern border.

GALY GAY   Well, why haven't I got a pack?

JESSE   Well, why hasn't he got a pack?
(*Soldiers bring his equipment*)

JESSE   Here's your kit, cap'n.
(*Some soldiers carry a large bundle wrapped in straw mats to the train*)

URIAH   He took his time, the bastard. But we'll get him yet.
(*Pointing to the bundle*) That was the Human Typhoon.
(*All go out*)

10

In the Moving Train

Just before dawn. The company are sleeping in hammocks. Jesse, Uriah and Polly are sitting up on guard. Galy Gay is asleep.

JESSE   It's a terrible world. No man can be relied on.

POLLY   The vilest and weakest thing alive is man.

JESSE   Through dust and water we've hiked down every road in this oversized country from the mountains of the Hindu Kush to the great plains of the southern Punjab, and from Benares to Calcutta, by sun and moon, we've seen nothing but treachery. This man we took under our wing has swiped our blankets and ruined our night's sleep, he's no better than a leaky oil can. Yes and no are the same to him. Today he says one thing, tomorrow another. Ah, Uriah, we've tried and failed. Let's go and see Widow Begbick, she's sitting up with the sergeant to keep him from falling off the platform. We'll ask her to lie down with this man. That way he'll feel good and won't ask questions. She may be old but there's still warmth in her, and when a man is lying with a woman he knows what's what. Get up, Polly. (*They go over to Widow Begbick*)

JESSE   Come in, Widow Begbick, we don't know which way to turn. We're afraid of falling asleep and we've got this sick man with us. Lie down with him, pretend he's spent the night with you, and make him feel good.

BEGBICK (*enters, half asleep*)   I'll do it for seven weeks' pay.

URIAH   We'll give you everything we make in seven weeks. (*Begbick lies down with Galy Gay. Jesse covers them with newspapers*)

GALY GAY (*waking up*)   What's shaking so?

URIAH (*to the others*)   It's the elephant nibbling at your hut, you grumbler.

GALY GAY   What's hissing so?

URIAH (*to the others*)   It's the fish boiling in the water, you agreeable man.

GALY GAY (*gets up with difficulty and looks out the window*) A woman. Sleeping bags. Telegraph poles. It's a train.

JESSE   Pretend you're all asleep.

(*The three pretend to be asleep*)

GALY GAY (*approaches a sleeping bag*)   Hey, you.

SOLDIER   What do you want?

GALY GAY   Where are you going?

SOLDIER (*opening one eye*)   To the front. (*Goes back to sleep*)

GALY GAY   They're soldiers. (*Looks out the window again, then wakes another*) Mr. Soldier, what time is it? (*No answer*) Almost morning. What day of the week is it?

SOLDIER   Between Thursday and Friday.

GALY GAY   I've got to get off. Hey, you. Stop the train.

SOLDIER   This train doesn't stop.

GALY GAY   If the train doesn't stop and everybody's asleep, I think I'll lie down too and sleep until it does. (*Sees Widow Begbick*) A woman is lying beside me. Who is this woman who's spent the night with me?

JESSE   Hello, comrade, good morning.

GALY GAY   Oh, I'm so glad to see you, Mr. Jesse.

JESSE   You old Casanova. Lying with a woman where everybody can see.

GALY GAY   Isn't it funny? Almost indecent, isn't it? But a man's a man, you know. He isn't always entirely his own master. For instance, here I wake up and there's a woman lying beside me.

JESSE   Yes, so there is.

GALY GAY   And would you believe it, sometimes I wake up in the morning and I don't even know the woman who's lying in bed with me? Frankly, as man to man, I don't know this woman. As one man to another, Mr. Jesse, could you tell me who she is?

JESSE   Oh, you bullshitter! This time it's Widow Leocadia Begbick, of course. If you duck your head in a pail of cold water, you'll know your lady friend all right. As it is, you probably don't even know your own name.

GALY GAY   Of course I do.

JESSE   All right, what is your name?

GALY GAY   (*is silent*)

JESSE   So you know your name?

GALY GAY   Yes.

JESSE   That's good. A man's got to know who he is when he's going off to war.

GALY GAY   It there a war on?

JESSE   Yes, the Tibetan War.

GALY GAY   Oh, the Tibetan War. But suppose a man didn't know who he was for the moment. Wouldn't it be funny, his going off to war?—Talking about Tibet, sir, that's a place I've always wanted to see. I once knew a man whose wife came from the province of Sikkim, that's on the border of Tibet. She says the people there are good people.

BEGBICK   Jippie, where are you?

GALY GAY   Who's she talking to?

JESSE   You, I think.

GALY GAY   Here.

BEGBICK   Come and give me a kiss, Jippie.

GALY GAY   I don't mind if I do, but I think you're kind of confusing me with somebody else.

BEGBICK   Jippie!

JESSE   This man claims his head isn't quite clear. He says he doesn't know you.

BEGBICK   Oh, how can you humiliate me so in front of this gentleman?

GALY GAY   If I duck my head into this pail of water, I'll know you right away. (*He sticks his head into the pail of water*)

BEGBICK   You know me now?

GALY GAY   (*lying*)   Yes.

POLLY   Then you must know who you are too.

GALY GAY   (*slyly*)   Didn't I know before?

POLLY   No. You were out of your mind and claimed to be somebody else.

GALY GAY   Who was I?

JESSE   I see you're still feeling no better. Moreover I think you're still a public menace, because last night when we called you by your right name, you got dangerously violent.

GALY GAY   All I know is that my name is Galy Gay.

JESSE   Did you hear that, it's starting in again. You'd better all call him Galy Gay like he says, or he'll throw another fit.

URIAH   Go on! Mr. Jip of Ireland, you have our permission to play the wild man until we tie you to a stake outside the canteen and it starts raining. We've been your comrades since the battle of the Chadze River, and we'd sell our shirts to help you in any way.

GALY GAY   Never mind your shirts.

URIAH   Call him what he wants to be called.

JESSE   Shut up, Uriah! Would you care for a glass of water, Galy Gay?

GALY GAY   Yes, that's my name.

JESSE   Of course it is, Galy Gay. What else could it be? Just take it easy. Lie down. Tomorrow they'll put you in the hospital, they'll give you a nice comfortable bed and plenty of castor oil. Then you'll feel better, Galy Gay. Quiet, boys, our comrade Jip, I mean Galy Gay, is sick.

GALY GAY   I'm telling you gentlemen, I don't get it. But when you've got a suitcase to carry, no matter how heavy it is, they say every suitcase has a soft spot somewhere.

POLLY (*ostensibly aside to Jesse*)   Just keep his hands off that pouch around his neck, or he'll read his right name in his paybook and throw another fit.

JESSE   What a fine thing a paybook is! It's so easy to forget some little thing. That's why we soldiers, who couldn't possibly keep everything in our heads, carry a pouch around our necks, and in the pouch each one of us has a paybook with his name in it. It's no good for people to think about their names too much.

GALY GAY (*goes to the rear, looks gloomily at his paybook, then to his corner*)   I'd better stop thinking. I'll just sit on my ass and count the telegraph poles.

THE VOICE OF SERGEANT FAIRCHILD   O misery, O awakening! Where is my name that was great from Calcutta to Cooch Behar? Even the uniform I wore is gone. They loaded me into this train as if they were sending a calf to the slaughterhouse. They've stopped my mouth with a civilian hat and

the whole train knows that I'm not Bloody Five any more.
When I'm through with this train, it will look like a
battered stovepipe on a junk pile. It stands to reason!

JESSE   Bloody Five! Wake up, Widow Begbick!

(*Fairchild enters in soiled civilian clothes*)

GALY GAY   Has something happened to your name?

FAIRCHILD   You're the most miserable specimen of them all,
I'll squash you first. Tonight I'll make mincemeat of all
of you. (*He sees the Widow Begbick sitting there, she
smiles*) I'll be damned! So, you're still here, you Gomorrah!
What have you done to me that I'm not Bloody Five any-
more? Go away! (*Begbick laughs*) What are these clothes
I've got on? Are they right for me? And what's this head
I've got on? Is it agreeable? Should I lie down with you
again, you Sodom?

BEGBICK   If you want to, go ahead.

FAIRCHILD   I don't want to! Go away! The eyes of this
country are on me. I was a big shot. My name is Bloody
Five. The history books are full of that name, in triplicate.

BEGBICK   Then don't, if you don't want to.

FAIRCHILD   Don't you realize that my manhood makes me
weak when you sit there like that?

BEGBICK   Then pluck out your manhood, my lad.

FAIRCHILD   Don't say that twice! (*He goes out*)

GALY GAY (*cries out after him*)   Stop! Don't do anything on
account of your name! A name is uncertain, you can't
build on a name.

FAIRCHILD'S VOICE   It stands to reason! That's the solution.
Here's a rope, here's an army revolver. Nothing can stop
me. Mutineers are shot. It stands to reason! "Johnny, pack
your kit." I'll never have to spend another penny on a
girl, not in this world. It stands to reason! I won't bat an
eyelash! I take full responsibility. I've got to do it if I'm to
go on being Bloody Five. Fire!

(*A shot is heard*)

GALY GAY (*who has been standing by the door for some time,
laughs*)   Fire!

SOLDIERS (*in the cars in front and behind*)   Did you hear that
scream—Who screamed?—Somebody must have got hurt.

They've all stopped singing, even way up in front—
Listen!

GALY GAY   I know who screamed and I know why. On account of his name, this gentleman has done something
bloody to himself. He's shot off his manhood. Seeing that
was a lucky thing for me: Now I see where it gets you to
be so stubborn, and what a bloody thing it is when a man
isn't satisfied with himself and makes such a fuss about his
name. (*He runs off to Widow Begbick*) Don't get the idea
that I don't know you, I know you very well. And it
doesn't matter anyway. But tell me quickly, how far away
is the city where we met?

BEGBICK   Many days' march and further every minute.

GALY GAY   How many days' march?

BEGBICK   At least a hundred at the moment you asked.

GALY GAY   And how many men here are on their way to
Tibet?

BEGBICK   A hundred thousand! One man is no man.

GALY GAY   Of course. A hundred thousand! And what do
they eat?

BEGBICK   Dried fish and rice.

GALY GAY   Everybody the same?

BEGBICK   Everybody the same.

GALY GAY   Of course. Everybody the same.

BEGBICK   They all have hammocks to sleep in; each man his
own, and cotton uniforms for the summer.

GALY GAY   And for the winter?

BEGBICK   Khaki for the winter.

GALY GAY   And women?

BEGBICK   Everybody the same.

GALY GAY   Everybody the same.

BEGBICK   And now you know who you are?

GALY GAY   Jeraiah Jip's my name. (*He runs over to the three
others and shows them his name in his paybook*)

JESSE (*and the others smile*)   Right. Always dragging your
name into it, aren't you Comrade Jip?

GALY GAY   How about food?
(*Polly brings him a dish of rice*)

GALY GAY   Yes, it's very important that I eat. (*Eats*) How

many days' march did you say the train covered in a
minute?

BEGBICK Ten.

POLLY Look how he makes himself at home. And gapes at
everything and counts the telegraph poles. He's happy because we're moving so fast.

JESSE I can't stand the sight of him. It's really loathsome
when a mammoth turns into a louse just because a couple
of rifles are shoved under his nose. Instead of doing the
decent thing and gathering himself to his forefathers.

URIAH No, that's a sign of vitality. If only Jip doesn't come
after us now, singing "A man's a man, that's what counts,
Goddam" I think we're over the hump.

A SOLDIER What's that noise?

URIAH (*smiling wickedly*) That's the roaring of the artillery;
we're coming to the hills of Tibet.

GALY GAY Any more rice?

11

Deep in Remote Tibet Lies the Mountain Fortress of Sir El-Djowr

*And on a hilltop Jeraiah Jip sits waiting amid the thunder of
cannon*

VOICES FROM BELOW This is as far as we can go.—This is the
fortress of Sir el-Djowr that blocks the pass to Tibet.

GALY GAY'S VOICE (*behind the hill*) At the double! At the
double! Or we'll be too late. (*He appears, carrying a gun
mount on his shoulders*) Out of the train and straight into
battle. That's for me. A cannon calls for action!

JIP Have you seen a machine-gun detachment with only
three men?

GALY GAY (*charging on irresistibly like a war elephant*)

There's no such thing, soldier. Our detachment, for instance, has four men. One man to the right of you, one to the left, and one behind you. That's the way it's got to be. Then you can fight your way through any pass.

BEGBICK (*appears, carrying a cannon barrel on her back*) Don't run so fast, Jippie. Just because you've got a heart like a lion.

(*The three soldiers appear, groaning as they drag their machine gun*)

JIP   Hello, Uriah; hello, Jesse; hello, Polly! I'm back. (*The three soldiers pretend not to see him*)

JESSE   Let's get this machine gun set up!

URIAH   Listen to those guns. You can't hear yourself talk.

POLLY   Keep a sharp eye on the fortress of Sir el-Djowr.

GALY GAY   I want to shoot first. Something's holding us up, it's got to go. All these gentlemen here can't be kept waiting. It won't hurt the mountain. Jesse, Uriah, Polly! The battle's starting, and already I feel the urge to sink my teeth into the enemy's throat. (*With Widow Begbick he assembles the cannon*)

JIP   Hello, Jesse; hello, Uriah; hello, Polly! How are you? I haven't seen you in a long time. I've been delayed, see? I hope you haven't had any trouble on my account. I couldn't make it any sooner. I'm mighty glad to be back though. But why don't you say something?

POLLY   What can we do for you, sir? (*Polly puts a dish of rice on the cannon for Galy Gay*) Don't you want to eat your rice ration? The battle will be starting soon.

GALY GAY   Let's have it! (*He eats*) Yes; first my rice ration, then my whisky ration, and while I'm eating and drinking, I'll take a good look at this mountain fortress and find its soft spot. Then it will be a piece of cake.

JIP   Your voice has changed, Polly, but you're still the same old joker. Me, I was employed in a flourishing business, but I had to leave. For your sakes of course. You're not angry, are you?

URIAH   We're sorry to have to tell you, but you seem to have come to the wrong address.

POLLY   We don't even know you.

JESSE   We may have met sometime, sir. There's an awful lot
of manpower in the army.

GALY GAY   I'd like another dish of rice. You haven't handed
over your ration yet, Uriah.

JIP   You know, you fellows have really changed.

URIAH   That's quite possible. That's army life.

JIP   But I'm Jip, your comrade.

(*The three laugh. When Galy Gay also begins to laugh, the
others stop*)

GALY GAY   One more ration. I'm ravenous now that we're
going into battle. This fortress appeals to me more and
more.

(*Polly gives him a third dish*)

JIP   Who's this man that's gobbling up your rations?

URIAH   That's our business.

JESSE   See here, you couldn't possibly be our Jip. Our Jip
would never have betrayed us and abandoned us. Nothing
would have delayed our Jip. So you can't be our Jip.

JIP   You know I am.

URIAH   Prove it! Prove it!

JIP   Won't a single one of you admit he knows me? Then
listen to me and mark my words. You're hard-hearted men,
and I can see right now what kind of an end you'll come to.
Give me back my paybook.

GALY GAY   (*goes up to Jip with his last dish of rice*)   You
must be mistaken. (*Turns back to the others*) He's not right
in the head. (*To Jip*) Is it a long time since you've eaten?
Care for a glass of water? (*To the others*) Mustn't do anything to upset him. (*To Jip*) You don't know where you
belong? That doesn't matter. Just sit down quietly over here
until we've won the battle. And please don't get any closer
to the roar of the cannon, that takes great strength of
character. (*To the three*) He doesn't know what he's at.
(*To Jip*) Of course you need a paybook. Nobody's going
to let you run around without a paybook. Polly, look in
that ammunition box where we keep the little megaphone
and take out Galy Gay's old papers, you remember, that
fellow you used to tease me about. (*Polly runs over to the
box*) Anybody who's lived in the lowlands where the tiger

asks the jaguar about his teeth knows how important it is to have something on you in black and white, because, you see, wherever you go nowadays, they try to take your name away. I know what a name is worth. Boys, boys, when you called me Galy Gay that time, why didn't you just call me Mr. Nobody? That kind of a joke is dangerous. It could have turned out very badly. But I say, let bygones be bygones. (*He gives Jip the papers*) Here are the papers. Take them. Is there anything else you want?

JIP   You're the best of the lot. You've got a heart at least. As for the rest of you, I'm going to curse you.

GALY GAY   Curses are hard to listen to. I think I'll make a little noise with the cannon to drown them out. Show me how this thing works, Widow Begbick.

(*The two of them aim the cannon at the fortress and begin to load*)

JIP   May the icy wind of Tibet freeze the marrow in your bones. May you never again hear the bell in Kilkoa harbor, you devils. May you march to the end of the world and back again, several times over. The Devil himself, your teacher, won't want you when you're old, you'll just have to go on marching through the Gobi desert by day and by night and the waving green rye fields of Wales. That's what you'll get for betraying a comrade in need. (*Goes out*)

(*The three are silent*)

GALY GAY   All set. And now I'll do it with five shots.

(*The first shot is fired*)

BEGBICK (*smoking a cigar*)   You're one of those great soldiers who made the Army so dreaded in times gone by. Five such men and a woman's life was in danger.

(*The second shot is fired*)

I have proof that a good many of those men, and not the worst in the company, thought of my kisses in the battle of the Chadze River. A man would go without whiskey and save up two weeks' pay for a night with Leocadia Begbick. They had names like Genghis Khan, known from Calcutta to Cooch Behar.

(*The third shot is fired*)

Their Irish colleen had only to embrace them once to

steady their blood. You can read in *The Times* how staunchly they fought in the battles of Bourabay, Camathura and Daguth.

(*The fourth shot is fired*)

GALY GAY   Anything that isn't part of the mountain will topple now.

(*Smoke begins to pour from the fortress of Sir el-Djowr*)

POLLY   Look!

(*Farchild enters*)

GALY GAY   That's terrific. Leave me alone. I've tasted blood.

FAIRCHILD   What do you think you're doing? Take a look over there. I'm going to bury you up to your neck in that anthill or you'll shoot the whole Hindu Kush to pieces. My hand is perfectly steady. (*He aims his army revolver at Galy Gay*) It's not shaking at all. There, it stands to reason. You're looking at the world for the last time.

GALY GAY (*loading with enthusiasm*)   One more shot! Just this one! The fifth and last!

(*The fifth shot is fired. A cry of joy is heard from the valley below*: "The fortress of Sir el-Djowr that blocked the pass to Tibet has fallen. The army is entering Tibet")

FAIRCHILD   Right! Once again I hear the familiar step of the Army on the march, and now I'll take some steps myself. (*Steps up to Galy Gay*) Who are you?

VOICE OF A SOLDIER (*from below*)   Who is the man who leveled the fortress of Sir el-Djowr?

GALY GAY   Just a second. Polly, hand me that little megaphone out of the ammunition box, so I can tell them who.

(*Polly brings the megaphone and hands it to Galy Gay*)

GALY GAY (*through the megaphone*)   It was me, one of you, Jeraiah Jip!

JESSE   Hurrah for Jeraiah Jip, the human fighting machine!

POLLY   Look!

(*The fortress has begun to burn. A thousand horrified voices cry out in the distance*)

DISTANT VOICE   The fortress of Sir el-Djowr is in flames. Seven thousand refugees from the province of Sikkim had found shelter there, peasants, artisans and shopkeepers, most of them friendly, hard-working people.

GALY GAY   Oh!—But what's that to me? The one cry and the other cry.

> Already I feel within me
> The lust to sink my teeth
> In the enemy's throat
> The instinct to kill
> The breadwinner
> To carry out the orders
> Of the conquerors.

> Hand me your paybooks!
> (*They do so*)

POLLY   Polly Baker.

JESSE   Jesse Mahoney.

URIAH   Uriah Shelley.

GALY GAY   Jeraiah Jip. At ease! We will now cross the borders of frozen Tibet.
(*All four go out*)

APPENDIX TO *A MAN'S A MAN*

The Baby Elephant

An Interlude for the Foyer

Translator: Gerhard Nellhaus

Theater

Under a group of rubber trees, a platform. In front of it, chairs.

POLLY (*before the curtain*) Wishing the dramatic art to have its full effect on you, we request you to smoke for all you are worth. Our actors are the best in the world, our drinks full strength and our chairs comfortable. Bets on the outcome will be accepted at the bar, and the curtain will be drawn for the end of an act every time the audience bets. Kindly refrain from shooting the piano player, he's doing his best. If you don't catch on to the plot right away, don't rack your brains, it defies understanding. If you insist on seeing something that makes sense, go to the toilet. Your admission will not be refunded under any circumstances. Here's our comrade Jip, who has the honor of playing the part of the Baby Elephant. If you think that's too difficult, let me tell you: an actor must be able to do anything.

A SOLDIER (*out front*) Bravo!

POLLY Here is Jesse Mahoney in the role of the Baby Elephant Jackie Pall's mother, and here's Uriah Shelley, the foremost living authority on international horse racing, cast as the moon. Last but not least, you will have the pleasure of seeing yours truly in the important role of the Banana Tree.

SOLDIERS Start the show, and don't forget that ten cents is a hell of a price for this tripe!

POLLY Permit me to assure you that your crude invective leaves us unruffled. The play deals mainly with a crime committed by the Baby Elephant. I'm telling you this so we won't have to keep interrupting.

URIAH (*from behind the curtain*)   Allegedly committed.

POLLY—Right! That's what comes of reading only my own part. Actually the Baby Elephant is innocent.

SOLDIERS (*in rhythm*)   Start the show! Start the show! Start the show!

POLLY As you wish. (*Steps behind the curtain*) I'm beginning to think we may have charged too much admission. What do you fellows think?

URIAH No use worrying about that now. We've just got to take the plunge.

POLLY It's only because the play's so poor. You see, Jesse, I'm sure you didn't remember exactly what it was like at the regular theater, and I suspect, Jesse, that what you forgot was all the main points. Hey, wait a minute, I've got to take a leak. (*The curtain rises*) I'm the Banana Tree.

A SOLDIER At last!

POLLY The Judge of the Jungle. Here I stand on the parched steppes of the southern Punjab, and here I've been standing ever since elephants were invented. Now and then, usually in the evening, the Moon comes over to me and brings charges against somebody, a Baby Elephant, for instance.

URIAH Not so fast! That's half the play! For ten cents! (*He rises*)

POLLY Hello, Moon. Where have you come from so late in the evening?

URIAH I've just heard a fine story about a baby elephant—

POLLY Are you bringing charges?

URIAH Of course.

POLLY Am I to assume that the Baby Elephant has committed a crime?

URIAH Your assumption is quite correct. One more proof of your perspicacity, which nothing can escape.

POLLY Oh, you haven't seen anything yet. Didn't the Baby Elephant murder his mother?

URIAH Exactly.

POLLY But that's dreadful.

URIAH It's abominable.

POLLY   If only I hadn't mislaid my horn-rimmed glasses!

URIAH   Oh, I just happen to have a pair on me, if they suit you.

POLLY   They'd suit me fine if only they had lenses. They haven't got any lenses.

URIAH   They're better than nothing.

POLLY   Why isn't anybody laughing?

URIAH   Yes, it is queer. That's why I'm bringing charges against the Moon, I mean the Baby Elephant.

(*The Baby Elephant enters slowly*)

POLLY   Ah, here's that nice little Baby Elephant. Where have you come from, eh?

GALY GAY   I am the Baby Elephant. Seven rajahs attended my cradle. What are you laughing at, Moon?

URIAH   Keep talking, Baby Elephant.

GALY GAY   My name is Jackie Pall. I'm taking a walk.

POLLY   I hear you beat your mother to death.

GALY GAY   No, I only smashed her milk jug.

URIAH   On her head. On her head.

GALY GAY   No, Moon, on a stone. On a stone.

POLLY   And I tell you, you did it, as sure as I'm the Banana Tree!

URIAH   And as sure as I'm the Moon, I'll prove it. My first proof is this woman here.

(*Enter Jesse as the Baby Elephant's mother*)

POLLY   Who's this?

URIAH   His mother.

POLLY   But isn't that rather strange?

URIAH   Not at all.

POLLY   All the same, it strikes me as odd. Her being here.

URIAH   Not me.

POLLY   In that case, she can stay. Only of course all this has to be proved.

URIAH   Yes, indeed. You're the judge.

POLLY   Well, then, Baby Elephant, prove you didn't murder your mother.

A SOLDIER (*out front*)   Christ! And her standing right there!

URIAH (*calling down to him*)   That's just it!

A SOLDIER   It stinks right from the start. With the mother

standing right there. I refuse to take any further interest in this play.

JESSE   I am the Baby Elephant's mother, and I bet my little Jackie will be able to prove very nicely that he's not a murderer. Won't you, Jackie?

URIAH   And I bet he won't be able to prove it in a million years.

POLLY (*bellowing*)   Curtain!
(*The audience goes silently to the bar and loudly and vehemently orders cocktails*)

POLLY (*behind the curtain*)   It went pretty well, not a single catcall!

GALY GAY   But why doesn't anybody applaud?

JESSE   Maybe they're too overwhelmed.

POLLY   It's so interesting, though!

URIAH   If we could only show them the legs of a few chorus girls they'd tear the house down. Go on out, let's see if we can get them to bet.

POLLY (*steps out*)   Gentlemen . . .

SOLDIERS   Wait a minute! The intermission's too short. Give us a chance to drink.—After watching you, we need it.

POLLY   We only thought you might like to place some bets, on one of the contenders, I mean, Mother versus Moon.

SOLDIERS   What nerve! Trying to squeeze more money out of us.—Oh well, let's wait till they really get going.—The beginning never amounts to much!

POLLY   All right. Anyone wishing to bet on the Mother, step this way. (*No one steps forward*) On the Moon, over here. (*No one steps forward. Looking worried, Polly goes behind the curtain*)

URIAH (*behind the curtain*)   Did they bet?

POLLY   Not so you can notice. They think the best is yet to come. That really has me worried.

JESSE   They're drinking themselves blind, as if they couldn't sit through it any other way.

URIAH   We'd better try some music. That will cheer them up.

POLLY (*steps out*)   From now on we'll play the Victrola. (*Steps back in, the curtain opens*) Step this way, Moon, Mother and Baby Elephant. You will now witness the complete solution of this mysterious crime. And so will you down there. How, Jackie Pall, can you hope to conceal the fact that you stabbed your venerable mother?

GALY GAY How can I have done such a thing when I'm only a weak little girl?

POLLY Indeed? In that case I maintain that you, Jackie Pall, are not a girl at all as you claim to be. Hear now my first conclusive proof. I remember a strange story that I heard as a child in Whitechapel—

A SOLDIER Southern Punjab!

(*Resounding laughter*)

POLLY—Southern Punjab. A man put on a woman's skirt because he didn't want to be a soldier. The sergeant came along with a bullet and tossed it in his lap. When he didn't spread his legs as a girl would to catch it in her skirt, the sergeant knew he was a man, and in the case before us, likewise. (*They act out the story*) Now you have all seen that the Baby Elephant is a man. Curtain!

(*Curtain. Feeble applause*)

POLLY Hear that? A triumph! Raise the curtain! Take your bows.

(*Curtain. No more applause*)

URIAH They're positively hostile. It's just hopeless.

JESSE We'll simply have to stop and give them their money back. It's touch and go already: to be lynched or not to be lynched, that is the question. It's a grim situation. Just take a look at them.

URIAH Their money back? Never! No theater in the world can exist like that!

A SOLDIER Tomorrow we're pulling out for Tibet. Georgie boy, these may be the last rubber trees you'll ever drink four-cent cocktails under. The weather isn't nice enough for a war or it would be pleasant to stay right here if only they weren't putting on that stupid show.

ANOTHER SOLDIER How about entertaining us with a little song? How about "Johnny, shine your boots."

SOLDIERS Bravo! (*They sing*) "Johnny, shine . . ."

URIAH Now they're doing their own singing. We'd better get on with the show.

POLLY   I wish I were sitting down there myself. I'm crazy about that Johnny song. Why didn't we think of that? Well, on with the show! (*Curtain*) Now that . . . (*fighting to make himself heard over the singing*) Now that the Baby Elephant . . .

A SOLDIER   Still talking about that Baby Elephant?

POLLY   As I was saying: Now that this . . .

A SOLDIER   This baby soldier!

POLLY   . . . this animal before us has been unmasked as an impostor by my first conclusive proof, I will bring forth my second and still more conclusive proof.

A SOLDIER   Can't you skip that one, Polly?

URIAH   Don't you dare, Polly!

POLLY   Baby Elephant, I contend you are a murderer. Therefore prove that you are incapable of murdering anybody— the Moon, for instance.

A SOLDIER   That's all wrong! The Banana Tree has to do the proving.

POLLY   That's just what I'm driving at. If only you'd pay attention. This is one of the most exciting moments in our drama. As I was saying: "Prove that you are incapable of murdering anybody, the Moon, for instance." Climb up that creeper and take a knife with you.

(*Galy Gay does so. The creeper is a rope ladder held up by the Moon*)

SOLDIERS   (*silencing those who want to go on singing*)   Quiet! —Climbing up there isn't so easy, as he can't see anything out of that elephant-head.

JESSE   Let's hope he doesn't piss! Put some vigor into your voice, Uriah!

(*Uriah lets out a scream*)

URIAH   Oh! Oh! Oh!

POLLY   What's the matter, Moon? Why are you yelling?

URIAH   Because it hurts something awful. It must be a murderer climbing up to me.

GALY GAY   Hang the ladder on a branch, Uriah. I'm very heavy.

URIAH   Oh, he's pulling my hand off! My hand! My hand! He's pulling my hand off!

POLLY   You see! You see!
(*Galy Gay has seized Uriah's artificial hand and shows it around*)

JESSE   That's bad, Jackie. I'd never have expected such a thing of you. You're no child of mine.

URIAH (*holding up the stump of his hand*)   I testify that he is a murderer.

POLLY   Do you all see that bloody stump? Isn't that living proof? And you, Baby Elephant, you haven't proved that you are incapable of committing murder. On the contrary. You've fixed the Moon so he'll certainly bleed to death before dawn. Curtain! (*Curtain. He steps out at once*) If you wish to bet now, you may do so at the bar.

SOLDIERS (*going to bet*)   A cent on the Moon.—Half a cent on the Baby Elephant.

URIAH   Look! They're biting! Now's the time to hit them with the Grieving Mother Soliloquy.
(*The curtain rises*)

JESSE
Do you all know what a mother is?
Ah, her heart as soft as butter is.
Tender your mother's heart as you lay in her
Tender the mother's hand that fed you dinner.
Tender the mother's eye that watched you play
Tender the mother's foot that led the way.
(*Laughter*)
And when a mother's heart is laid beneath the turf
(*Laughter*)
A noble soul will vanish from this earth.
(*Laughter*)
Hark to a mother's plaint ere she depart
(*Laughter*)
This calf once nestled 'neath this mother's heart.

(*Prolonged, unroarious laughter*)

SOLDIERS   Encore! That's worth ten cents by itself!—Bravo!— Three cheers! Three cheers for the mother! Hurrah! Hurrah! Hurrah!

(*The curtain falls*)

URIAH Go on! It's a hit! Get out on that stage!

(*The curtain rises*)

POLLY I have proved that you are a man capable of committing murder. And now, Baby Elephant, I ask you: Do you claim that this woman is your mother?

SOLDIERS That's a rank injustice they're putting on up there. It goes against the grain.—But it's philosophical all right. They must have some happy ending up their sleeves, that's a sure thing.—Quiet!

POLLY Never, of course, would I wish to maintain that any child in the whole world would touch a hair of his own mother's head in a country governed by Old England. (*Cries of "Bravo!"*) Rule Britannia! (*All sing "Rule Britannia"*) Thank you, gentlemen. As long as that soul-stirring song rises from rugged, manly throats, all's well with Old England. But let's get on with the play! In view of the fact that you, O Baby Elephant, have murdered this universally beloved woman and great actress (*cries of "Bravo!"*), you, Jackie Pall, cannot possibly be this celebrated woman's (*cries of "Bravo!"*) son or daughter. And when a Banana Tree makes allegations he proves them. (*Applause*) Therefore, O Moon of Cooch Behar, take a piece of billiard chalk and draw a full circle in the middle of the stage. Then take an ordinary rope and wait until this Mother, who has been wounded to the very heart, has stepped into the center of this most incompetently drawn circle. Then place the rope ever so gently around her snow-white neck.

SOLDIERS Around her beautiful snow-white neck. Her beautiful snow-white mother's neck.

POLLY Exactly. And you, the alleged Jackie Pall, take the other end of this rope of justice and stand outside the circle, facing the Moon. That's it. And now I ask you, woman: Did you give birth to a murderer? No answer? There, you see. I only wished to show you, gentlemen, that Jackie Pall's own mother, whose role is here enacted before you, disowns her fallen child. But in a moment I shall show you still more, for presently the terrible sun of justice will cast a light into the most secret depths.

(*Applause*)

SOLDIERS   Don't overdo it, Polly—Shh!

POLLY   For the last time, Jackie Pall: do you still claim to be this unhappy woman's son?

GALY GAY   Yes.

POLLY   I see. You're her son, are you? A moment ago you claimed to be her daughter. But when it comes to testifying, you're no stickler for accuracy. We now proceed to our last and most important super-duper proof, which surpasses all previous proofs and will, I am sure, fully satisfy you gentlemen. Jackie Pall, if you are this mother's child, you must have the power to draw this woman, your alleged mother, out of the circle. That's quite clear.

(*Applause*)

SOLDIERS   As clear as day! As clear as a foggy day!—Stop! He's all wrong!—Stick to the truth, Jackie!

POLLY   Pull when I say three.

ALL   One—two—three—

POLLY   Pull!

(*Galy Gay pulls Jesse out of the circle*)

JESSE   Stop, damn it! What do you think you're doing? My neck!

SOLDIERS   Forget about your neck! Pull, Jackie!—Stop!—He's as blue as a mackerel!

JESSE   Help!

GALY GAY   I pulled her out! I pulled her out!

POLLY   Well? What do you all say now? Did you ever see such brutality? Unnatural deceit has now received its just reward.

(*Tumultuous applause*)

POLLY   You see, you've made a big mistake. You haven't proved what you thought you were proving. All you've proved with your brutal pulling is that you couldn't possibly be the son or daughter of this poor martyred mother. You have pulled the truth to light, Jackie Pall.

SOLDIERS   Christ!—Bravo!—Disgusting! Nice family!—Clear

out, Jackie, you're through!—Put-up job!—Stick to the
truth, Jackie!

POLLY   Well, gentlemen, I think that will suffice. Our clinch-
ing super-duper proof has, I believe, been brought home.
Pay close attention, gentlemen. I especially ask the attention
of those who felt called upon to raise such a row at the
beginning and of those who bet their good pennies that
this Baby Elephant, now punctured by proofs, was not a
murderer. This Baby Elephant *is* a murderer. This Baby
Elephant is not the daughter of this revered mother as he
maintained, but her son, as I have demonstrated, and, as you
have seen, not her son either. He is not even the child of
this matron, whom in fact he has murdered, although she
stands here before your eyes, acting as if nothing had
happened, which is perfectly natural though unprecedented,
as I will prove, in fact I will now prove everything and
assert still more, nor will I let anything deter me, but will
stand by my opinion, and prove that too, for I ask you:
what is anything without proof?

(*The applause grows more and more frenetic*)

POLLY   Without proof a man isn't a man at all, but an
orang-utan as Darwin demonstrated, and what becomes of
progress then, and if you dare to bat an eyelash, you miserable insignificant Baby Elephant, dripping with lies and
false to the marrow, I will prove to the hilt, I was going to
do so anyway—yes, gentlemen, this is the main point—
that this Baby Elephant is not a Baby Elephant at all, but
at the very most Jeraiah Jip from Tipperary.

(*Tumultuous applause*)

SOLDIERS   Hurrah!

GALY GAY   That's not fair.

POLLY   Why not? What's not fair about it?

GALY GAY   It's not in the play. Take it back.

POLLY   But you are a murderer.

GALY GAY   That's not true.

POLLY   But I've proved it. I've proved it. I've proved it!

(*Galy Gay groans and hurls himself at the Banana Tree,
whose pedestal gives way under the onslaught*)

POLLY (*falling*)   You see! You see!

URIAH   There. Now you *are* a murderer.

POLLY (*groaning*)   And I've proved it.

(*Curtain*)

URIAH   Quick! The song!

(*All four actors come quickly out in front of the curtain and sing*)

What good times we had in old Uganda
Seven cents a seat on the veranda.
Ah, the poker hands we played with that old tiger
And how we played! I well remember that.
When we bet the hide of Papa Krueger
And he bet nothing but his battered hat.
 How peacefully the moon shone in Uganda!
 Through the cool night we sat about
 Until sunrise.
 The train pulled out.
 A man needs money to be able
 To sit at the poker table
 With a tiger in disguise.
 (Seven cents a seat on the veranda.)

SOLDIERS   All over? Rank injustice I call it.—Call that a happy ending? You can't let it end like that.—Keep the curtain up. Go on with the play.

POLLY   What's this? There's no more script. Be reasonable. The play's over.

A SOLDIER   What nerve! Dirtiest trick I ever saw! It's rubbish of the first water, it's an affront to common sense.

(*A group of soldiers climb resolutely up on the stage*)

SOLDIERS (*earnestly*)   We want our money back.—See here, Moon of Cooch Behar, either the Baby Elephant comes to a decent end or you'd better hand over every penny of our money in two seconds flat.

(*Stormy protests*)

POLLY   Seriously, gentlemen: what you've witnessed here is the naked truth.

A SOLDIER   I'm afraid it's you who'll have to look the naked truth straight in the eye right now.

POLLY   It's all because you don't know anything about art, and have no respect for artists.

A SOLDIER   Don't waste your breath!

GALY GAY (*after a dangerous pause*)   Don't get me wrong, I wouldn't want you to think that I'm not foursquare behind this show of ours.

POLLY   That's telling them, cap'n.

GALY GAY   To come straight to the point, I should like to invite the man who has been the most insistent about getting his money back, I mean to say, I should like to invite that peculiar gentleman to join me in a little eight-round boxing match with four-ounce gloves.

SOLDIERS   Go to it, Townley!—Give that Baby Elephant's snout a good wiping!

GALY GAY   Well, my friends, now we will see, I think, whether it was the truth we presented to you this evening and whether it was good or bad theater.

(*All go off to the boxing match*)

The Rise and Fall of
the City of Mahagonny

Opera

Collaborators: E. Hauptmann, C. Neher, K. Weill

Translator: Michael Feingold

CHARACTERS

JIM MACINTYRE
BANK ACCOUNT BILL
JACK O'BRIEN } Lumberjacks
ALASKA WOLF JOE
LEOCADIA BEGBICK

TRINITY MOSES   JENNY SMITH
FATTY THE BOOKKEEPER   MEN AND GIRLS OF MAHAGONNY
TOBBY HIGGINS

The Founding of the City of Mahagonny

A large truck in very bad shape stops in a desolate place.

FATTY THE BOOKKEEPER
  Hey, we gotta keep going!
TRINITY MOSES
  But the motor's had it.
FATTY THE BOOKKEEPER
  Yeah, then we can't keep going.
  (*Pause*)
TRINITY MOSES
  But we gotta keep going.
FATTY THE BOOKKEEPER
  But there's only desert up ahead.
TRINITY MOSES
  Yeah, then we can't keep going.
  (*Pause*)
FATTY THE BOOKKEEPER
  In that case we gotta turn back.
TRINITY MOSES But the constables are after us, and they
  know our faces from one pore to the next.
FATTY THE BOOKKEEPER
  Yeah, then we can't turn back.
  (*They sit down on the running board and smoke*)
TRINITY MOSES
  You know they've found gold up on the coast.
FATTY THE BOOKKEEPER
  Yeah, that's one long coast.

TRINITY MOSES
  Yeah, then we can't head up that way.

FATTY THE BOOKKEEPER
  But they have found gold up there.

TRINITY MOSES
  Yeah, but the coast is too long.

MRS. LEOCADIA BEGBICK (*appears on the truck*)
  Can't we keep going?

TRINITY MOSES
  No.

BEGBICK   Okay, then we'll stay right here. I've got an idea:
  If we can't make it up there, let's stay down here. Look,
  everybody who comes back from up there says those rivers
  don't give up their gold so easy. It's tough work and we're
  not cut out for working. But I've seen those guys, and let
  me tell you, they're very free with their gold. It's easier to
  get gold out of men than out of rivers!

  So we might as well build a city here
  And we'll call it Mahagonny
  That means: Spiderweb!
  It will be like a web
  Spun out to catch all the plump juicy insects.
  All the world's full of labor and sorrow
  But down here we'll have fun.
  For it is a man's greatest pleasure
  Not to suffer and do what he feels like.
  That is what money gets you.
  Gin and whiskey
  Young girls and young boys.
  And every week here will be seven days away from working
  And the big hurricanes don't travel northward this far.
  Calmly in perfect peace our men
  Will sit around and smoke while they wait for the sunset.
  Then every other day we'll have boxing
  Lots of noise and violence, but the fights will be fair.
  So stick this fishing rod in the ground right here and run
  This old rag up it for a flag, so the ships heading down
      from the gold coast

Can see us.
Set the bar up there
Under that rubber tree:
This is the town.
This will be its center
And it's called "At the Sign of the Rich Man."

(*The red Mahagonny-pennon is run up a long fishing rod*)

WILLY AND MOSES

Still, we're only building Mahagonny
Because the world is so rotten
Because there is no peace
And no contentment
And there is nothing
A man can depend upon.

2.

The city grew quickly in the weeks that followed and the first "sharks" drifted into town

Enter Jenny and six girls carrying large suitcases, they sit down on the suitcases and sing the "Alabama Song."

Oh, show us the way to the next whiskey bar!
Oh, don't ask why!
For we must find the next whiskey bar
For if we don't find the next whiskey bar
I tell you we must die!
Oh, moon of Alabama
We now must say good-bye
We've lost our good old mama
And must have whiskey
Oh, you know why.

Oh, show us the way to the next pretty boy!
Oh, don't ask why!

For we must find the next pretty boy
For if we don't find the next pretty boy
I tell you we must die!
Oh, moon of Alabama
We now must say good-bye
We've lost our good old mama
And must have boys
Oh, you know why.

Oh, show us the way to the next little dollar!
Oh, don't ask why!
For we must find the next little dollar
For if we don't find the next little dollar
I tell you we must die!
Oh, moon of Alabama
We now must say good-bye
We've lost our good old mama
And must have dollars
Oh, you know why.

(*The girls leave with their suitcases*)

3

Reports of a new paradise reach the big cities

A projection shows the view of a city of millions and photographs of many men.

THE MEN
We live in giant cities. They have sewers below them
And nothing inside, only smoke overhead.
Life may have joys, but city men don't know them.
Rapidly we die and slowly they also go dead.

(*Fatty the Bookkeeper and Trinity Moses come on with posters*)

FATTY THE BOOKKEEPER
Far from the cares of the world . . .

TRINITY MOSES
—The noisy diesel trains don't stop nearby—

FATTY THE BOOKKEEPER
. . . paved with gold brick: Mahagonny!

TRINITY MOSES
Just yesterday they asked about you there.

FATTY THE BOOKKEEPER   In these troubled times you can find, in every city, millions longing for a better life. Wise men set out for Mahagonny, the golden.

TRINITY MOSES
Where the booze is a bargain.

FATTY THE BOOKKEEPER
In your giant cities full of noise and smoke
There's no peace and no contentment
There's nothing you can depend upon.

TRINITY MOSES
The world is so rotten.

FATTY AND MOSES
But once you sit among the
People of Mahagonny
Sipping your rum and coke
Your skin will turn yellow like honey
And smoke.
Skies blue as mountain lakes
Mellow Sweet Cap!
When San Francisco quakes
You'll see its joys are fakes.
Cities are big mistakes
They end in scrap.

THE MEN
They have sewers below them
There's nothing inside and only smoke overhead
Life may have joys, but city men don't know them.
Rapidly we die and slowly they also go dead.

FATTY THE BOOKKEEPER
  Then off to Mahagonny!
TRINITY MOSES
  Just yesterday they asked about you there.

4

In the next few years, the discontented of all the continents headed for Mahagonny, city of gold

Four men—Jim, Jack, Bill, Joe—come on with suitcases.

Off to Mahagonny!
The air is clean and fresh
They've booze and poker tables there
Good whores and good horseflesh.
Shine on, harvest
Moon of Alabama
Light the South!
Tucked into our shirts today
We've the dollar bills to pay
For a great big grin
Upon your great big stupid mouth.

Off to Mahagonny!
The wind is blowing free
Fresh meat for sale on every street
And no bureaucracy.
Shine on, harvest
Moon of Alabama
Light the South!
Tucked into our shirts today
We've the dollar bills to pay
For a great big grin
Upon your great big stupid mouth.

Off to Mahagonny!
The ship is leaving shore
And there Our civ-civ-syphilis
We soon will see no more.
Shine on, harvest
Moon of Alabama
Light the South!
Tucked into our shirts today
We've the dollar bills to pay
For a great big grin
Upon your great big stupid mouth.
(*The men go out*)

5

**Among the many who came to Mahagonny at that
time was Jim MacIntyre, and it is his story we want
to tell you**

*Wharf at Mahagonny. Four men stand before a sign pointing
"To Mahagonny," with a price list hanging from it.*

JIM
   When you're a stranger in the city
   Then at first you are always slightly nervous.
JACK
   You're not exactly sure just where to go.
BILL
   Or just who you can yell at.
JOE
   And to whom you take your hat off.
JIM
   You have that problem
   When you're a stranger in the city.
   (*Mrs. Leocadia Begbick appears with a long list*)

BEGBICK

　Gentlemen, welcome
　You've finally made it.
　(*Looks at her list*)
　You must be Mister Jimmy MacIntyre
　Who is famous for switchblade throwing.
　Every night before you go to bed
　You like a gin with pepper.

JIM

　Glad to meet you.

BEGBICK

　Widow Begbick.
　(*Salutations*)
　And for your arrival
　Mister O'Brien
　We have raked the gravel path.

JACK

　Thanks a lot, ma'am.

BEGBICK

　And you must be Billy?

JIM (*introducing*)

　Bank Account Billy.

BEGBICK

　And this must be Joe?

JIM (*same*)

　Alaska Wolf Joe.

BEGBICK

　Just to show you that we want to make you happy, we're
　　prepared
　To offer a small discount.
　(*She changes the price list*)

BILL, JOE

　Thank you kindly!
　(*Salutations*)

BEGBICK

　Maybe you'd like some nice clean girls for a starter?

TRINITY MOSES (*brings pictures of girls and stands them up.
like a sandwich board*)　Gentlemen, every man carries in
his heart the picture of his true love. What's plump and

juicy to one man may be scrawny to another. Those
swinging hips might be the thing for you, Mister Joe.

JACK

Might be just the thing for me.

JOE

I had something darker in mind, anyway.

BEGBICK

And you, Mister Bill?

BILL

Never mind about me.

BEGBICK

And Mister Jim?

JIM

No, I can't tell from pictures. I've got to touch flesh before
    I know
If I'm in love or not.
Come out, you beauties of Mahagonny!
We've got the dough, and what's with you?

JACK, BILL, JOE

Seven years up in Alaska
Where there's money, where it's cold
Come out, you beauties of Mahagonny
If we like you, we'll pay in gold.

JENNY AND THE SIX GIRLS

Well, hello, you big boys from Alaska
Was it cold there, did you get rich?

JIM

Well hello, you beauties of Mahagonny.

JENNY AND THE SIX GIRLS

We are the beauties of Mahagonny
If you can pay you'll get what pleases your itch.

BEGBICK (*indicating Jenny*)

This is the girl for you, Mister O'Brien.
If her hips don't swing enough
Your fifty bucks ain't worth an outhouse crap.

JACK

Thirty bucks!

BEGBICK (*shrugging, to Jenny*)

Thirty bucks!

JENNY
Won't you bear in mind, Mister O'Brien
Won't you bear in mind a girl can't live on thirty bucks!
That won't keep her in stockings.
I come from Havana
But my mother was white and well-born
She used to say to me:
"My child, don't sell yourself
For a few dollar bills the way I used to do
Look at me, at what my life did to me."
Won't you change your mind, Mister O'Brien.

JACK
In that case, twenty bucks.

BEGBICK
Thirty, mister, thirty.

JACK
Forget it.

JIM
Maybe I'll take her. (*To Jenny*) What's your name?

JENNY
Jenny Smith from Oklahoma.
I got here about two months ago.
I was working down in the big cities.
And there's not one thing that I refuse to do.
I know those Jimmys, Jimmys, Jimmys from Alaska's snow
The dead don't have it half so bad as they did
That's how they made their dough, that's how they made
    their dough
They stuffed their pockets full of greenbacks and paraded
Down to the train and off to Mahagon they go.
Oh, Jimmy, darling Jimmy mine
The men all think my legs are fine
My legs are yours alone now, Jimmy.
Oh Jimmy, sit here on my knee
I've never found the man for me
Oh, do drink from my glass now, Jimmy!

JIM
Okay, I'll take you.

JENNY

Chin up, Jimmy!

(*All are about to set out for Mahagonny when people with suitcases arrive from there*)

JOE

What kind of people are they?

THE PEOPLE WITH SUITCASES (*rushing past*)

Has the ship left yet?

Thank God! No, it's still here!

(*The people with suitcases rush off to the wharf*)

BEGBICK (*cursing after them*)

Idiots, blockheads! Look at them, running for the ship. And their pockets still loaded with cash. What a bunch of lowlifes! No sense of humor!

JACK

Now I wonder why they're leaving.

Where it's nice, wise folks settle.

I'm afraid there's something fishy.

BEGBICK

Now listen, my good fellows

Just come along to Mahagonny.

It won't mean nothing to me

To once again reduce the price of whiskey.

(*She puts a third sign with even lower prices over the previous sign*)

JOE

Seems this Mahagonny, after all we've heard about it

Is too cheap, I don't like it.

BILL

To me, it's all much too expensive.

JACK

And you, Jimmy, does the place look good to you?

JIM

Wherever we are is good.

JENNY

Oh, Jimmy, sit here on my knee.

THE SIX GIRLS

Oh, Jimmy, sit here on my knee.

JENNY AND THE SIX GIRLS
  I've never found the man for me
  Oh, do drink from my glass now, Jimmy!
JENNY, THE SIX GIRLS, BEGBICK, JIM, JACK, BILL, JOE
  Those are the Jimmys, Jimmys, Jimmys from Alaska's snow.
JENNY AND THE SIX GIRLS
  The dead don't have it half so bad as they did.
JIM, JACK, BILL, JOE
  That's how we made our dough, that's how we made our dough.
JENNY AND THE SIX GIRLS
  They stuffed their jackets full of greenbacks and paraded
  Down to the train and off to Mahagon they go.
  (*All go off to Mahagonny*)

6

Instruction

Map of Mahagonny. Jim and Jenny walking.

JENNY   I've learned in my trade when you meet a man for the first time, you must ask him just how he likes things. So please tell me how you want me to be, sir.
JIM   You look fine to me just as you are. Drop the "sir," call me Jimmy, and I might begin to think you like me.
JENNY   Tell me, Jimmy, how would you like my hair done? In bangs or comb it back?
JIM   You might wear it different ways, depending on where we are.
JENNY   Then there's the matter of my lingerie, Jim. Should it be fancy underwear or should I just skip the undies?
JIM
  Skip the undies.
JENNY
  It's for you to say, sir.

JIM
And what do you want?

JENNY
Perhaps it is too soon to talk about it.

7

All great enterprises have their crises

A projection shows the statistics of crime and of cash flow in Mahagonny. Seven different price lists. Inside the "Sign of the Rich Man," Fatty the bookkeeper and Trinity Moses are sitting at the bar. Begbick rushes in, her face made up white.

BEGBICK
Fatty and Moses! Fatty and Moses, have you seen that people are leaving? They're down at the harbor. I've seen them.

FATTY THE BOOKKEEPER
What's to keep them here? A few bars and a big pile of silence . . .

TRINITY MOSES
What kind of people are they, anyway? They catch a fish and they're happy! They sit on the porch smoking and they're contented . . .

BEGBICK, FATTY, MOSES
Oh damn, this Mahagonny
Turned out to be a failure.

BEGBICK
Today whiskey is twelve dollars.

FATTY THE BOOKKEEPER
Tomorrow it will surely go down to eight.

TRINITY MOSES
And it won't ever recover!

BEGBICK, FATTY, MOSES
Oh damn, this Mahagonny
Turned out to be a failure.

BEGBICK   I don't know what to do any more! Everybody wants something from me, and I have nothing left to give. What can I offer them to make them stay and let me go on living?

BEGBICK, FATTY, MOSES
Oh damn, this Mahagonny
Turned out to be a failure.

BEGBICK
I too once tarried beside a wall in the springtime
With a young man
We had pretty phrases to trade
And our great passion to talk of.
But when the cash was gone
Who had time to be passionate?

FATTY, MOSES
Cash breeds passion
Cash breeds passion.

BEGBICK   Nineteen years of misery. The struggle for existence turned me into an empty shell. This was my last big plan; we called it Mahagonny, the spiderweb. But nothing's been caught in our web . . .

BEGBICK, FATTY, MOSES
Oh damn, this Mahagonny
Turned out to be a failure.

BEGBICK
Well, it's time for us to turn around
Go back in our tracks, driving through a thousand cities
And count backwards, wiping out
This nineteen-year stretch.
We're leaving right now!

FATTY THE BOOKKEEPER   Sure, Widow Begbick! Sure, Widow Begbick, that's just what they'd like you to do! (*Reading from a newspaper*) A squad of constables has been seen in Pensacola, inquiring for a female suspect known as Leocadia Begbick. They made a thorough search of every building there and then traveled onward . . .

BEGBICK
Damn! Now nothing can save us.

FATTY, MOSES
>Sure, Widow Begbick
>Crime won't pay, I tell you, in the long run
>And those who lead a life of crime
>Always die young!

BEGBICK
>If we had money!
>If we had made some money
>Out of this spiderweb which is no web
>Then who'd care if the constables came!
>Didn't some new suckers turn up today?
>They looked as if they had money.
>If we don't get their dough we're lost.

8

All true seekers shall be disappointed

Wharf of Mahagonny. Jim—like the men with suitcases earlier—comes from the city. His friends try to hold him back.

JACK
>Jimmy, why are you running away?

JIM
>Give me one good reason for staying.

BILL
>Come on, what are you looking so gloomy for?

JIM
>Because I saw a notice posted
>That said "Not allowed here."

JOE
>Don't you have gin and cheap whiskey?

JIM
>Too cheap!

BILL
  And peace and contentment?
JIM
  Too peaceful!
JACK
  If you want a fish for dinner
  You just go and catch one.
JIM
  That doesn't make me happy.
JOE
  You smoke.
JIM
  You smoke.
BILL
  You sleep a bit.
JIM
  You sleep.
JACK
  You swim.
JIM (*mimicking him*)
  You go pick a banana!
JOE
  You look at the water.
  (*Jim only shrugs his shoulders*)
BILL
  You forget.
JIM
  But there's something wrong.
JACK, BILL, JOE
  Wonderful to contemplate the falling twilight
  And beautiful the converse of men among themselves.
JIM
  But there's something wrong.
JACK, BILL, JOE
  Beautiful things are peace and quiet
  And a blessing is contentment.
JIM
  But there's something wrong.

JACK, BILL, JOE
  Great is the simple life in its glory
  And Mother Nature's grandeur is beyond compare.

JIM
  But there's something wrong.

  I think that I just might eat my hat
  I think that will see me through
  Tell me, why shouldn't I simply eat my hat
  When there's nothing else to do?
    The ABC's of drinking now are yours
    You've seen the moon aloft all night till dawn
    The Mandalay Saloon has closed its doors
    And face it, nothing is going on.
    Oh fellas, face it, nothing is going on!

  I think I'd just better drive to Georgia
  I hear they've got something new
  Tell me why shouldn't I simply drive to Georgia
  When there's nothing else to do?
    The ABC's of drinking now are yours
    You've seen the moon aloft all night till dawn
    The Mandalay Saloon has closed its doors
    And face it, nothing is going on.
    Oh fellas, face it, nothing is going on.

JACK, BILL, JOE
  Oh, Jimmy, don't get in a state
  The Mandalay bar's open late.

JOE
  Jimmy thinks he should eat his hat.

BILL
  Now why, Jim, would you want to eat your hat?

JACK, BILL, JOE
  You must be going bats, Jimmy!

JACK
  You can't eat any hats, Jimmy!

JACK, BILL, JOE
Don't be such a dope!
Jimmy, we've got a rope!
(*All three shouting*)
We're beating you black and blue, Jim
Until you decide that you, Jim
Are human!

JIM
Oh, fellas, I'm sick of being human.

JOE All right, you've had your say, and now you'll come
back to Mahagonny with us like a good boy.
(*They lead him back to town*)

9

*Under the open sky, in front of the "Sign of the Rich Man,"
sit the men of Mahagonny, smoking, rocking, and drinking,
our four friends among them. They listen to music and
dreamily contemplate a white cloud traveling across the
sky from left to right, then back again and so on. There are
signs standing about reading: "Kindly be careful with my
chairs," "No rough stuff," "Avoid offensive songs."*

JIM
Deep in Alaska's snow-covered woodland
My three pals and I cut all the timber we could, and
Worked as a team to haul the logs to the stream
Lived on rotten horsemeat and hoarded money.
Seven years I sweated and slaved
In order to come here.

Trapped in that cabin for seven freezing winters
Carving our curses in the one crummy table.
We talked about all the places we'd go to
All the places we'd go to, if we had enough money.
I put up with all that hardship
In order to come here.

When our time was over, we took out our money
Picked as our target of all places this damned Mahagonny
Headed this way just as fast as we could
With no rest at all
And what we found was this place.
There wasn't any place worse than this
It was the stupidest thing we could do
Deciding to come here.

(*He jumps up*) Hey, you, who do you think you are? You think you can treat us like dirt? That's where you're wrong! (*He shoots off his revolver*) Come on out, you "not-allowed-here" bitch! This is Jimmy MacIntyre from Alaska! He don't like it here!

BEGBICK (*rushing from the house*)
Just what don't you like here?

JIM
This shit-hole!

BEGBICK
I believe I heard the word "shit-hole"! Did you happen to say "shit-hole"?

JIM
Yeah, I said it, me, Jimmy MacIntyre.
(*The white cloud shudders and disappears quickly*)

JIM
Seven winters, seven winters, cutting down the trees like a fiend.

THE SIX GIRLS, JACK, BILL, JOE
He cut down trees like a fiend.

JACK
Calm down, Jim!

JIM
And the river, and the river, and the river frozen every day.

THE SIX GIRLS, JACK, BILL, JOE
The river frozen every day.

JIM
I put up with all that hardship, all of that so I could come here.

But I just don't like it here where
Nothing's going on!

JENNY

Jimmy baby, Jimmy baby
Do what we say, put the knife away.

JIM

Try and hold me back!

JACK, BILL, JOE

Do what we say, put the knife away.

JENNY

Jimmy baby, come along with us and please behave.

JIM

Try and hold me back!

JACK, JOE, BILL

Come along with us and please behave.

JIM

Seven winters cutting timber
Seven years of freezing weather
I put up with all that hardship
And all I could find was this place.

BEGBICK, FATTY, MOSES

You have quiet, friendship, whiskey, women.

JIM

Quiet, friendship, whiskey, women!

JENNY, JACK, BILL, JOE

Leave the switchblade in your pocket!

CHORUS

Qui-et! Qui-et!

BEGBICK, FATTY, MOSES

Think of sleeping, smoking, fishing, swimming!

JIM

Sleeping, smoking, fishing, swimming!

JENNY, THE SIX GIRLS, JACK, JOE, BILL

Jimmy, put the knife away! Jimmy, put the knife away!

CHORUS

Qui-et! Qui-et!

BEGBICK, FATTY, MOSES

Those are the Jimmys from Alaska
Those are the Jimmys from Alaska.

JIM

Try and hold me back, or there may be bloodshed!
Try and hold me back!

JACK, JOE, BILL

Try and hold him back! Or there may be bloodshed!
Try and hold him back!

CHORUS

Those are the Jimmys, Jimmys, Jimmys from Alaska's snow
The dead don't have it half so bad as they did.
That's how they made their dough! That's how they
made their dough!

BEGBICK, FATTY, MOSES   If these stupid jerks would only stay
in the Alaskan forest, because all they want to do is to
destroy our quiet and our contentment. Throw the bastard
out, go throw him out!

JIM

Try and hold me back or there'll be bloodshed
It's just too dull here!
It's just too dull here!
(*He stands on a table*)
Nothing in your whole damn Mahagonny
Will ever make people happy
Because there's too much peace
Too much contentment
And there is too much
A man can depend upon.
(*Lights out. All remain on stage, standing in the dark*)

10

On the backdrop appears a sign in giant letters: "A TYPHOON,"
then a second sign: "A HURRICANE IS MOVING TOWARD MAHA-
GONNY."

ALL

How frightful! A disaster!
The town of pleasure will be doomed

On the mountain peaks the hurricanes hover
Sudden death rises up out of the sea.
How frightful! A disaster!
Oh, horror, what a fate!

Where is there a wall that will keep me safe?
Where is there a cavern to protect me?
How frightful! A disaster!
Oh, horror! What a fate!

11

On this night of horrors a simple lumberjack named Jim MacIntyre discovered the laws of human happiness

Night of the hurricane. Sitting on the ground, leaning against a wall, are Jenny, Begbick, Jim, Jack, Bill, and Joe. All are in great despair, except Jim, who is laughing. From the background are heard the voices of processions passing behind the wall.

THE MEN OF MAHAGONNY (*outside*)
Stand proudly, brothers, conquer your fright
Even if chaos should darken the light
Tears are unavailing
What's the use of wailing
When you've got a hurricane to fight?

JENNY (*softly and sadly*)
Oh, moon of Alabama
We now must say good-bye
We've lost our good old mama
And must have whiskey
Oh, you know why.

JACK

    Don't try to escape it
    There's no use.
    Go where you like
    It will catch you.
    The best thing you can do
    Is to sit still
    Awaiting
    That last moment.

THE MEN OF MAHAGONNY (*outside*)

    Stand proudly, brothers, conquer your fright
    Even if chaos should darken the light
    Tears are unavailing
    What's the use of wailing
    When you've got a hurricane to fight?
    (*Jim laughs*)

BEGBICK (*to Jim*)

    What's so funny?

JIM

    Look now, this is your world:
    Peace and contentment, they don't exist
    But of hurricanes we've got plenty
    Not to mention typhoons and waterspouts.
    And it's just the same way with man:
    He will destroy what's around him.
    Why on earth do we need hurricanes?
    You think a typhoon is frightening
    Compared with man when he starts acting funny?
    (*From the distance: "Stand proudly, brothers," etc.*)

JACK

    Pipe down, Jim!

JOE

    You talk too much.

BILL

    Sit down and have a smoke and forget.

JIM

    Why build walls and towers tall as the Himalayas
    If we can't destroy them again
    Because that's how we get our kicks?

What's straight must be twisted out of shape
And what stands high must fall in the dust.
We do not need a hurricane
Let cyclones do what they can
Because devastation, fright and pain
Can also be caused by man.
(*From the distance: "Stand proudly, brothers," etc.*)

BEGBICK

Fierce is the hurricane
Fiercer still the typhoon
But the worst of all is man.

JIM (*to Begbick*)

Now look, you've put signs all around
With instructions on them:
This is forbidden
And that you may not do.
That's not the way to promote happiness.
Look on that wall, fellas, there's a signboard
It says here: Tonight it is forbidden
To sing any joyous songs.
But before two o'clock strikes
You'll hear me, Jimmy MacIntyre
Singing a joyous song
So you can see
That it's not forbidden!

JACK

We do not need a hurricane
Let cyclones do what they can
Because devastation, fright and pain
Can also be caused by man.

JENNY

Pipe down, Jimmy! You talk too much. Come outside with
me and love me up.

JIM

No, there's more to say:

Don't let false hopes blind you
There is no eternal life
The night creeps up behind you

Let each day's end remind you
Night's wind cuts like a knife.

Don't let harsh words chill you
Or think that Life's too tough
But gorge and let it fill you
The day death comes to still you
You won't have had enough.

Drop the dreams they've sold you
There isn't that much time
Don't let death's rot enfold you
Let Life's great flow uphold you
To waste it is a crime.

Let not hope confound you
To labor on and on
Or fear and trembling hound you.
Just like the beasts around you
You die and you are gone.

(*He steps forward onto the apron*)

If you're short of cash
For a thing you want to buy
Then go get the cash.
Just head for the street and find a rich man
Hit him on the head and take all his cash:
Just do it!

See a house where you'd like to live?
Just go in that house
And lie down in a bed.
When the wife comes home, give her shelter and love
When the roof starts to leak, then pack your bag!
Just do it!

If you should ever find a thought
That's new to you

Go ahead and think it.
If it costs you money or ruins your home:
Think that thought! Think that thought!
Just do it!

In the interest of order
For the good of the state
For the future of mankind
And for your personal satisfaction
Do it!

(*All have got up and taken off their hats. Jim steps back and receives their congratulations*)

THE MEN OF MAHAGONNY (*outside*)
Tears are unavailing
What's the use of wailing
When you've got a hurricane to fight . . .

BEGBICK (*motions Jim toward her and goes into a corner with him*) Then you think it was wrong of me to forbid anything?!

JIM   Sure, because when I feel like it, I just naturally ignore your signs and your laws, and kick down your walls. Just like the hurricane does. You can make money out of it. Have some.

BEGBICK (*to everyone*)
So do whatever you enjoy
Or typhoons will do it for you
For when hurricanes start to destroy
There's nothing that we can't do.

JIM, JACK, BILL, JOE
We'll live out our everyday lives
As if each day were our last one
Taking each new joy as it arrives
Never lingering over a past one.
Who can say
Any day
Nature may pull a fast one.

(*Fatty the Bookkeeper and Trinity Moses rush in, very excited*)

FATTY AND MOSES

All dead in Pensacola!
All dead in Pensacola!
And the hurricane's now moving straight ahead
For Mahagonny!

BEGBICK (*triumphantly*)

Pensacola!
Pensacola!
The constables have been struck down for good
And just and unjust alike will perish all together.
They all must go to their death.

JIM

So I say what I said before:
Now's the time to indulge in forbidden acts
When the hurricane strikes, no laws will stop it!
So, sing, for a change, because they've forbidden it.

THE MEN OF MAHAGONNY (*very near, behind the wall*)

Don't worry. Don't worry.

JIM WITH JENNY AND JOE

Therefore sing with us
Let us sing all the gay songs we know
We are forbidden to sing
So let's sing!

JIM (*jumps on top of the wall*)

Your life in this world's what you make it
And no one will carry you through
If there's got to be kicks, then I'll give them
And the kicked one, believe me, will be you.

ALL

Your life in this world's what you make it
And no one will carry you through
If there's got to be kicks, then I'll give them.
And the kicked one, believe me, will be you.

(*Blackout. The posters in the background show a geo-graphical drawing, with an arrow slowly moving toward Mahagonny, indicating the path of the hurricane*)

CHORUS (*from a distance*)

Stand proudly, brothers, conquer your fright.

12

In the pale light men and girls wait on the road outside Mahagonny. As at the end of Scene Eleven, the posters in the background again show the arrow slowly moving toward Mahagonny.
Periodic announcements over a loudspeaker during the orchestra's ritornello:
Hurricane approaching Atsena at 120 miles per hour.

Second announcement:
Atsena in ruins. No further news. Communication with Atsena impossible.

Third announcement:
Speed of hurricane increasing, hurricane heading straight for Mahagonny. Wire service with Mahagonny cut off. 11,000 dead in Pensacola.

All stare horrified at the arrow. Now, one minute away from Mahagonny, the arrow stops moving. Dead silence. Then the arrow makes a quick half-circle around Mahagonny and moves on. Loudspeakers: Hurricane has moved around Mahagonny and is continuing on its way.

CHORUS
    Oh glory, what a rescue!
    The town of pleasure has been saved.
    The mighty hurricanes have retreated beyond the mountains
    Sudden death has sunk back into the sea.
    Oh glory, what a rescue!

From then on the motto of the people of Mahagonny was "Anything goes!" As they had learned in their night of trial.

13

Hectic activity in Mahagonny, about a year after the great hurricane

The Men step out on the apron and sing.

CHORUS
First, don't forget the joys of eating
Second, comes the sexual act.
Third, go and watch the boxers fighting
Fourth comes drinking as per pact.
But mainly get it through your head
That nothing is prohibited.

(*The men move back upstage and participate in the activities. On the posters in the background the word "*EATING*" is projected in giant letters. A number of men sit, each at his own table. The tables are piled with meat. Jim among them. Jack, now nicknamed "The Glutton," sits at a table in the center and eats without stopping. To one side are the two musicians*)

JACK THE GLUTTON
I've eaten two calves, head to crupper
And now I shall eat one more calf
Not enough by half
I may eat myself for supper.

JIM
Brother, with pleasures like that
Brother, never stop at half.

A FEW MEN
O'Brien! Why fight your fat?
Stay and eat one more calf.

JACK THE GLUTTON
Brothers, watch me, doing my best
I'll eat my fill of it yet.

When it's gone, I'll be at rest
Then I can forget.
Brothers, give me more . . .
(*He falls down dead*)
THE MEN (*form a semicircle behind him, doffing their hats*)
Brother Jack has departed!
See his look of sheer ecstasy
See his look of complete satisfaction
His whole face is shining!
That man went the whole hog
That man never stopped himself
A man without fear!
(*The men put their hats back on*)
THE MEN (*filing along the apron*)
Second, comes the sexual act.

14

The posters in the background show the giant word "LOVING."
*A simple room is arranged on a podium. Begbick sits in the
center of the room, flanked by a girl, left, and a man, right.
At the foot of the podium the men of Mahagonny are standing
in line. Music in the background.*

BEGBICK (*turning toward the man beside her*)
Spit out your chewing gum first
Then give your hands a good washing.
Give the kid time
Be patient and say a few words.
THE MEN (*without looking up at them*)
Spit out your chewing gum first
Then give your hands a good washing.
Give the kid time
Be patient and say a few words.
(*The room slowly darkens*)

Quick, fellas, hey!
Now strike up the song of Mandalay:
Love doesn't have days and weeks to be reckoned
Fellas, move fast, we don't dare waste a second.
Will the moon shine every night over you, Mandalay?

(*The room has slowly been lit again. The man's chair is empty. Begbick turns to the girl*)

BEGBICK
Cash alone won't breed passion.

THE MEN (*without looking up*)
Cash alone won't breed passion.
(*The room is darkened again*)

Quick fellas, hey!
Now strike up the song of Mandalay:
Love doesn't have days and weeks to be reckoned
Fellas, move fast, we don't dare waste a second.
Will the moon shine every night over you, Mandalay?

(*The room is lit again. Another man enters the room, hangs his hat on the wall, and sits down on the empty chair. Slowly it grows dark in the room*)

THE MEN
Will the moon shine every night over you, Mandalay?
(*As it grows light again, Jim and Jenny are sitting on two chairs at some distance from each other. He is smoking, she is applying make-up*)

JENNY
See those two cranes in a great circle wheeling!

JIM
The clouds that ride beside them in the distance

JENNY
Joined them when from their nest they first were stealing

JIM
From their old life into a new existence.

JENNY
At equal heights they fly, with equal daring

JIM
Each seems to give the other its assistance.
JENNY
They fly, the crane and cloud together sharing
The lovely sky, through which their flight is fleeting.
JIM
Neither dares lag behind and end their pairing
JENNY
And neither feels a thing except the beating
The wind gives both. Each sees its partner quaking
As they fly side by side, their motions meeting.
JIM
Letting the wind abduct them with its shaking
As long as they can touch and see each other
JENNY
During which time they are immune from aching
JIM
And can be driven from one place to another
When thunder warns of rain and guns of danger.
JENNY
So under sun and moon, each orb much like its brother
They fly along, enthralled by one another.
JIM
To go where?
JENNY
                    Anywhere.
JIM
                              In flight from whom?
JENNY
                                              From
strangers.
JIM
          You ask how long these two have been together?
JENNY
Just briefly.
JIM
          And when these two will be parting?
JENNY
                                        Soon.

BOTH

So love to lovers seems a strength and boon.

(*Men are parading along the apron*)

THE MEN

First, don't forget the joys of eating
Second, comes the sexual act.
Third, go and watch the boxers fighting
Fourth comes drinking as per pact.
But mainly get it through your head
That nothing is prohibited.
(If you have money.)

15

The Men move back upstage where the word on a backdrop is now "FIGHTING" and a boxing ring is being set up. On a podium to one side a wind band is playing.

JOE (*standing on a chair*)

Now, friends and neighbors, the management proposes
Right here a prizefight, ending in k.o.
And on the card it's Trinity Moses
Versus me, big Alaska Wolf Joe.

FATTY THE BOOKKEEPER

What! You're challenging Trinity Moses?
Fella! You better throw in the towel!
We don't care who wins or who loses
But homicide is strictly foul!

JOE

I'm still alive and I'm pretty limber
All the dough that I made cutting timber
I'm gonna bet that I will come through!
And I hope my pals won't con me
You better put your money on me

Jimmy, I'm counting especially on you!
If you value brains over brawn in a fight
And speed over strength in facing a foe
Then if your wits are about you tonight
You'll bet your cash on Alaska Wolf Joe.

THE MEN

If you value brains over brawn in a fight
And speed over strength in facing a foe
Then if your wits are about you tonight
You'll bet your cash on Alaska Wolf Joe.
(*Joe has stepped over to Bill*)

BILL

Joe, you know how much I care
But when cash comes into question
I develop indigestion
When I see Trinity Moses there.
(*Joe goes to Jim*)

JIM

Joe, we'll always be friends, come what may
Unto death you are my brother
All my dough is on you today
You're a true friend like no other.

JOE

Jim, you're so good I can't bear it
And Alaska comes in view.
The seven winters, the freezing weather
The giant pine trees we felled together.

JIM

Joe, and cross my heart, I swear it
I'd give all I own to you:
The seven winters, the freezing weather
The giant pine trees we felled together.
Oh, Alaska, I can't bear it
Makes your image come in view.

JOE

Your dough will be safe, I swear it
I would kill myself for you.
(*In the meantime the boxing ring has been set up. Trinity Moses enters the ring*)

THE MEN
> Give three cheers for Trinity Moses!
> Hiya, Moses! Lay him out flat!

A WOMAN'S VOICE
> This is foul!

TRINITY MOSES
> > Sorry 'bout that!

THE MEN
> Give the weakling double doses!

REFEREE (*presenting the fighters*)
> The white trunks is Moses, muscle and guts
> The black trunks is Joe, pale and skinny.

A MAN (*shouts*)
> > > Nuts!

> (*Final preparations for the fight*)

JIM (*from below*)
> Hiya, Joe!

JOE (*greets him from the ring*)
> > Hiya, Jim!

JIM
> Don't swallow a tooth!

JOE
> > Don't look so grim!

> (*The fight begins*)

THE MEN (*severally*)
> Let's go! It's fixed!
> Crap! No clinches!
> Watch it! Keep moving! That's low! No holding!
> Got him! Like hell! Right on the kisser!
> At him, Joe! Fat chance! Yeah, he's sinking!
> (*Trinity Moses and Joe are boxing in rhythm*)
> Moses, go get him!
> Chop him up for hash!
> Moses, make him suffer!
> Give him one more bash!
> (*Joe falls*)

REFEREE
> The man is dead.
> (*Great prolonged laughter. The crowd breaks up*)

THE MEN (*drifting out*)
  A k.o.'s a k.o. After all, he knocked him flat.
REFEREE
  The winner: Trinity Moses!
TRINITY MOSES

                              Sorry 'bout that.
  (*Goes out*)
BILL (*To Jim. They are alone in the ring*)
  I told you so.
  Now he's out for good.
JIM (*softly*)
  Hiya, Joe!
  (*Men are parading along the apron*)
THE MEN
  First, don't forget the joys of eating
  Second, comes the sexual act.
  Third, go and watch the boxers fighting.
  Fourth comes drinking as per pact.
  But mainly get it through your head
  That nothing is prohibited.

16

*The Men are on stage again. The posters in the background
show the large sign "DRINKING." The men sit down, rest their
feet on the table, and drink. In the foreground Jim, Bill, and
Jenny are playing pool.*

JIM
  Bottoms, up, friends! Have one on me!
  Time we all got drunk
  You can see how easily
  A guy like Joe gets sunk.
  Widow Begbick, set 'em up for all the guys!

THE MEN
   Here's to Jimmy! Now he's talking! He's a prize!

   If you had five bucks a day
   You could stay in Mahagonny
   But a guy who liked to play
   Needed lots of extra money.
   Guys would go there for the action
   The big saloon was Mahagonny's pride
   Though they never got satisfaction
   Still, they all felt satisfied.

   On the sea
   And on land
   Everybody's getting skinned in one big operation
   All the people sit around
   And sell their skin because they've found
   That every little bit they sell brings in some dollars
      compensation.

JIM
   Widow Begbick, a second round for the gentlemen!
THE MEN
   Here's to Jimmy! Bring the whiskey! He's a prize!

   On the sea
   And on land
   People sell their skin because their needs are so intensive.
   There's a big demand for skin
   But these poor suckers never win
   Because they sell their hides so cheap, and then buy whiskey
      that's expensive.

   If you had five bucks a day
   You could stay in Mahagonny
   But a guy who liked to play
   Needed lots of extra money.
   Guys would go there for the action
   The big saloon was Mahagonny's pride

Though they never got satisfaction
Still, they all felt satisfied.

BEGBICK
Time to pay up now, gentlemen!
JIM (*softly to Jenny*)
Jenny, come here!
Jenny, I'm out of money.
We'd better beat it, you know
And it don't matter where we go!
(*Aloud to all, while pointing at the pool table*)
Friends, why don't you get on board here with me?
We'll have a little sail on the open sea.
(*Softly again*)
Better stay right here next to me, Jenny
For the deck is rocking like an earthquake
And, please, you too, Billy, better stick with me
For I'm going to head back up to Alaska
Because I do not like this town
(*Aloud*)
Look, my friends, tonight I'm sailing on this ship back to
    Alaska.
(*All have built a "ship" out of the pool table, a curtain rod
and other materials. Jim, Bill, and Jenny now get on board.
Standing on the pool table, the three imitate sailors*)
JIM
We poured all our whiskey straight down the toilet
We pulled those chintzy pink curtains down.
We had a good time and nothing to spoil it
Alaska's next if we don't drown.
(*The Men are sitting below enjoying the spectacle*)
THE MEN
Hello, Jimmy, master navigator!
Just watch him running all those sails up the mast.
Jenny, take your clothes off, we're near the Equator!
Don't lose your hat, Bill, in the Gulf Stream blast!
JENNY
My God! I can see a typhoon out yonder!

THE MEN (*solemnly, like a glee club*)
　Look at how black
　The sky over yonder is getting.
　(*The Men make the sounds of a storm, whistling and howling*)

JENNY, JIM (*roaring*)
　This ship's no velveteen settee!
　Stormy the night and raging the sea
　The boat is rocking, the night is thick
　Six of us three are getting very sick.

THE MEN
　How black the sky is now.
　Look at how black . . .

JENNY (*nervously clinging to the mast*)
　We'd better sing "Stormy the Night" to keep our courage up.

BILL
　"Stormy the Night" is terrific, when you feel your courage sinking.

JIM
　Whatever happens, we'd better sing right away.

JENNY, JIM, BILL
　"Stormy the night and the waves roll high
　Bravely the ship doth ride.
　Hark! while the light-house bell's solemn cry
　Rings over the sullen tide."

JENNY
　Pick up your speed and mind your tiller. Don't ever sail against the wind, and for God's sake don't try any new tricks.

THE MEN
　Hearken
　Hark how the wind in the fo'c'sle roars!
　Look there
　Look how the sky has turned black over yonder!

BILL
　Shouldn't we lash ourselves to the mast if the storm gets any worse?

JIM

    No, those are no storm clouds, don't you worry

    Those are the woodlands of Alaska.

    Now we're home

    Now you can all relax.

    (*He disembarks and calls out*)

    Hello, is this Alaska?

TRINITY MOSES (*suddenly appearing next to him*)

    Let's have the money for those drinks!

JIM (*deeply disappointed*)

    Oh, it's Mahagonny!

    (*The Men come forward with their drinks*)

THE MEN

    Jimmy, you have been a most splendid host here

    Jimmy, just for that we'll drink you a toast here

    You offered us food and good liquor too

    Both food and drink were a gift from you.

BEGBICK

    Well, suppose you pay me now.

JIM

    Sure, Widow Begbick, but here's something funny

    Seems all my cash has just gone somehow

    There's no way I can pay your money.

BEGBICK

    What, you don't want to pay me?

JENNY

    Jimmy, take another look.

    I bet you've got something somewhere.

JIM

    Just this minute as I took . . .

TRINITY MOSES

    What, the gentleman is out of change?

    What, the gentleman does not wish to pay?

    Do you know what that means for you?

FATTY THE BOOKKEEPER

    Fella, now you're really through.

    (*All except Bill and Jenny have moved away from him*)

BEGBICK (*to Bill and Jenny*)

    Isn't there something you could arrange?

(*Bill goes off in silence*)
How about you, Jenny?

JENNY

Me?

BEGBICK

Sure, why not?

JENNY

You're kidding!
The things they ask us girls to do!

BEGBICK

Nothing doing then?

JENNY

No, if you really want to know.

TRINITY MOSES

Tie him up!
(*While Jenny sings her song, walking back and forth across
the apron, Jim is being tied up*)

JENNY

Gents, when I was young my mother painted
My future completely black:
She said I'd end up on a stone slab
Or at any rate flat on my back.
Well, things like that aren't hard to say.
But I'm telling you it won't be like that!
You can't do a thing like that to me!
And what becomes of me, just wait and see!
A girl's not a dog!
  Your life in this world's what you make it
  And no one will carry you through.
  If there's got to be kicks, then I'll give them
  And the kicked one, believe me, will be you.

Let me tell you, once my boyfriend told me
While gazing in my eyes
"In life love is all that's important"
And "Who cares if the morning will rise?"
Well, love's a word that can be rashly said:
But we're getting older every day

And suddenly love will be dead
And you have to use your time as best you can.
A girl's not a dog!
    Your life in this world's what you make it
    And no one will carry you through.
    If there's got to be kicks, then I'll give them
    And the kicked one, believe me, will be you.

TRINITY MOSES
    Everybody come get a thrill!
    Look at the man who can't pay his bill!
    Rudeness, vice and all that mean stuff
    Worst of all, he has no green stuff!
    (*Jim is being led away*)
    The penalty's the noose, no doubt
    But, gentlemen, don't let that put you out!
    (*All go back to their seats. More drinking and pool*)
THE MEN
    You won't need five bucks a day
    If you stay inside your boxes
    And if you've a wife to lay
    You won't have to spend on extras.
    But today they get their action
    Sitting in the good Lord's run-down barroom fried.
    And they all call it satisfaction
    (*They stamp the time with their feet*)
    But they don't feel satisfied.
    (*They stop and calmly put their feet on the tables again*)

(*Men are parading along the apron before they disappear in the rear*)
THE MEN
    First, don't forget the joys of eating
    Second, comes the sexual act.
    Third, go and watch the boxers fighting
    Fourth comes drinking as per pact.
    But mainly get it through your head
    That nothing is prohibited.

17

Jim MacIntyre, handcuffed. It is night.

JIM
When the sky turns brighter
Then we start an accursed day.
But for now there is darkness in the heavens.
May the night
Last forever.
May the day
Never dawn.

I am afraid they'll be here shortly.

I will have to lie down on the ground
When they get here.
They'll have to pry me loose if they expect
To take me away.
May the night
Last forever
May the day
Never dawn.

Put it in your pipe now
Jim, old fellow
Smoke it up.
Every day you lived
Was good enough for you
And what's coming
Put that in your pipe too.

Surely, the sky will stay dark for a long time.
(*It becomes light*)
Don't let the light come
For then we start an accursed day.

18

The courts in Mahagonny were no worse than anywhere else

Law court in a tent. A table and three chairs, and a small amphitheater-like gallery of the kind seen in operating rooms. In it spectators reading newspapers, smoking, chewing gum. Begbick is in the judge's chair, Fatty the Bookkeeper acts as counsel for the defense. In the dock on one side, a man.

MOSES (*as prosecutor, at the entrance*)
Everyone step up and buy your tickets
We've got a few seats left for just five dollars.
Two really entertaining trials
Only five dollars for a seat.
Only a fin, gentlemen
To see the wheels of Justice in motion.
(*As no one else comes in, he goes back to the prosecutor's chair*)
First comes the case of Tobby Higgins.
(*The man in the dock rises*)
You are charged with premeditated murder
For the purpose of trying out an old revolver.
Till today
The world has never known a deed
So frankly brutal.
Every normal human feeling
You have shamelessly defied.
And the mortally offended heart of justice
Raises loud cries of retribution.
Hence I demand for the prosecution
That in view of the defendant's unrepentant stance
Which proves his unbelievable depravity
Justice be given free rein
(*hesitating*)

And he . . .
Conceivably . . .
Be acquitted!
(*During the prosecutor's speech a silent battle has been
going on between the accused and Begbick. By putting up
his fingers he has shown how large a bribe he is willing to
pay. In the same way Begbick has led him to up his offer
again and again. The prosecutor's hesitation at the end of
his speech marks the point at which the accused raises his
offer for the last time*)

BEGBICK
Let the defense present its argument!

FATTY THE BOOKKEEPER
Will the injured party rise?
(*Silence*)

THE MEN (*audience on the gallery*)
The dead don't tell no tales.

BEGBICK
If no injured party comes forward
Then it is our duty to acquit the man.
(*The accused joins the spectators in the gallery*)

TRINITY MOSES (*continues reading*)
Second, the case of Jimmy MacIntyre
Charged with petty larceny and defaulting on debt.
(*Jim has appeared in handcuffs, led in by Bill*)

JIM (*before taking his seat in the dock*)
Please, Bill, let me have a hundred dollars
So my case can get a decent hearing.

BILL
Jim, you know how much I care
But with cash it's quite another matter.

JIM
Bill, won't you try to remember
The time we spent up in Alaska.
The seven winters, the freezing weather
The giant pine trees we felled together
And give me the dough.

BILL
Jim, I'll remember forever

The time we spent up in Alaska.
The seven winters, the freezing weather
The giant pine trees we felled together
And how hard it was
To earn all that money
Yes, Jim, and that's why I
Can't give you any.

TRINITY MOSES

You, the defendant, are charged with never paying
For whiskey and a curtain rod you took.
Till today
The world has never known a deed
So frankly brutal.
Every normal human feeling
You have shamelessly defied
And the mortally offended heart of justice
Raises loud cries of retribution.
Hence I demand for the prosecution
That justice be given free rein.
(*During the prosecutor's speech, Jim has not responded to Begbick's finger-signals. Begbick, Fatty the Bookkeeper, and Moses exchange meaningful glances*)

BEGBICK

Good. Let's begin. I now will read the charges
Against you, Jimmy MacIntyre!
When you first came here to Mahagonny
You did seduce a girl named Jenny Smith
And did compel her with cash
To commit a carnal act with you.

FATTY THE BOOKKEEPER

Will the injured party rise?

JENNY (*coming forward*)

I'm the one.
(*Murmurs among the spectators*)

BEGBICK

And on the night of the great typhoon
In our hour of doubt and confusion
You sang an illegal, joyous song.

FATTY THE BOOKKEEPER
>Will the injured party rise?

THE MEN
>No injured party is speaking up
>Because no injury has been done.
>If no injury has been done
>Maybe there's some hope left for you, Jimmy MacIntyre!

TRINITY MOSES (*interrupting*)
>But on that aforesaid night
>The accused behaved
>As though the typhoon were in him
>And he seduced the entire town
>And destroyed their peace and contentment.

THE MEN
>Bravo! Yay, Jimmy!

BILL (*rising in the gallery*)
>He's a simple lumberjack from Alaska
>Who discovered the laws of human happiness
>By which you all have lived in Mahagonny
>You, the people of Mahagonny.

THE MEN
>That's why they must acquit our hero, Jimmy MacIntyre
>The lumberjack from Alaska.

BILL
>Jim, I'm doing this for you
>Because I think of Alaska.
>The seven winters, the freezing weather
>The giant pine trees we felled together.

JIM
>Bill, what you did for me just now
>Brings me memories of Alaska.
>The seven winters, the freezing weather
>The giant pine trees we felled together.

TRINITY MOSES (*pounds the table*)
>But during a boxing match
>This so-called "simple lumberjack from Alaska"
>So as to win a lot of money
>Sent his best friend to a certain death.

BILL (*jumps up*)
>   Ah, but who, I ask Your Honor
>   Just who really killed the aforesaid friend?

BEGBICK
>   Who did kill the said Alaska Wolf Joe?

TRINITY MOSES (*after a pause*)
>   That is not known to the court.

BILL
>   But of all the men who stood around and watched
>   Not a single one bet on Joe
>   When he gave up his life in fighting.
>   Only Jimmy MacIntyre who's standing here.

THE MEN (*severally*)
>   That's why they've got to fry this bastard Jimmy MacIntyre
>   That's why they must acquit our hero, Jimmy MacIntyre
>   The lumberjack from Alaska.
>   (*The men cheer and boo*)

TRINITY MOSES
>   Now comes the main count against you.
>   You consumed three bottles of whiskey
>   And you entertained yourself with a curtain rod.
>   Then why, oh why, Jimmy MacIntyre
>   When it came time to pay did you refuse?

JIM
>   Because I am broke.

THE MEN (*severally*)
>   Because he's broke
>   He can't pay for his expenses.
>   That's it for Jimmy MacIntyre!
>   That's it for him!

BEGBICK
>   Now, will the injured parties rise?
>   (*Begbick, Fatty the Bookkeeper, and Trinity Moses rise*)

THE MEN
>   Look at the three injured parties there
>   Aha, so they are the injured ones.

FATTY THE BOOKKEEPER
>   Your Honor, what is the verdict?

BEGBICK   In view of the deplorable state of the economy, the
Court grants itself extenuating cirmumstances.
You, Jimmy MacIntyre, hereby are sentenced—

TRINITY MOSES
As accessory to the murder of a friend—

BEGBICK
To two days in jail.

TRINITY MOSES
For disturbing our peace and contentment—

BEGBICK
Two year's loss of civil rights.

TRINITY MOSES
For the seduction of a girl known as Jenny—

BEGBICK
To four years probation.

TRINITY MOSES
For the singing of illegal songs during a hurricane—

BEGBICK
To ten years in prison.
But because you drank three bottles of whiskey
And used my curtain rod without paying
You are condemned to death, Jimmy MacIntyre.

BEGBICK, FATTY, MOSES
In the whole human race
There is no greater criminal
Than a man without money.
(*A storm of applause*)

[Benares song]

19

Execution and death of Jimmy MacIntyre. Many people may prefer not to witness the execution of Jimmy MacIntyre here following; but in our opinion even they would not want to pay his bill. So great is the respect for money in our times

A projection in the background shows a general view of Mahagonny peacefully lit up. Many people are standing around in scattered groups. When Jim appears, led by Trinity Moses, Jenny, and Bill, the men doff their hats. On the right an electric chair is being made ready.

TRINITY MOSES (*to Jim*)
  Greet them!
  Can't you see they're greeting you?
  (*Jim greets the Men*)
  Settle all your worldly affairs right now
  Because the gentlemen who wish to witness your downfall
  Will not want to be bothered with your private affairs.

JIM
  Darling Jenny
  I'm leaving now.
  The days that I spent with you
  Were pleasant ones.
  And pleasant too
  Was their ending.

JENNY
  Darling Jimmy
  I also enjoyed the little time I had
  With you
  And I don't know
  What will happen to me.

JIM
  Take my word
  There's many more around like me.

JENNY
  That is not true.
  I know nothing ever will be like it.

JIM
  You're even wearing a white dress, aren't you
  Like a widow?

JENNY
  Yes, I'm your widow.
  And I'll never forget you
  When I go back
  To the girls.

JIM
  Kiss me, Jenny!

JENNY
  Kiss me, Jimmy!

JIM
  Think of me.

JENNY
  Sure will.

JIM
  Don't think badly of me.

JENNY
  Why would I?

JIM
  Kiss me, Jenny.

JENNY
  Kiss me, Jimmy.

JIM
  And now I'll leave you, my dear
  To my close companion Billy
  He's the only one left
  Of us four musketeers
  Who came down from Alaska.

BILL
  So long, Jim!

JIM
    So long, Bill!
    (*They walk to the execution site*)
SEVERAL MEN (*walking past them say to each other*)
    First, don't forget the joys of eating
    Second, comes the sexual act.
    Third, go and watch the boxers fighting
    Fourth comes drinking as per pact.
    (*Jim has stopped and is looking after them*)
TRINITY MOSES
    Do you have anything else to say?
JIM
    Yes. Do you really want to execute me?
BEGBICK
    Yes. It's the custom.
JIM
    Maybe you don't know that there's a God?
BEGBICK
    A what?
JIM
    A God!
BEGBICK   Oh! You want to know if we think there's a God?
    We have an answer for that: For his benefit, let's put on the
    God in Mahagonny Play! And you, sit down in that electric
    chair!
    (*Four Men and Jenny Smith place themselves in front of
    Jim MacIntyre and enact the God in Mahagonny Play*)

THE FOUR MEN
    One morning when the sky was gray
    Smack in our whiskey
    God came to Mahagonny
    Smack in our whiskey
    We saw God had come to Mahagonny.

TRINITY MOSES (*who plays the role of God, separates himself
    from the others, steps forward, and covers his face with
    his hat*)
    Must you swill like sponges

All my precious rye year after year?
Did you think that I was never coming?
Are you ready now that I am here?

JENNY

At one another they looked, the men of Mahagonny.
Yes, they said, the men of Mahagonny.

THE FOUR

One morning when the sky was gray
Smack in our whiskey
God came to Mahagonny
Smack in our whiskey
We saw God had come to Mahagonny.

TRINITY MOSES

Did you laugh on Friday evening?
I saw Mary Weeman in the lake
Floating belly up like some dead codfish
And she won't dry out, make no mistake.

JENNY

At one another they looked, the men of Mahagonny.
Yes, they said, the men of Mahagonny.

THE FOUR (*acting as though they had heard nothing*)

One morning when the sky was gray
Smack in our whiskey
God came to Mahagonny
Smack in our whiskey
We saw God had come to Mahagonny.

TRINITY MOSES

Does this gun look familiar?
Did you shoot a man who served me well?
Do I have to live with you in Heaven
With your dirty hair and drunken smell?

JENNY

At one another they looked, the men of Mahagonny.
Yes, they said, the men of Mahagonny.

THE FOUR

One morning when the sky was gray
Smack in our whiskey

God came to Mahagonny
Smack in our whiskey
We saw God had come to Mahagonny.

TRINITY MOSES
You can all go to Hell now!
Put away your stogies. Off you go!
Double-time it down to Hell, you meat-heads!
Soon you'll all be burning there below.

JENNY
At one another they looked, the men of Mahagonny.
No, they said, the men of Mahagonny.

THE FOUR
One morning when the sky was gray
Smack in our whiskey
You come to Mahagonny
Smack in our whiskey
You start out in Mahagonny!

Boys, sit square on your asses
We are on strike. Hold it steady!
You can't drag us down to hell, you nitwit
'Cause we've been in hell for years already.

JENNY (*yells through a megaphone*)
At God they looked, the men of Mahagonny.
No, they said, the men of Mahagonny.

JIM   Now I realize that my doom was sealed when I first
came to this city, trying to buy myself happiness with
money. Here I sit now, and I've had nothing. I was the
one who said: Everybody must carve out a piece of meat
for himself, with any knife. But the meat was rotten! The
happiness I bought was no happiness and the freedom money
gives is no freedom. I ate and was still hungry, I drank and
was still thirsty. Could somebody give me a glass of water?

TRINITY MOSES (*putting the helmet on him*)
Ready!

20

And amid increasing confusion, rising prices, and
the hostility of all against all, those not yet killed
demonstrated during the last weeks of Spiderweb
City for their ideals.—They had learned nothing

The posters in the background show Mahagonny in flames.
Then the columns of demonstrators march in: they intersect,
collide, and continue to the end.

First column: Begbick, Fatty the Bookkeeper, Trinity Moses,
and their friends. The signs of the first column say:

FOR HIGHER PRICES

FOR THE FIGHT OF ALL AGAINST ALL

FOR THE CHAOTIC CONDITION OF OUR CITIES

FOR THE CONTINUATION OF THE GOLDEN AGE

FIRST COLUMN
This enchanting town of Mahagonny
Is great if you've got the money
It offers everything
'Cause everything's for sale
And there is nothing on earth that can't be bought.

The signs of the second column say:

FOR PROPERTY

FOR THE EXPROPRIATION OF OTHERS

FOR THE JUST DISTRIBUTION OF UNWORLDLY GOODS

FOR THE UNJUST DISTRIBUTION OF WORLDLY GOODS

FOR LOVE

FOR THE VENALITY OF LOVE

FOR THE NATURAL DISORDER OF THINGS

FOR THE CONTINUATION OF THE GOLDEN AGE

SECOND COLUMN
> We do not need a hurricane
> Let cyclones do what they can
> Because devastation, fright and pain
> Can also be caused by man.

> *The signs of the third column say:*
> FOR THE FREEDOM OF THE RICH
> FOR BRAVERY AGAINST THE DEFENSELESS
> FOR THE HONOR OF MURDERERS
> FOR THE IDEALIZATION OF FILTH
> FOR THE IMMORTALITY OF BASENESS
> FOR THE CONTINUATION OF THE GOLDEN AGE

THIRD COLUMN
> Your life in this world's what you make it
> And no one will carry you through.
> If there's got to be kicks, then I'll give them
> And the kicked one, believe me, will be you.

FIRST COLUMN (*coming back with its signs*)
> This enchanting town of Mahagonny
> Is dismal when there's no money
> For cash does wonders
> You're sunk without it
> It's only money a man can depend upon.

FOURTH COLUMN (*girls carrying on a linen cushion Jim Mac-Intyre's watch, revolver, and checkbook, and on a pole his shirt*)
> Oh, moon of Alabama
> We now must say good-bye
> We've lost our good old mama
> And must have dollars
> Oh, you know why.

> *Fifth column with Jim MacIntyre's body. Close behind a sign:*
> FOR THE RULE OF LAW

FIFTH COLUMN
    You can wet his mouth with vinegar
    You can wipe the sweat off his brow
    You can go get a pair of pincers
    Gently draw his tongue out of his mouth
    Nothing you can do will help a dead man.

Sixth column, with a small sign:
FOR STUPIDITY

SIXTH COLUMN
    You can try to sweet-talk him
    Or you can yell at him
    Or you can let him lie there
    Or you can drag him with you
    You can never give a dead man any orders
    You can press cash into his hand
    You can dig a hole for him
    You can stuff him down in it
    You can throw the shovel at him
    Nothing you can do will help a dead man.

Seventh column, with a giant sign:
FOR THE CONTINUATION OF THE GOLDEN AGE

SEVENTH COLUMN
    You can reminisce about his shining hour
    You can let his shining hour be forgotten
    Nothing you can do will help a dead man.

(Endless columns in constant motion)
ALL COLUMNS
    Nothing will help him or us or you now.

The Threepenny Opera

After John Gay:
The Beggar's Opera

Collaborators: E. Hauptmann, K. Weill

Translators: Ralph Manheim and John Willett

CHARACTERS

MACHEATH, called Mac the Knife

JONATHAN JEREMIAH PEACHUM,
    proprietor of "Beggar's
    Friend Ltd."

CELIA PEACHUM, his wife

POLLY PEACHUM, his daughter

BROWN, High Sheriff of London

LUCY, his daughter

LOW-DIVE JENNY

SMITH

THE REVEREND KIMBALL

FILCH

A BALLAD SINGER

THE GANG

BEGGARS

WHORES

CONSTABLES

Prologue

The Ballad of Mac the Knife

Fair in Soho

The beggars are begging, the thieves are stealing, the whores are whoring. A ballad singer sings a ballad:

See the shark with teeth like razors.
All can read his open face.
And Macheath has got a knife, but
Not in such an obvious place.

See the shark, how red his fins are
As he slashes at his prey.
Mac the Knife wears white kid gloves which
Give the minimum away.

By the Thames's turbid waters
Men abruptly tumble down.
Is it plague or is it cholera?
Or a sign Macheath's in town?

On a beautiful blue Sunday
See a corpse stretched in the Strand.
See a man dodge round the corner . . .
Mackie's friends will understand.

And Schmul Meier, reported missing
Like so many wealthy men:
Mack the Knife acquired his cash box.
God alone knows how or when.

(Peachum goes walking across the stage from left to right with his wife and daughter)

Jenny Towler turned up lately
With a knife stuck through her breast
While Macheath walks the Embankment
Nonchalantly unimpressed.

Where is Alfred Gleet the cabman?
Who can get that story clear?
All the world may know the answer
Just Macheath has no idea.

And the ghastly fire in Soho—
Seven children at a go—
In the crowd stands Mac the Knife, but he
Isn't asked and doesn't know.

And the child-bride in her nightie
Whose assailant's still at large
Violated in her slumbers—
Mackie, how much did you charge?

(Laughter among the whores. A man steps out from their midst and walks quickly away across the square)

LOW-DIVE JENNY   That was Mac the Knife!

ACT ONE

1

To combat the increasing callousness of mankind, J. Peachum, businessman, has opened a shop where the poorest of the poor can acquire an exterior that will touch the hardest of hearts.

Jonathan Jeremiah Peachum's outfitting shop for beggars

PEACHUM'S MORNING HYMN

You ramshackle Christian, awake!
Go on with your sinful employment
Show what an old crook you could make.
The Lord will soon cut your enjoyment.

Betray your own brother, you rogue
And sell your old woman, you rat.
You think the Lord God's just a joke?
He'll give you His Judgment on that.

PEACHUM (*to the audience*) Something must be done. My business is too hard, for my business is arousing human sympathy. There are a few things that stir men's souls, just a few, but the trouble is that after repeated use they lose their effect. Because man has the abominable gift of being able to deaden his feelings at will, so to speak. Suppose, for instance, a man sees another man standing on the corner with a stump for an arm; the first time he may be shocked enough to give him tenpence, but the second time it will only be fivepence, and if he sees him a third time he'll hand him over to the police without batting an eyelash. It's the same with the spiritual approach. (*A large sign saying "It is more blessed to give than to receive" is lowered from the grid*) What good are the most beautiful, the most poignant sayings, painted on the most enticing little signs, when they get expended so quickly? The Bible has four or five sayings that stir the heart; once a man has expended them, there's nothing for it but starvation. Take this one, for instance— "Give and it shall be given unto you"—how threadbare it is after hanging here a mere three weeks. Yes, you have to keep on offering something new. So it's back to the good old Bible again, but how long can it go on providing? (*Knocking. Peachum opens. Enter a young man by the name of Filch*)

FILCH   Messrs. Peachum & Co.?

PEACHUM   Peachum.

FILCH   Are you the proprietor of the "Beggar's Friend Ltd."? I've been sent to you. Fine slogans you've got there! Money in the bank, that is. Got a whole library full of them, I suppose? That's what I call really something. What chance has a bloke like me got to think up ideas; and how can business flourish without education?

PEACHUM   What's your name?

FILCH   It's like this, Mr. Peachum, I've been down on my luck since I was a boy. My mother drank, my father gambled. Left to my own resources at an early age, without a mother's tender hand, I sank deeper and deeper into the quicksands of the big city. I've never known a father's care or the blessings of a happy home. So now you see me . . .

PEACHUM   So now I see you . . .

FILCH   (*confused*)   . . . bereft of all support, a prey to my base instincts.

PEACHUM   Like a derelict on the high seas and so on. Now tell me, derelict, which district have you been reciting that fairy story in?

FILCH   What do you mean, Mr. Peachum?

PEACHUM   You deliver that speech in public, I take it?

FILCH   Well, it's like this, Mr. Peachum, yesterday there was an unpleasant little incident in Highland Street. There I am, standing on the corner quiet and miserable, holding out my hat, no suspicion of anything nasty . . .

PEACHUM (*leafs through a notebook*) Highland Street. Yes, yes, right. You're the bastard that Honey and Sam caught yesterday. You had the impudence to be molesting passers-by in District 10. We let you off with a thrashing because we had reason to believe you didn't know what's what. But if you show your face again it'll be the ax for you. Got it?

FILCH Please, Mr. Peachum, please. What can I do, Mr. Peachum? The gentlemen beat me black and blue and then they gave me your business card. If I took off my coat, you'd think you were looking at a fish on a slab.

PEACHUM My friend, if you don't look like a bloater, then my men haven't been doing their job. Along come these young whippersnappers, imagining they've only got to hold out their paws to land a steak. What would you say if somebody started fishing the best trout out of your pond?

FILCH It's like this, Mr. Peachum—I haven't got a pond.

PEACHUM Licenses are issued to professionals only. (*Points in a businesslike way to a map of the city*) London is divided into fourteen districts. Any man who intends to practice the craft of begging in any of them needs a license from Jonathan Jeremiah Peachum & Co. Why, anybody could come along—a prey to his base instincts.

FILCH Mr. Peachum, only a few shillings stand between me and utter ruin. Something must be done. With two shillings in my pocket I . . .

PEACHUM One pound.

FILCH Mr. Peachum!

(*Points imploringly at a sign saying "Do not turn a deaf ear to misery!" Peachum points to the curtain over a show-case, on which is written: "Give and it shall be given unto you!"*)

FILCH Ten bob.

PEACHUM Plus fifty percent of your take. Settle up once a week. With outfit seventy percent.

FILCH What does the outfit consist of?

PEACHUM That's for the firm to decide.

FILCH Which district could I start in?

PEACHUM   Baker Street. Numbers 2 to 104. That comes even cheaper. Only fifty percent, including the outfit.

FILCH   Very well. (*He pays*)

PEACHUM   Your name?

FILCH   Charles Filch.

PEACHUM   Right. (*Shouts*) Mrs. Peachum! (*Mrs. Peachum enters*) This is Filch. Number three-fourteen. Baker Street district. I'll do his entry myself. Trust you to pick this moment to apply, just before the Coronation, when for once in a lifetime there's a chance of making a little something. Outfit C. (*He opens a linen curtain before a show-case in which there are five wax dummies*)

FILCH   What's that?

PEACHUM   Those are the five basic types of misery, those most likely to touch the human heart. The sight of such types puts a man into that unnatural state where he is willing to part with money.

Outfit A: Victim of the traffic speed-up. The merry cripple, always cheerful (*he acts it out*), always carefree, emphasized by arm-stump.

Outfit B: Victim of the Higher Strategy. The Tiresome Trembler, molests passers-by, operates by inspiring nausea (*he acts it out*), attenuated by medals.

Outfit C: Victim of modern Technology. The Pitiful Blind Man, the Cordon Bleu of Beggary. (*He acts it out, staggering toward Filch. The moment he bumps into Filch, Filch cries out in horror. Peachum stops at once, looks at him with amazement and suddenly roars*) He's *sorry* for me! You'll never be a beggar as long as you live! You're only fit to be begged from! Very well, outfit D! Celia, you've been drinking again. And now you can't see straight. Number one-thirty-six has complained about his outfit. How often do I have to tell you that a gentleman doesn't put on filthy clothes? Number one-thirty-six paid for a brand-new suit. The only thing about it that could inspire pity was the stains and they should have been added by just ironing in candle wax. Use your head! Have I got to do everything myself? (*To Filch*) Take off your clothes and put this on, but mind you, look after it!

FILCH   What about my things?

PEACHUM   Property of the firm. Outfit E: young man who has seen better days or, if you'd rather, never thought it would come to this.

FILCH   Oh, you use them again? Why can't *I* do the better days act?

PEACHUM   Because nobody can make his own suffering sound convincing, my boy. If you have a bellyache and say so, people will simply be disgusted. Anyway, you're not here to ask questions but to put these things on.

FILCH   Aren't they rather dirty? (*After Peachum has given him a penetrating look*) Excuse me, sir, please excuse me.

MRS. PEACHUM   Shake a leg, son, I'm not standing here holding your trousers till Christmas.

FILCH   (*suddenly emphatic*)   But I'm not taking my shoes off! Absolutely not. I'd sooner drop the whole business. They're the only present my poor mother ever gave me, I may have sunk pretty low, but never . . .

MRS. PEACHUM   Stop driveling. We all know your feet are dirty.

FILCH   Where am I supposed to wash my feet? In mid-winter? (*Mrs. Peachum leads him behind a screen, then she sits down on the left and starts ironing candle wax into a suit*)

PEACHUM   Where's your daughter?

MRS. PEACHUM   Polly? Upstairs.

PEACHUM   Has that man been here again? The one who always comes round when I'm out?

MRS. PEACHUM   Don't be so suspicious, Jonathan, there's no finer gentleman. The Captain takes a real interest in our Polly.

PEACHUM   I see.

MRS. PEACHUM   And if I've got half an eye in my head, Polly thinks he's very nice too.

PEACHUM   Celia, the way you chuck your daughter around anyone would think I was a millionaire. Wanting to marry her off? The idea! Do you think this lousy business of ours would survive a week if those ragamuffins our customers had nothing better than *our* legs to look at? A husband! He'd have us in his clutches in three shakes! In his clutches like this! Do you think your daughter can hold her tongue in bed any better than you?

MRS. PEACHUM   A fine opinion of your daughter you have.

PEACHUM   The worst. The very worst. A lump of sensuality, that's what she is.

MRS. PEACHUM   If so, she didn't get it from you.

PEACHUM   Marriage! I expect my daughter to be to me as bread to the hungry (*he leafs in the Book*); it even says so in the Bible somewhere. Anyway marriage is disgusting. I'll teach her to get married.

MRS. PEACHUM   Jonathan, you're just a barbarian.

PEACHUM   Barbarian! What's this gentleman's name?

MRS. PEACHUM   They never call him anything but "the Captain."

PEACHUM   So you haven't even asked him his name? Interesting.

MRS. PEACHUM   We wouldn't be so rude as to ask him for his birth certificate when he's so distinguished and invited the two of us to the Cuttlefish Hotel for a little hop.

PEACHUM   Where?

MRS. PEACHUM   To the Cuttlefish for a little hop.

PEACHUM   Captain? Cuttlefish Hotel? Hm, hm, hm . . .

MRS. PEACHUM   A gentleman who has always handled my daughter and me with kid gloves.

PEACHUM   Kid gloves!

MRS. PEACHUM   It's quite true, he always does wear gloves, white ones: white kid gloves.

PEACHUM   I see. White gloves and a cane with an ivory handle and spats and patent-leather shoes and an overpowering personality and a scar . . .

MRS. PEACHUM   On his neck. What! Isn't there anybody you don't know? (*Filch crawls out from behind the screen*)

FILCH   Mr. Peachum, couldn't you give me some tips, I've always believed in having a system and not just shooting off my mouth any old how.

MRS. PEACHUM   A system!

PEACHUM   Let him be a half-wit. Come back this evening at six, we'll teach you the rudiments. Now clear out!

FILCH   Thank you very much indeed, Mr. Peachum. Many thanks. (*Goes out*)

PEACHUM   Fifty percent!—And now I'll tell you who this gentleman with the gloves is—Mac the Knife! (*He runs up the stairs to Polly's bedroom*)

MRS. PEACHUM   God in Heaven! Mac the Knife! Lord alive! For what we are about to receive, the Lord—Polly! What's become of Polly?

(*Peachum comes down slowly*)

PEACHUM   Polly? Polly's not come home. Her bed is untouched.

MRS. PEACHUM   Then she's gone to supper with that wool merchant. That'll be it.

PEACHUM   Let's hope to God it is the wool merchant!

(*Mr. and Mrs. Peachum step before the curtain and sing. Song lighting: golden glow. The organ is lit up. Three lamps are lowered from above on a pole, and the signs say:*)

The "No They Can't" Song

1

PEACHUM

No, they can't
Bear to be at home all tucked up tight in bed.
It's fun they want
You can bet they've got some fancy notions brewing up
   instead.

MRS. PEACHUM

So that's your Moon over Soho
That is your infernal "d'you feel my heart beating?" line.
That's the old "wherever you go I shall be with you, honey"
When you first fall in love and the moonbeams shine.

2

PEACHUM

No, they can't
See what's good for them and set their mind on it.

It's fun they want
So they end up on their arses in the shit.

BOTH
Then where's your Moon over Soho?
What's come of your infernal "d'you feel my heart beating?"
    bit?
Where's the old "wherever you go I shall be with you,
    honey"?
When you're no more in love and you're in the shit.

2

Deep in the heart of Soho the bandit Mac the Knife is
celebrating his marriage to Polly Peachum, the beggar
king's daughter

Bare Stable

MATTHEW (*known as Matt of the Mint, holds out his revolver
and examines the room with a lantern*)   Hey, hands up if
anybody's here!
    (*Macheath enters and makes a tour of inspection along the
    footlights*)
MACHEATH   Well, is anybody here?
MATTHEW   Not a soul. Just the place for our wedding.
POLLY (*enters in wedding dress*)   But it's a stable!
MAC   Sit on the feed-bin for the moment, Polly. (*To the
audience*) Today this stable will witness my marriage to
Miss Polly Peachum, who has followed me for love in order
to share my life with me.
MATTHEW   All over London they'll be saying this is the most
daring job you've ever pulled, enticing Mr. Peachum's only
child from his home.
MAC   Who's Mr. Peachum?

MATTHEW   He'll tell you he's the poorest man in London.

POLLY   But you surely don't intend to have our wedding here? Why, it is a common stable. You can't ask the vicar to a place like this. Besides, it isn't even ours. We really oughtn't to start our new life with a burglary, Mac. Why, this is the biggest day of our life.

MAC   Dear child, everything shall be done as you wish. We can't have you embarrassed in any way. The trimmings will be here in a moment.

MATTHEW   That'll be the furniture.

(*Large vans are heard driving up. Half a dozen men come in, carrying carpets, furniture, dishes, etc., with which they transform the stable into an exaggeratedly luxurious room*[1])

MAC   Junk.

(*The gentlemen put the presents down left, congratulate the bride, and report to the bridegroom*)[2]

JAKE (*known as Crook-fingered Jake*)   Congratulations! At 14 Ginger Street there were some people on the second floor. We had to smoke them out.

BOB (*known as Bob the Saw*)   Congratulations! A copper got bumped in the Strand.

MAC   Amateurs.

NED   We did all we could, but three people in the West End were past saving. Congratulations!

MAC   Amateurs and bunglers.

JIMMY   An old gent got hurt a bit, but I don't think it's anything serious. Congratulations.

MAC   My orders were: avoid bloodshed. It makes me sick to think of it. You'll never make businessmen! Cannibals, yes, but not businessmen!

WALTER (*known as Dreary Walt*)   Congratulations. Only half an hour ago, madam, that harpsichord belonged to the Duchess of Somerset.

POLLY   What is this furniture anyway?

MAC   How do you like the furniture, Polly?

POLLY (*in tears*)   Those poor people, all for a few sticks of furniture.

---

* The notes in the text refer to the "Hints for Actors," p. 327.

MAC   And what furniture! Junk! You have a perfect right to be angry. A rosewood harpsichord with a Renaissance sofa. That's unforgivable. What about a table?

WALTER   A table?

(*They lay some planks over the bins*)

POLLY   Oh, Mac, I'm so miserable! I only hope the vicar doesn't come.

MATTHEW   Of course he'll come. We gave him exact directions.

WALTER (*introduces the table*)   A table!

MAC (*seeing Polly in tears*)   My wife is very much upset. Where are the rest of the chairs? A harpsichord and no chairs! Use your heads! For once I'm having a wedding, and how often does that happen? Shut up, Dreary! How often does it happen that I leave you to do something on your own? And when I do you make my wife unhappy right at the start.

NED   Dear Polly . . .

MAC (*knocks his hat off his head*)[3]   "Dear Polly"! I'll bash your head through your kidneys with your "dear Polly," you squirt. Have you ever heard the like? "Dear Polly"! I suppose you've been to bed with her?

POLLY   Mac!

NED   I swear . . .

WALTER   Dear madam, if any items of furniture should be lacking, we'll be only too glad to go back and . . .

MAC   A rosewood harpsichord and no chairs. (*Laughs*) Speaking as a bride, what do you say to that?

POLLY   It could be worse.

MAC   Two chairs and a sofa and the bridal couple has to sit on the floor.

POLLY   Something new, I'd say.

MAC (*sharply*)   Get the legs sawn off this harpsichord! Go on!

FOUR MEN (*saw the legs off the harpsichord and sing*)

Bill Lawgen and Mary Syer
Were made man and wife a week ago.
When it was over and they exchanged a kiss

He was thinking "Whose wedding dress was this?"
While his name was a thing she would have liked to know.
Hooray!

WALTER   The final result, madam: there's your bench.

MAC   May I now ask the gentlemen to take off those filthy rags and put on some decent clothes? After all this isn't just anybody's wedding. Polly, may I ask you to look after the grub?

POLLY   Is this our wedding feast? Was the whole lot stolen, Mac?

MAC   Of course. Of course.

POLLY   I wonder what you will do if there's a knock at the door and the sheriff steps in.

MAC   I'll show you what your husband will do in such a situation.

MATTHEW   It couldn't happen today. The mounted police are all sure to be in Daventry. They'll be escorting the Queen back to town for Friday's Coronation.

POLLY   Two knives and fourteen forks! One knife per chair.

MAC   What incompetence! That's the work of apprentices, not experienced men! Haven't you any sense of style? Fancy not knowing the difference between Chippendale and Louis Quatorze.

(*The gang comes back. The gentlemen are now wearing fashionable evening dress, but unfortunately their movements are not in keeping with it*)

WALTER   We only wanted to bring the most valuable stuff. Look at that wood! Really first class.

MATTHEW   Ssst! Ssst! Permit us, Captain . . .

MAC   Polly, come here a minute.

(*Mac and Polly assume the pose of a couple prepared to receive congratulations*)

MATTHEW   Permit us, Captain, on the greatest day of your life, in the bloom of your career, or rather the turning point, to offer you our most indispensable and at the same time most sincere congratulations, and so forth. That posh talk don't half make me sick. So to cut a long story short (*shakes Mac's hand*)—keep a stiff upper lip, old mate.

MAC   Thank you, that was kind of you, Matthew.

MATTHEW (*shaking Polly's hand after embracing Mac with emotion*)   It was spoken from the heart, all right! Anyway, keep a stiff upper lip, old girl, I mean (*grinning*) he should keep it stiff.

(*Roars of laughter from the guests. Suddenly Mac with a deft movement sends Matthew to the floor*)

MAC   Shut your trap. Keep that filth for your Kitty, she's the kind of slut that appreciates it.

POLLY   Mac, don't be so vulgar.

MATTHEW   Here, I don't like that. Calling Kitty a slut . . . (*stands up with difficulty*)

MAC   Oh, so you don't like that?

MATTHEW   And besides, I never use filthy language with her. I respect Kitty a lot too much for that. But maybe you wouldn't understand that, the way you are. You're a fine one to talk about filth. Do you think Lucy didn't tell me the things you've told her? Compared to that, I'm a kid glove.

(*Mac stares at him*)

JAKE   Cut it out, this is a wedding. (*They pull him away*)

MAC   Fine wedding, isn't it, Polly? Having to see trash like this around you on the day of your marriage. You wouldn't have thought your husband's friends would let him down so. Let it be a lesson to you.

POLLY   I think it's nice.

ROBERT   Blarney. Nobody's letting you down. What's a difference of opinion between friends? Your Kitty's as good as the next girl. But now bring out your wedding present, mate.

ALL   Yes, hand it over!

MATTHEW (*offended*)   Here.

POLLY   Oh, a wedding present. How kind of you, Mr. Matt of the Mint. Look, Mac, what a lovely nightgown.

MATTHEW   Another bit of filth, eh, Captain?

MAC   Forget it. I didn't mean to hurt your feelings on this festive occasion.

WALTER   What do you say to this? Chippendale! (*He unveils an enormous Chippendale grandfather clock*)

MAC   Quatorze.

POLLY   It's wonderful. I'm so happy. Words fail me. You're so unbelievably kind. Oh, Mac, isn't it a shame we haven't got a flat to put it in?

MAC   Hm, it's a start in the right direction. The great thing is to get started. Thank you kindly, Walter. Go on, clear the stuff away now. Food!

JAKE   (*while the others start setting the table*)   Trust me to come empty-handed again. (*Intensely to Polly*) Believe me, young lady, I find it most distressing.

POLLY   It doesn't matter in the least, Mr. Crook-fingered Jake.

JAKE   Here are the boys flinging presents right and left, and me standing here like a fool. What a situation to be in! It's always the way with me. Situations! It's enough to make your hair stand on end. The other day I meet Low-Dive Jenny; well, I say, you old cow . . . (*Suddenly he sees Mac standing behind him and goes off without a word*)

MAC   (*leads Polly to her place*)   This is the best food you'll taste today, Polly. Gentlemen! (*All sit down to the wedding feast*)[4]

NED   (*indicating the china*)   Beautiful dishes. Savoy Hotel.

JAKE   The plover's eggs are from Selfridge's. There was supposed to be a bucket of foie gras. But Jimmy ate it on the way, he was mad because it had a hole in it.

WALTER   We don't talk about holes in polite society.

JIMMY   Don't bolt the eggs like that, Ned, not on a day like this.

MAC   Couldn't somebody sing something? Something delectable?

MATTHEW   (*choking with laughter*)   Something delectable? That's a first-class word. (*He sits down in embarrassment under Mac's withering glance*)

MAC   (*knocks a bowl out of someone's hand*)   I didn't intend us to start eating yet. Instead of seeing you people wade straight into the trough, I would have liked a little something for the heart. That's what other people do on an occasion like this.

JAKE   What, for instance?

MAC   Am I supposed to think of everything myself? I'm not

asking you to put on an opera. But you might have arranged for something else besides stuffing your bellies and making filthy jokes. Oh well, it's a day like this that you find out who your friends are.

POLLY   The salmon is marvelous, Mac.

NED   I bet you've never eaten anything like it. You get that every day at Mac the Knife's. You've landed in the honey pot all right. That's what I've always said: Mac is the right match for a girl with a feeling for higher things. As I was saying to Lucy only yesterday.

POLLY   Lucy? Mac, who is Lucy?

JAKE (*embarrassed*)   Lucy? Oh, nothing serious, you know.
(*Matthew has risen; standing behind Polly, he is waving his arms to shut Jake up*)

POLLY (*sees him*)   Do you want something? Salt perhaps . . . ? What were you saying, Mr. Jake?

JAKE   Oh, nothing, nothing at all. The main thing I wanted to say really was nothing at all. I'm always putting my foot in it.

MAC   What have you got in your hand, Jake?

JAKE   A knife, Captain.

MAC   And what have you got on your plate?

JAKE   A trout, Captain.

MAC   I see. And with the knife you are eating the trout, are you not? It's incredible. Did you ever see the like of it, Polly? Eating his fish with a knife! Anybody who does that is just a plain swine, do you get me, Jake? Let that be a lesson to you. You'll have your hands full, Polly, trying to turn trash like them into human beings. Have you boys got the least idea what that means?

WALTER   A human being or a human pee-ing?

POLLY   Really, Mr. Walter!

MAC   So you won't sing a song, something to brighten up the day? Has it got to be a miserable gloomy day like any other? And come to think of it, is anybody guarding the door? I suppose you want me to attend to that myself too? Do you want me on this day of days to guard the door so you lot can stuff your bellies at my expense?

WALTER (*sullenly*)   What do you mean at your expense?

JIMMY   Stow it, Walter boy. I'm on my way. Who's going to come here anyway? (*Goes out*)

JAKE   A fine joke on a day like this if all the wedding guests were pulled in.

JIMMY (*rushes in*)   Hey, Captain. The cops!

WALTER   Tiger Brown!

MATTHEW   Nonsense, it's the Reverend Kimball.
 (*Kimball enters*)

ALL (*roar*)   Good evening, Reverend Kimball!

KIMBALL   So I've found you after all. I find you in a lowly hut, a humble place but your own.

MAC   Property of the Duke of Devonshire.

POLLY   Good evening, reverend. Oh, I'm so glad that on the happiest day of our life you . . .

MAC   And now I request a rousing song for the Reverend Kimball.

MATTHEW   How about Bill Lawgen and Mary Syer?

JAKE   Good. Bill Lawgen might be the right thing.

KIMBALL   Be nice if you'd do a little number, boys.

MATTHEW   Let's have it, gentlemen.
 (*Three men rise and sing hesitantly, weakly and uncertainly:*)

Wedding Song for the Less Well-off

Bill Lawgen and Mary Syer
Were made man and wife a week ago.
(Three cheers for the happy couple: hip, hip, hooray!)
When it was over and they exchanged a kiss
He was thinking "Whose wedding dress was this?"
While his name was a thing she would have liked to know.
Hooray!

Do you know what your wife's up to? No!
Do you like her sleeping round like that? No!
(Three cheers for the happy couple: hip, hip, hooray!)
Billy Lawgen told me recently
Just one part of her will do for me.
The swine.
Hooray!

MAC   Is that all? Paltry!

MATTHEW   (*chokes again*) Paltry is the word, gentlemen. Paltry.

MAC   Shut your trap!

MATTHEW   Oh, I only meant no gusto, no fire, and so on.

POLLY   Gentlemen, if none of you wishes to perform, I myself will sing a little song; it's an imitation of a girl I saw once in some twopenny halfpenny dive in Soho. She was washing the glasses, and everybody was laughing at her, and then she turned to the guests and said things like the things I'm going to sing to you. All right. This is a little bar, I want you to think of it as filthy. She stood behind it morning and night. This is the bucket and this is the rag she washed the glasses with. Where you are sitting, the customers were sitting laughing at her. You can laugh too, to make it exactly the same; but if you can't, you don't have to. (*She starts pretending to wash glasses, muttering to herself*) Now, for instance, one of them—it might be you (*pointing at Walter*)—says: Well, when's your ship coming in, Jenny?

WALTER   Well, when's your ship coming in, Jenny?

POLLY   And another says—you, for instance: Still washing up glasses, Jenny the pirate's bride?

MATTHEW   Still washing up glasses, Jenny the pirate's bride?

POLLY   Good. And now I'll begin.

(*Song lighting: golden glow. The organ is lit up. Three lamps are lowered from above on a pole, and the signs say:*)

Pirate Jenny

1

Now you gents all see I've the glasses to wash
If a bed's to be made I make it.
You may tip me with a penny, and I'll thank you very well
And you see me dressed in tatters, and this tatty old hotel
And you never ask how long I'll take it.
But one of these evenings there will be screams from the harbor

And they'll ask: what can all that screaming be?
And they'll see me smiling as I do the glasses
And they'll say: how she can smile beats me.
   And a ship with eight sails and
   All its fifty guns loaded
   Has tied up at the quay.

2

They say: get on, dry your glasses, my girl
And they tip me and don't give a damn.
And their penny is accepted, and their bed will be made
(Although nobody is going to sleep there, I'm afraid)
And they still have no idea who I am.
But one of these evenings there will be explosions from the
   harbor,
And they'll ask: what kind of a bang was that?
And they'll see me as I stand beside the window
And they'll say: what's she got to smile at?
   And that ship with eight sails and
   All its fifty guns loaded
   Will lay siege to the town.

3

Then, you gents, you aren't going to find it a joke
For the walls will be knocked down flat
And in no time the town will be razed to the ground.
Just one tatty old hotel will be left standing safe and sound
And they'll ask: did someone special live in that?
Then there'll be a lot of people milling round the hotel
And they'll ask: what made them let that place alone?
And they'll see me as I leave the door next morning
And they'll say: don't tell us she's the one.
   And that ship with eight sails and
   All its fifty guns loaded
   Will run up its flag.

4

And a hundred men will land in the bright midday sun
Each stepping where the shadows fall.
They'll look inside each doorway and grab anyone they see

And put him in irons and then bring him to me
And they'll ask: which of these should we kill?
In that noonday heat there'll be a hush round the harbor
As they ask which has got to die.
And you'll hear me as I softly answer: the lot!
And as the first head rolls I'll say: hoppla!
   And that ship with eight sails and
   All its fifty guns loaded
   Will vanish with me.

MATTHEW   Very pretty. Cute, eh? And the way the missus puts it across!

MAC   What do you mean pretty? It's not pretty, you idiot! It's art, it's not pretty. You did that marvelously, Polly. But it's wasted on trash like this, if you'll excuse me, Your Reverence. (*In an undertone to Polly*) Anyway, I don't like you play-acting; let's not have any more of it. (*Laughter at the table. The gang is making fun of the parson*) What you got in your hand, Your Reverence?

JAKE   Two knives, Captain.

MAC   What you got on your plate, Your Reverence?

KIMBALL   Salmon, I think.

MAC   And with that knife you are eating the salmon, are you not?

JAKE   Did you ever see the like of it, eating fish with a knife? Anybody who does that is just a plain . . .

MAC   Swine. Do you understand me, Jake? Let that be a lesson to you.

JIMMY   (*rushing in*)   Hey, Captain, cops. The sheriff in person.

WALTER   Brown. Tiger Brown!

MAC   Yes, Tiger Brown, exactly. It's Tiger Brown himself, the high sheriff of London, that pillar of the Old Bailey, who will now enter Captain Macheath's humble cabin. Let that be a lesson to you.
   (*The bandits creep away*)

JAKE   It'll be the gallows for us!
   (*Brown enters*)

MAC   Hullo, Jackie.

BROWN   Hullo, Mac! I haven't much time, got to be leaving in a minute. Does it have to be somebody else's stable? Why, this is breaking and entering again!

MAC   But Jackie, it's so conveniently located. I'm glad you could come to old Mac's wedding. Let me introduce my wife, née Peachum. Polly, this is Tiger Brown, what do you say, old man? (*Slaps him on the back*) And these are my friends, Jackie, I imagine you've seen them all before.

BROWN (*pained*)   I'm here unofficially, Mac.

MAC   So are they. (*He calls them. They come in with their hands up*) Hey, Jake.

BROWN   That's Crook-fingered Jake. He's a dirty dog.

MAC   Hey, Jimmy; hey Bob; hey, Walter!

BROWN   Well, just for today I'll turn a blind eye.

MAC   Hey, Ned; hey, Matthew.

BROWN   Be seated, gentlemen, be seated.

ALL   Thank you, sir.

BROWN   I'm delighted to meet my old friend Mac's charming wife.

POLLY   Don't mention it, sir.

MAC   Sit down, ya old blighter, and pitch into the whiskey!— Polly and gentlemen! You have today in your midst a man whom the king's inscrutable decree has placed high above his fellow men and who has none the less remained my friend throughout the storms and perils, and so on. You know whom I mean, and you too know whom I mean, Brown. Ah, Jackie, do you remember how we served in India together, soldiers both of us? Ah, Jackie, let's sing the Cannon Song right now.
(*They sit down on the table*)

(*Song lighting: golden glow. The organ is lit up. Three lamps are lowered from above on a pole, and the signs say:*)

The Cannon Song

1

John was all present and Jim was all there
And Georgie was up for promotion.
Not that the army gave a bugger who they were

When confronting some heathen commotion.
The troops live under
The cannon's thunder
From Sind to Cooch Behar.
Moving from place to place
When they come face to face
With men of a different color
With darker skins or duller
They quick as winking chop them into
     beefsteak tartare.

2

Johnny found his whiskey too warm
And Jim found the weather too balmy
But Georgie took them both by the arm
And said: never let down the army.
The troops live under
The cannon's thunder
From Sind to Cooch Behar.
Moving from place to place
When they come face to face
With men of a different color
With darker skins or duller
They quick as winking chop them into
     beefsteak tartare.

3

John is a write-off and Jimmy is dead
And they shot poor old Georgie for looting
But young men's blood goes on being red
And the army goes on recruiting.
The troops live under
The cannon's thunder
From Sind to Cooch Behar.
Moving from place to place
When they come face to face
With men of a different color
With darker skins or duller
They quick as winking chop them into
     beefsteak tartare.

MAC Though life with its raging torrents has carried us boyhood friends far apart, although our professional interests
are very different, some people would go so far as to say
diametrically opposed, our friendship has come through un-
impaired. Let that be a lesson to all of you. Castor and
Pollux, Hector and Andromache and so on. Seldom have
I, the humble bandit, well, you know what I mean, made
even the smallest haul without giving him, my friend, a
share, a sizable share, Brown, as a gift and token of my
unswerving loyalty, and seldom has he, take that knife out
of your mouth, Jake, the all-powerful police chief, staged
a raid without sending me, his boyhood friend, a little tip-
off. Well, and so on and so forth, it's all a matter of give
and take. Let that be a lesson to you. (*He takes Brown by
the arm*) Well, Jackie, old man, I'm glad you've come, I
call it real friendship. (*Pause, because Brown has been looking sadly at a carpet*) Genuine Shiraz.

BROWN From the Oriental Carpet Company.

MAC Yes, we never go anywhere else. Do you know, Jackie,
I had to have you here today, I hope it's not too unpleasant
for you in your position.

BROWN You know, Mac, that I can't refuse you anything.
I must be going, I've really got so much on my mind;
if the slighest thing should go wrong at the Queen's
Coronation . . .

MAC See here, Jackie, my father-in-law is a rotten old stinker.
If he tries to make trouble for me, is there anything on
record against me at Scotland Yard?

BROWN There's nothing whatsoever on record against you
at Scotland Yard.

MAC I knew it.

BROWN I've taken care of all that. Good night.

MAC Aren't you fellows going to stand up?

BROWN (*to Polly*) Best of luck. (*Goes out accompanied by
Mac*)

JAKE (*who along with Matthew and Walter has meanwhile
been conferring with Polly*) I must admit I couldn't re-
press a certain alarm a while ago when I heard Tiger Brown
was coming.

MATTHEW   You see, dear lady, we have connections with the top authorities.

WALTER   Yes, Mac always has an iron in the fire that the rest of us don't even suspect. But we have our own little iron in the fire. Gentlemen, it's half-past nine.

MATTHEW   And now comes the high point.
(*All go upstage behind the carpet that conceals something. Mac enters*)

MAC   I say, what's going on?

MATTHEW   Hey, Captain, another little surprise.
(*Behind the carpet they sing the Bill Lawgen song softly and with much feeling. But at* "his name was a thing she would have liked to know" *Matthew pulls down the carpet and all go on with the song, bellowing and pounding on the bed that has been disclosed*)

MAC   Thank you, friends, thank you.

WALTER   And now we shall quietly take our leave. (*The gang go out*)

MAC   And now the time has come for softer sentiments. Without them man is a mere working animal. Sit down, Polly.
(*Music*)

MAC   Look at the moon over Soho.

POLLY   I see it, dearest. Feel my heart beating, my beloved.

MAC   I feel it, beloved.

POLLY   Where'er you go I shall be with you.

MAC   And where you stay, there too shall I be.

BOTH (*sing*)
And though we've no paper to say we're wed
And no altar covered with flowers
And nobody knows for whom your dress was made
And even the ring is not ours—
That platter off which you are eating your bread
Give it one brief look; fling it far.
For love will endure or not endure
Regardless of where we are.

3

To Peachum, aware of the hardness of the world, the loss of his daughter means utter ruin

Peachum's Outfitting Shop for Beggars

To the right Peachum and Mrs. Peachum. In the doorway stands Polly in her coat and hat, holding her traveling bag.

MRS. PEACHUM   Married? First you rig her fore and aft in dresses and hats and gloves and parasols, and when she's cost as much as a sailing ship, she throws herself in the garbage like a rotten pickle. Are you really married?

(Song lighting: golden glow. The organ is lit up. Three lamps are lowered from above on a pole and the signs say:)

In a little song Polly gives her parents to understand that she has married the bandit Macheath

Barbara Song

1
I once used to think, in my innocent youth
(And I once was as innocent as you)
That someone someday might come my way
And then how would I know what best to do?
And if he'd got money
And seemed a nice chap
And his workday shirts were white as snow
And if he knew how to treat a girl with due respect
I'd have to tell him: No.
That's where you must keep your head screwed on
And insist on going slow.

Sure, the moon will shine throughout the night
Sure, the boat is on the river, tied up tight.
That's as far as things can go.
Oh, you can't lie back, you must stay cold at heart
Oh, you must not let your feelings show.
Oh, whenever you feel it might start
Ah, then your only answer's: No.

2
The first one that came was a man of Kent
And all that a man ought to be.
The second one owned three ships down at Wapping
And the third was crazy about me.
And as they'd got money
And all seemed nice chaps
And their workday shirts were white as snow
And as they knew how to treat a girl with due respect
Each time I told them: No.
That's where I still kept my head screwed on
And I chose to take it slow.
Sure, the moon could shine throughout the night
Sure, the boat was on the river, tied up tight
That's as far as things could go.
Oh, you can't lie back, you must stay cold at heart
Oh, you must not let your feelings show.
Oh, whenever you feel it might start
Ah, then your only answer's: No.

3
But then one day, and that day was blue
Came someone who didn't ask at all
And he went and hung his hat on the nail in my little attic
And what happened I can't quite recall.
And as he'd got no money
And was not a nice chap
And his Sunday shirts, even, were not like snow
And as he'd no idea of treating a girl with due respect
I could not tell him: No.
That's the time my head was not screwed on

And to hell with going slow.
Oh, the moon was shining clear and bright
Oh, the boat kept drifting downstream all that night
That was how it simply had to go.
Yes, you must lie back, you can't stay cold at heart
In the end you have to let your feelings show.
Oh, the moment you know it must start
Ah, then's no time for saying: No.

PEACHUM   So now she's associating with criminals. That's lovely. That's delightful.

MRS. PEACHUM   If you're immoral enough to get married, did it have to be a horse thief and a highwayman? That'll cost you dear one of these days! I ought to have seen it coming. Even as a child she had a swelled head like the Queen of England.

PEACHUM   So she's really got married!

MRS. PEACHUM   Yes, yesterday, at five in the afternoon.

PEACHUM   To a notorious criminal. Come to think of it, it shows that the fellow is really audacious. If I give away my daughter, the last prop of my old age, my house will cave in and my last dog will run off. I'd think twice about giving away the dirt under my fingernails, it would mean risking starvation. If the three of us can get through the winter on one log of wood, maybe we'll live to see the new year. Maybe.

MRS. PEACHUM   What got into you? This is our reward for all we've done, Jonathan. I'm going mad. My head is swimming. I'm going to faint. Oh! (she faints) A glass of Cordial Médoc.

PEACHUM   You see what you've done to your mother. Quick! Associating with criminals, that's lovely, that's delightful! Interesting how the poor woman takes it to heart. (Polly brings in a bottle of Cordial Médoc) That's the only consolation your poor mother has left.

POLLY   Go ahead, give her two glasses. My mother can take twice as much when she's not quite herself. That will put her back on her feet. (During the whole scene she looks very happy)

MRS. PEACHUM (*wakes up*) Oh, there she goes again, pretending to be so loving and sympathetic!
(*Five men enter*)[5]

BEGGAR I'm making a complaint, see, this thing is a mess, it's not a proper stump, it's a botch-up, and I'm not wasting my money on it.

PEACHUM What do you expect? It's as good a stump as any other; it's only that you don't keep it clean.

BEGGAR Then why don't I take as much money as the others? Naw, you can't do that to me. (*Throws down the stump*) If I wanted crap like this, I could cut off my real leg.

PEACHUM What do you fellows want anyway? Is it my fault if people have hearts of flint? I can't make you five stumps. In five minutes I can turn any man into such a pitiful wreck it would make a dog weep to see him. Can I help it if people don't weep? Here's another stump for you if one's not enough. But look after your equipment!

BEGGAR This one will do.

PEACHUM (*tries a false limb on another*) Leather is no good, Celia; rubber is more repulsive. (*To the third*) That swelling is going down and it's your last. Now we'll have to start all over again. (*Examining the fourth*) Obviously natural scabies is never as good as the artificial kind. (*To the fifth*) You're a sight! You've been eating again. I'll have to make an example of you.

BEGGAR Mr. Peachum, I really haven't eaten anything much. I'm just abnormally fat, I can't help it.

PEACHUM Nor can I. You're fired. (*Again to the second beggar*) My dear man, there's an obvious difference between "tugging at people's heart strings" and "getting on people's nerves." What I need is artists. Only an artist can tug at anybody's heart strings nowadays. If you fellows performed properly, your audience would be forced to applaud. You just haven't any ideas! So obviously I can't extend your engagement.
(*The beggars go out*)

POLLY Look at him. Is he particularly handsome? No. But he makes a living. He can support me. He is not only a first-class burglar but a farsighted and experienced stick-up man as well. I've been into it, I can tell you the exact amount of his savings to date. A few successful ventures and we shall be able to retire to a little house in the country just like that Mr. Shakespeare father admires so much.

PEACHUM It's all perfectly simple. You're married. What does a girl do when she's married? Use your head. Well, she gets divorced, see, is that so hard to figure out?

POLLY I don't know what you're talking about.

MRS. PEACHUM Divorce.

POLLY But I love him. How can I think of divorce?

MRS. PEACHUM Really, have you no shame?

POLLY Mother, if you've ever been in love . . .

MRS. PEACHUM In love! Those damn books you've been reading have turned your head. Why, Polly, everybody's doing it.

POLLY Then I'm an exception.

MRS. PEACHUM Then I'm going to tan your behind, you exception.

POLLY Oh yes, all mothers do that, but it doesn't help because love goes deeper than a tanned behind.

MRS. PEACHUM Don't strain my patience.

POLLY I won't let my love be taken away from me.

MRS. PEACHUM One more word out of you and you'll get a clip on the ear.

POLLY But love is the finest thing in the world.

MRS. PEACHUM Anyway, he's got several women, the blackguard. When he's hanged, like as not half a dozen widows will turn up, each of them like as not with a brat in her arms. Oh, Jonathan!

PEACHUM Hanged, what made you think of that, that's a good idea. Run along, Polly. (*Polly goes out*) Quite right. That'll earn us forty pounds.

MRS. PEACHUM I see. Report him to the sheriff.

PEACHUM Naturally. And besides, that way we get him hanged free of charge . . . Two birds with one stone. Only we've got to find out where he's holed up.

MRS. PEACHUM I can tell you that, my dear, he's holed up with his tarts.

PEACHUM But they won't turn him in.

MRS. PEACHUM   Just let me attend to that. Money rules the
world. I'll go to Turnbridge right away and talk to the
girls. Give us a couple of hours, and after that if he meets
a single one of them he's done for.

POLLY (*has been listening behind the door*)   Dear mama, you
can spare yourself the trip. Mac will go to the Old Bailey
of his own accord sooner than meet any of those ladies.
And even if he did go to the Old Bailey, the sheriff would
serve him a cocktail; they'd smoke their cigars and have
a little chat about a certain shop in this street where a little
more goes on than meets the eye. Because, papa dear, the
sheriff was very cheerful at my wedding.

PEACHUM   What's this sheriff called?

POLLY   He's called Brown. But you probably know him as
Tiger Brown. Because everyone who has reason to fear
him calls him Tiger Brown. But my husband, you see, calls
him Jackie. Because to him he's just dear old Jackie. They're
boyhood friends.

PEACHUM   Oh, so they're friends, are they? The sheriff and
Public Enemy No. 1, ha, they must be the only friends in
this city.

POLLY (*poetically*)   Every time they drank a cocktail together, they stroked each other's cheeks and said: "If you'll
have the same again, I'll have the same again." And every
time one of them left the room, the other's eyes grew moist
and he said: "Where'er you go I shall be with you." There's
nothing on record against Mac at Scotland Yard.

PEACHUM   I see. Between Tuesday evening and Thursday
morning Mr. Macheath, a gentleman who has assuredly
been married many times, enticed my daughter from her
home on pretext of marriage. Before the week is out, he
will be taken on that account to the gallows, which he has
deserved. "Mr. Macheath, you once had white kid gloves,
a cane with an ivory handle, and a scar on your neck, and
frequented the Cuttlefish Hotel. All that is left is your
scar, undoubtedly the least valuable of your distinguishing
marks, and today you frequent nothing but prison cells. and
within the foreseeable future no place at all . . ."

MRS. PEACHUM   Oh, Jonathan, you'll never bring it off. Why, he's Mac the Knife, whom they call the biggest criminal in London. He takes what he pleases.

PEACHUM   Who's Mac the Knife? Get ready, we're going to see the Sheriff of London. And you're going to Turnbridge.

MRS. PEACHUM   To see his whores.

PEACHUM   For the villainy of the world is great, and a man needs to run his legs off to keep them from being stolen from under him.

POLLY   I, papa, shall be delighted to shake hands with Mr. Brown again.

(*All three step forward and sing the first finale. Song lighting. On the signs is written:*)

First Threepenny Finale

Concerning the Insecurity of the Human State

POLLY
　　Am I reaching for the sky?
　　All I'm asking from this place is
　　To enjoy a man's embraces.
　　Is that aiming much too high?

PEACHUM (*with a Bible in his hands*)
　　Man has a right, in this our brief existence
　　To call some fleeting happiness his own
　　Partake of worldly pleasures and subsistence
　　And have bread on his table rather than a stone.
　　Such are the basic rights of man's existence.
　　But do we know of anything suggesting
　　That when a thing's a right one gets it? No!
　　To get one's rights would be most interesting
　　But in our present state this can't be so.

MRS. PEACHUM
　　How I want what's best for you
　　How I'd deal you all the aces
　　Show you things and take you places
　　As a mother likes to do.

PEACHUM

Let's practice goodness: who would disagree?
Let's give our wealth away: is that not right?
Once all are good His Kingdom is at hand
Where blissfully we'll bask in His pure light.
Let's practice goodness: who would disagree?
But sadly on this planet while we're waiting
The means are meagre and the morals low.
To get one's record straight would be elating
But in our present state this can't be so.

POLLY AND MRS. PEACHUM

And that is all there is to it.
The world is poor, and man's a shit.

PEACHUM

Of course that's all there is to it.
The world is poor, and man's a shit.
Who wouldn't like an earthly paradise?
Yet our condition's such it can't arise.
Out of the question in our case.
Let's say your brother's close to you
But if there's not enough for two
He'll kick you smartly in the face.
You think that loyalty's no disgrace?
But say your wife is close to you
And finds she's barely making do
She'll kick you smartly in the face.
And gratitude: that's no disgrace
But say your son is close to you
And finds your pension's not come through
He'll kick you smartly in the face.
And so will all the human race.

POLLY AND MRS. PEACHUM

That's what you're all ignoring
That's what's so bloody boring.
The world is poor, and man's a shit
And that is all there is to it.

PEACHUM

    Of course that's all there is to it
    The world is poor, and man's a shit.
    We should aim high instead of low
    But in our present state this can't be so.

ALL THREE

    Which means He has us in a trap:
    The whole damn thing's a load of crap.

PEACHUM

    The world is poor, and man's a shit
    And that is all there is to it.

ALL THREE

    That's what you're all ignoring
    That's what's so bloody boring.
    That's why He's got us in a trap
    And why it's all a load of crap.

ACT TWO

Thursday afternoon: Mac the Knife takes leave of his wife and flees from his father-in-law to the heaths of Highgate.

The Stable

POLLY (*enters*)   Mac! Mac, don't be frightened.

MAC (*lying on the bed*)   Well, what's up? Polly, you look a wreck.

POLLY   I've been to see Brown, my father went too, they decided to pull you in; my father made some terrible threats and Brown stood up for you, but then he weakened, and now he thinks too that you'd better bestir yourself and make yourself scarce for a while, Mac. You must pack right away.

MAC   Pack? Nonsense. Come here, Polly. You and I have got better things to do than pack.

POLLY   No, we mustn't now. I'm so frightened. All they talked about was hanging.

MAC   I don't like it when you're moody, Polly. There's nothing on record against me at Scotland Yard.

POLLY   Perhaps there wasn't yesterday, but today there's suddenly a terrible lot. You—I've brought the charges with me, I don't even know if I can get them straight, the list goes on and on—you've killed two shopkeepers, more than thirty burglaries, twenty-three hold-ups, and God knows how many acts of arson, attempted murder, forgery and perjury, all within eighteen months. You're a dreadful man. And in Winchester you seduced two sisters under the age of consent.

MAC   They told me they were over twenty. What did Brown say? (*He stands up slowly and goes whistling to the right along the footlights*)

POLLY   He caught up with me in the corridor and said there was nothing he could do for you now. Oh, Mac! (*She throws herself on his neck*)

MAC   All right, if I've got to go away, you'll have to run the business.

POLLY   Don't talk about business now, Mac, I can't bear it. Kiss your poor Polly again and swear that you'll never never be . . .

(*Mac interrupts her brusquely and leads her to the table where he pushes her down in a chair.*)

MAC   Here are the ledgers. Listen carefully. This is a list of the personnel. (*Reads*) Right. First of all, Crook-fingered Jake, a year and a half in the business. Let's see what he's brought in. One, two, three, four, five gold watches, not much, but clean work. Don't sit on my lap, I'm not in the mood right now. Here's Dreary Walter, an unreliable dog. Sells stuff on the side. Give him three weeks grace, then get rid of him. Just turn him in to Brown.

POLLY (*sobbing*)   Just turn him in to Brown.

MAC   Jimmy II, an impertinent bastard; good worker but impertinent. Swipes bed sheets right out from under ladies of the best society. Give him a rise.

POLLY   Give him a rise.

MAC   Robert the Saw: small potatoes, not a glimmer of genius. Won't end on the gallows, but he won't leave any estate either.

POLLY   Won't leave any estate either.

MAC   In all other respects you will carry on exactly the same as before. Get up at seven, wash, bathe once a week and so on.

POLLY   You're perfectly right, I've got to grit my teeth and attend to the business. What's yours is mine now, isn't it, Mackie? What about your rooms, Mac? Should I let them go? I don't like having to pay the rent.

MAC   No, I still need them.

POLLY   What for, it's just a waste of our money!

MAC   You seem to think I'm never coming back.

POLLY   What do you mean? You can rent other rooms.[6] Mac . . . Mac, I can't go on. I keep looking at your lips and then I don't hear what you say. Will you be faithful to me, Mac?

MAC   Of course I'll be faithful, I'll do as I'm done by. Do you think I don't love you? It's only that I see farther ahead than you.

POLLY   I'm so grateful to you, Mac. Worrying about me when they're after you like bloodhounds . . .

(*Hearing the word "bloodhounds" he goes stiff, stands up, goes to the right, throws off his coat and washes his hands*)

MAC (*hastily*)   You will go on sending the profits to Jack Poole's banking house in Manchester. Between you and me it's only a matter of weeks before I go over to banking altogether. It's safer and it's more profitable. In two weeks at the most the money will have to be taken out of this business, then off you go to Brown and give the list to the police. Within four weeks all this scum of humanity will be safely in the cells at the Old Bailey.

POLLY   Why, Mac! How can you look them in the eye when you've written them off and they're as good as hanged? How can you shake hands with them?

MAC   With who? Robert the Saw, Matt of the Mint, Crook-fingered Jake? Those jailbirds?

(*Enter the gang*)

MAC   Gentlemen, it's a pleasure to see you.

POLLY   Good evening, gentlemen.

MATTHEW   Captain, I've got hold of the Coronation program. It looks to me like we have some days of very hard work ahead of us. The Archbishop of Canterbury is arriving in half an hour.

MAC   When?

MATTHEW   Five thirty. We'd better be shoving off, Captain.

MAC   Yes, you'd better be shoving off.

ROBERT   What do you mean: you?

MAC   For my part, I'm afraid I'm obliged to take a little trip.

ROBERT   Good God, are they out to nab you?

MATTHEW   It would be just now, with the Coronation coming up! A Coronation without you is soup without a spoon.

MAC   Shut your trap! In view of that, I am temporarily handing over the management of the business to my wife. (*He pushes her forward and goes to the rear where he observes her*)

POLLY   Well, boys, I think the Captain can go away with an easy mind. We'll swing this job, you bet. What do you say, boys?

MATTHEW   It's not for me to say. But at a time like this I'm not so sure that a woman . . . I'm not saying anything against you, Ma'am.

MAC (*from upstage*)   What do you say to that, Polly?

POLLY   You shit, that's a fine way to start in. (*Screaming*) Of course you're not saying anything against me! If you were, these gentlemen would have ripped your pants off long ago and tanned your arse for you. Wouldn't you, gentlemen?

(*Brief pause, then all clap like mad*)

JAKE   Yes, there's something in that, you can take her word for it.

WALTER   Hurrah, the missus knows how to lay it on! Hurrah for Polly!

ALL   Hurrah for Polly!

MAC   The rotten part of it is that I won't be here for the Coronation. There's a gilt-edged deal for you. In the daytime nobody's home and at night the toffs are all drunk. That reminds me, you drink too much, Matthew. Last week you were implying that it was you who set the Greenwich Children's Hospital on fire. If such a thing happens again, you're out. Who set the Children's Hospital on fire?

MATTHEW   I did.

MAC (*to the others*)   Who set it on fire?

THE OTHERS   You, Mr. Macheath.

MAC   So who did it?

MATTHEW (*sulkily*)   You, Mr. Macheath. At this rate our sort will never rise in the world.

MAC (*with a gesture of stringing up*)   You'll rise all right if you think you can compete with me. Who ever heard of one of those professors at Oxford College letting some assistant put his name to his errors? He puts his own.

ROBERT   Ma'am, while your husband is away, you're the boss. We settle up every Thursday, ma'am.

POLLY   Every Thursday, boys.
(*The gang goes out*)

MAC   And now farewell, my heart. Look after your complexion, and don't forget to make up every day, exactly as if I were here. That's very important, Polly.

POLLY   And you, Mac, promise me you won't look at another woman and that you'll leave town right away. Believe me, it's not jealousy that makes your little Polly say that; no, it's very important, Mac.

MAC   Oh, Polly, why should I go round drinking up the empties? I love only you. As soon as the twilight is deep enough I'll take my black stallion from somebody's stable and before you can see the moon from your window, I'll be the other side of Highgate Heath.

POLLY   Oh, Mac, don't tear the heart out of my body. Stay with me and let us be happy.

MAC   But I must tear my own heart out of my body, for I must go away and no one knows when I shall return.

POLLY   It's been such a short time, Mac.

MAC   Does it have to be the end?

POLLY   Oh, last night I had a dream. I was looking out of the window and I heard laughter in the street, and when I looked out I saw our moon and the moon was all thin like a worn-down penny. Don't forget me, Mac, in strange cities.

MAC   Of course I won't forget you, Polly. Kiss me, Polly.

POLLY   Good-bye, Mac.

MAC   Good-bye, Polly. (*On his way out*)
For love will endure or not endure
Regardless of where we are.

POLLY (*alone*)   He never will come back. (*She sings*)
Nice while it lasted, and now it is over
Tear out your heart, and good-bye to your lover!
What's the use of grieving, when the mother that bore you

(Mary, pity women!) knew it all before you?
(*The bells start ringing*)

POLLY
Into this London the Queen now makes her way.
Where shall we be on Coronation Day?

Interlude

(*Mrs. Peachum and Low-Dive Jenny step out before the curtain*)

MRS. PEACHUM   So if you see Mac the Knife in the next few days, run to the nearest constable and turn him in; it'll get you ten shillings.

JENNY   Shall we see him, though, if the constables are after him? If the hunt is on, he won't go spending his time with us.

MRS. PEACHUM   Take it from me, Jenny, even with all London at his heels, Macheath is not the man to give up his habits. (*She sings*)

The Ballad of Sexual Obsession

1
There goes a man who's won his spurs in battle
The butcher, he. And all the others, cattle.
The cocky sod! No decent place lets him in.
Who does him down, that's done the lot? The women.
Want it or not, he can't ignore that call.
Sexual obsession has him in its thrall.
   He doesn't read the Bible. He sniggers at the law.
   Sets out to be an utter egoist
   And knows a woman's skirts are what he must resist
   So when a woman calls he locks his door.
   So far, so good, but what's the future brewing?
   As soon as night falls he'll be up and doing.

2

Thus many a man watched men die in confusion:
A mighty genius, stuck on prostitution!
The watchers claimed their urges were exhausted
But when they died who paid the funeral? Whores did.
Want it or not, they can't ignore that call.
Sexual obsession has them in its thrall.
> Some fall back on the Bible. Some set out to change the
> law.
> Some turn to Christ. Others turn anarchist.
> At lunch you pick the best wine on the list
> Then meditate till half past four.
> At tea: what high ideals you are pursuing!
> Then soon as night falls you'll be up and doing.

5

Before the coronation bells had died away, Mac the
Knife was sitting with the whores of Turnbridge. The
whores betray him. It is Thursday evening.

Whorehouse in Turnbridge

*An afternoon like any other; the whores, mostly in their
shifts, are ironing clothes, playing draughts, or washing: a
bourgeois idyll.[7] Crook-fingered Jake is reading the newspaper.
No one is paying attention to him. He is rather in the way.*

JAKE   He won't come today.
WHORE   No?
JAKE   I don't think he'll ever come again.
WHORE   That would be too bad.
JAKE   Think so? If I know him, he's out of town by now.
This time he's cleared out.

(*Enter Macheath, hangs his hat on a nail, sits down on the sofa behind the table*)

MAC   My coffee!

VIXEN (*repeats admiringly*)   "My coffee!"

JAKE (*horrified*)   How come you're not in Highgate?

MAC   It's my Thursday. Do you think I can let such trifles interfere with my habits? (*Throws the warrant on the floor*) Anyhow, it's raining.

JENNY (*reads the warrant*)   In the name of the Queen, Captain Macheath is charged with three . . .

JAKE (*takes it away from her*)   Am I in it too?

MAC   Naturally, the whole team.

JENNY (*to the other whore*)   Look, that's the warrant. (*Pause*) Mac, let's see your hand.

(*He gives her his hand*)

DOLLY   That's right, Jenny, read his palm, you're so good at it. (*Holds up an oil lamp*)

MAC   Coming into money?

JENNY   No, not coming into money.

BETTY   What's that look for, Jenny? It gives me the shivers.

MAC   A long journey?

JENNY   No, no long journey.

VIXEN   What do you see?

MAC   Only the good things, not the bad, please.

JENNY   Oh well, I see a narrow dark place and not much light. And then I see a big T, that means a woman's treachery. And then I see . . .

MAC   Stop. I'd like some details about that narrow dark place and the treachery. What's this treacherous woman's name?

JENNY   All I see is it begins with a J.

MAC   Then you've got it wrong. It begins with a P.

JENNY   Mac, when the Coronation bells start ringing at Westminster, you'll be in for a sticky time.

MAC   Go on! (*Jake laughs uproariously*) What's the matter? (*He runs over to Jake, and reads*) They've got it wrong, there were only three.

JAKE (*laughs*)   Exactly.

MAC   Nice underwear you've got there.

WHORE   From the cradle to the grave, underwear first, last and all the time.

OLD WHORE   I never wear silk. Makes gentlemen think you've got something wrong with you.

(*Jenny slips stealthily out by the door*)

SECOND WHORE (*to Jenny*)   Where are you off to, Jenny?

JENNY   You'll see. (*Goes out*)

MOLLY   But homespun underwear can put them off, too.

OLD WHORE   I've had very good results with homespun underwear.

VIXEN   It makes the gentlemen feel at home.

MAC (*to Betty*)   Have you still got the black lace border?

BETTY   Still the black lace border.

MAC   What kind of underwear do you have?

SECOND WHORE   Oh, I don't like to tell you. I can't take anybody to my room because my aunt is so crazy about men, and in doorways, you know, I just don't wear any.

(*Jake laughs*)

MAC   Finished?

JAKE   No, I've just got to the rapes.

MAC (*back by the sofa*)   But where's Jenny? Ladies, long before my star rose over this city . . .

VIXEN   "Long before my star rose over this city . . ."

MAC   . . . I lived in the most impoverished circumstances with one of you, dear ladies. And though today I am Mac the Knife, my good fortune will never lead me to forget the companions of my dark days, especially Jenny, whom I loved the best of all. Now listen, please.

(*While Mac sings, Jenny stands to the right outside the window and beckons to Constable Smith. Then Mrs. Peachum joins her. The three stand under the street lamp and watch the house*)

Ballade of Immoral Earnings

1

MAC

There was a time, now very far away
When we set up together, I and she.

I'd got the brain, and she supplied the breast.
I saw her right, and she supported me—
A way of life then, if not quite the best.
And when a client came I'd slide out of our bed
And treat him nice, and go and have a drink instead
And when he paid up I'd address him: Sir
Come any time you feel you fancy her.
That time's long past, but what would I not give
To see that whorehouse where we used to live?

(*Jenny appears in the door, Smith behind her*)

2

JENNY

That was the time, now very far away
He was so sweet and bashed me where it hurt.
And when the cash ran out the feathers really flew
He'd up and say: I'm going to pawn your skirt.
A skirt is nicer, but no skirt will do.
Just like his cheek, he had me fairly stewing
I'd ask him straight to say what he thought he was doing
Then he'd lash out and would knock me headlong
    downstairs.
I had the bruises off and on for years.

BOTH

That time's long past, but what would I not give
To see that whorehouse where we used to live?

3

BOTH (*together and alternating*)

That was the time, now very far away[8]

MAC

Not that the bloody times seem to have looked up.

JENNY

When afternoons were all I had for you

MAC

I told you she was generally booked up.
    (The night's more normal, but daytime will do.)

JENNY

Once I was pregnant, so the doctor said.

MAC

So we reversed positions on the bed.

JENNY

He thought his weight would make it premature.

MAC

But in the end we flushed it down the sewer.

That could not last, but what would I not give

To see the whorehouse where we used to live?

(*Dance. Mac picks up his sword stick, she hands him his hat,
he is still dancing when Smith lays a hand on his shoulder*)

SMITH   Coming quietly?

MAC   Is there still only one way out of this dump?

(*Smith tries to put the handcuffs on Macheath; Mac gives
him a push in the chest and he reels back. Mac jumps out of
the window. Outside stands Mrs. Peachum with constables*)

MAC (*with poise, very politely*)   Good afternoon, ma'am.

MRS. PEACHUM   My dear Mr. Macheath. My husband says the
greatest heroes in history have tripped over this humble
threshold.

MAC   May I ask how your husband is doing?

MRS. PEACHUM   Better, thank you. I'm so sorry, you'll have
to be bidding the charming ladies good-bye now. Come,
constable, escort the gentleman to his new home. (*He is
led away. Mrs. Peachum through the window*) Ladies, if
you wish to visit him, you'll invariably find him in. From
now on the gentleman's address will be the Old Bailey. I
knew he'd be in to see his whores. I'll settle the bill. Good-
bye, ladies. (*Goes out*)

JENNY   Wake up, Jake, something has happened.

JAKE (*who has been too immersed in his reading to notice
anything*)   Where's Mac?

JENNY   The coppers were here.

JAKE   Good God! And me just reading, reading, reading . . .
Boy, oh boy, oh boy! (*Goes out*)

6

Betrayed by the whores, Mac is freed from prison by
the love of yet another woman.

The Old Bailey, a cage

Enter Brown.

BROWN If only my men don't catch him! Good God, I only
hope he's riding out beyond Highgate Heath, thinking of
his Jackie. But he's so frivolous, like all great men. If they
bring him in now and he looks at me with his faithful
friendly eyes, I won't be able to bear it. Thank God, at
least the moon is shining; if he is riding across the heath, at
least he won't stray from the path. (*Sounds backstage*)
What's that? Oh, my God, they're bringing him in.

MAC (*tied with heavy ropes, accompanied by six constables,
enters with head erect*) Well, flatfeet, thank God we're
home again. (*He notices Brown who has fled to the far
corner of the cell*)

BROWN (*after a long pause, under the withering glance of his
former friend*) Oh, Mac, it wasn't me . . . I did everything
in my . . . don't look at me like that, Mac . . . I can't stand
it . . . Your silence is killing me. (*Shouts at one of the constables*) Stop tugging at that rope, you swine . . . Say
something, Mac. Say something to your poor Jackie . . . A
kind word in his tragic . . . (*Rests his head against the wall
and weeps*) He doesn't deem me worthy even of a word.
(*Goes out*)

MAC That miserable Brown. The living picture of a bad
conscience. And he calls himself a chief of police. It was
a good idea not shouting at him. I was going to at first. But
then it occurred to me in the nick of time that a deep
withering stare would send much colder shivers down his

spine. It worked. I looked at him and he wept bitterly. That's a trick I got from the Bible. .
(*Enter Smith with handcuffs*)

MAC Well, Mr. Warder, I suppose these are the heaviest you've got? With your kind permission I should like to apply for a more comfortable pair. (*He takes out his checkbook*)

SMITH Of course, Captain, we've got them here at every price. It all depends how much you want to spend. From one guinea to ten.

MAC How much would none at all cost?

SMITH Fifty.

MAC (*writes a check*) But the worst of it is that now this business with Lucy is bound to come out. If Brown hears that I've been carrying on with his daughter behind his friendly back, he'll turn into a tiger.

SMITH As you make your bed, so must you lie on it.

MAC I'll bet you the tart is waiting outside right now. I can see happy days between now and the execution.

Is this a life for one of my proud station?
I take it, I must frankly own, amiss.
From childhood up I heard with consternation:
One must live well to know what living is!

(*Song lighting: golden glow. The organ is lit up. Three lamps are lowered on a pole, and the signs say:*)

Ballade of Good Living[9]

I

I've heard them praising single-minded spirits
Whose empty stomachs show they live for knowledge
In rat-infested shacks awash with ullage.
I'm all for culture, but there are some limits.
The simple life is fine for those it suits.
I don't find, for my part, that it attracts.
There's not a bird from here to Halifax
Would peck at such unappetizing fruits.

What use is freedom? None, to judge from this.
One must live well to know what living is.

2
The dashing sort who cut precarious capers
And go and risk their necks just for the pleasure
Then swagger home and write it up at leisure
And flog the story to the Sunday papers—
If you could see how cold they get at night
Sullen, with chilly wife, climbing to bed
And how they dream they're going to get ahead
And how they see time stretching out of sight—
Now tell me, who would choose to live like this?
One must live well to know what living is.

3
There's plenty that they have. I know I lack it
And ought to join their splendid isolation
But when I gave them more consideration
I told myself: my friend, that's not your racket.
Suffering ennobles, but it can depress.
The paths of glory lead but to the grave.
You once were poor and lonely, wise and brave.
You ought to try to bite off rather less.
The search for happiness boils down to this:
One must live well to know what living is.

(*Enter Lucy*)

LUCY   You dirty dog, you—how can you look me in the face after all there's been between us?

MAC   Have you no bowels, no tenderness, my dear Lucy, seeing a husband in such circumstances?

LUCY   A husband! You monster! So you think I haven't heard about your goings-on with Miss Peachum! I could scratch your eyes out!

MAC   Seriously, Lucy, you're not fool enough to be jealous of Polly?

LUCY   You're married to her, aren't you, you beast?

MAC   Married! It's true, I go to the house, I chat with the girl. I kiss her, and now the silly jade goes about telling everyone that I'm married to her. I am ready, my dear Lucy, to give you satisfaction—if you think there is any in marriage. What can a man of honor say more? He can say nothing more.

LUCY Oh, Mac, I only want to become an honest woman.

MAC If you think marriage with me will . . . all right. What can a man of honor say more? He can say nothing more. (*Enter Polly*)

POLLY Where is my dear husband? Oh, Mac, there you are. Why do you turn away from me? It's your Polly. It's your wife.

LUCY Oh, you miserable villain!

POLLY Oh, Mackie in prison! Why didn't you ride across Highgate Heath? You told me you wouldn't see those women any more. I knew what they'd do to you; but I didn't say anything, because I believed you. Mac, I'll stay with you till death.—Not one kind word. Mac? Not one kind look? Oh, Mac, think what your Polly must be suffering to see you in this condition.

LUCY Oh, the slut.

POLLY What does this mean, Mac? Who on earth is that? You might at least tell her who I am. Tell her I'm your wife, will you? Aren't I your wife? Look at me. Tell me, aren't I your wife?

LUCY You low-down sneak! Have you got two wives, you monster?

POLLY Say something, Mac. Aren't I your wife? Haven't I done everything for you? I was innocent when I married, you know that. Why, you even put me in charge of the gang, and I've done everything the way we arranged, and Jake wants me to tell you that he . . .

MAC If you two could only shut your traps for two minutes I'll explain everything.

LUCY No, I won't shut my trap, I can't bear it. It's more than flesh and blood can bear.

POLLY Yes, my dear, naturally the wife has . . .

LUCY The wife!!

POLLY . . . the wife deserves some preference. Or at least the appearance of it, my dear. All this fuss and bother will drive the poor man mad.

LUCY Fuss and bother, that's a good one. What have you gone and picked up now? This filthy little tart! So this is your great conquest! So this is your Rose of Old Soho!

(*Song lighting: golden glow. The organ is lit up. Three lamps are lowered on a pole and the signs say:*)

Jealousy Duet

1

LUCY

Come on out, you Rose of Old Soho!
Let us see your legs, my little sweetheart!
I hear you have a lovely ankle
And I'd love to see such a complete tart.
They tell me that Mac says your behind is so provoking.

POLLY

Did he now, did he now?

LUCY

If what I see is true he must be joking.

POLLY

Is he now, is he now?

LUCY

Ho, it makes me split my sides!

POLLY

Oh, that's how you split your side?

LUCY

Fancy you as Mackie's bride!

POLLY

Mackie fancies Mackie's bride.

LUCY

Ha ha ha! Catch him sporting
With something that the cat brought in.

POLLY

Just you watch your tongue, my dear.

LUCY

Must I watch my tongue, my dear?

BOTH

Mackie and I, see how we bill and coo, man
He's got no eyes for any other woman.
The whole thing's an invention
You mustn't pay attention
To such a bitch's slanders.
Poppycock!

2

POLLY

Oh, they call me Rose of Old Soho
And Macheath appears to find me pretty.

LUCY

Does he now?

POLLY

They say I have a lovely ankle
And the best proportions in the city.

LUCY

Little whippersnapper!

POLLY

Who's a little whippersnapper?
Mac tells me that he finds my behind is most provoking.

LUCY

Doesn't he? Doesn't he?

POLLY

I do not suppose that he is joking.

LUCY

Isn't he, isn't he?

POLLY

Ho, it makes me split my sides!

LUCY

Oh, that's how you split your side?

POLLY

Being Mackie's only bride!

LUCY

Are you Mackie's only bride?

POLLY (to the audience)

Can you really picture him sporting
With something that the cat brought in?

LUCY
> Just you watch your tongue, my dear.

POLLY
> Must I watch my tongue, my dear?

BOTH
> Mackie and I, see how we bill and coo, man
> He's got no eyes for any other woman.
> The whole thing's an invention
> You cannot pay attention
> To such a bitch's slanders.
> Poppycock!

MAC All right, Lucy. Calm down. You see it's just a trick of Polly's. She wants to come between us. I'm going to be hanged and she wants to parade as my widow. Really, Polly, this isn't the moment.

POLLY Have you the heart to disclaim me?

MAC And have you the heart to go on about my being married? Oh, Polly, why must you add to my misery? (*Shakes his head reproachfully*) Polly! Polly!

LUCY It's true, Miss Peachum, you're putting yourself in a bad light. Quite apart from the fact that it's barbarous of you to worry a gentleman in his situation!

POLLY The most elementary rules of decency, my dear young lady, ought to teach you, it seems to me, to treat a man with a little more reserve when his wife is present.

MAC Seriously, Polly, that's carrying a joke too far.

LUCY And if, my dear lady, you start raising a row here in this prison, I shall be obliged to send for the warder to show you the door. I'm sorry, my dear Miss Peachum.

POLLY Mrs., if you please! Mrs. Macheath. Just let me tell you this, young lady. The airs you give yourself are most unbecoming. My duty obliges me to stay with my husband.

LUCY What's that? What's that? Oh, she won't leave! She stands there and we throw her out and she won't leave! Must I speak more plainly?

POLLY You—you just hold your filthy tongue, you slut, or I'll knock your block off, my dear young lady.

LUCY   You've been thrown out, you interloper! I suppose that's not clear enough. You don't understand nice manners.

POLLY   You and your nice manners! Oh, I'm forgetting my dignity! I shouldn't stoop to . . . no, I shouldn't. (*She starts to bawl*)

LUCY   Just look at my belly, you slut! Did I get that from out of nowhere? Haven't you eyes in your head?

POLLY   Oh! So you're in the family way! And you think that gives you rights? A fine lady like you, you shouldn't have let him in!

MAC   Polly!

POLLY   (*in tears*)   This is really too much. Mac, you shouldn't have done that. Now I don't know what to do.
        (*Enter Mrs. Peachum*)

MRS. PEACHUM   I knew it. She's with her man. You little trollop, come here immediately. When they hang your man, you can hang yourself too. A fine way to treat your respectable mother, making her come and get you out of jail. And he's got two of them, what's more—the Nero!

POLLY   Leave me here, mama; you don't know . . .

MRS. PEACHUM   You're coming home this minute.

LUCY   There you are, it takes your mama to tell you how to behave.

MRS. PEACHUM   Get going.

POLLY   Just a second. I only have to . . . I only have to tell him something . . . Really . . . it's very important.

MRS. PEACHUM   (*giving her a box on the ear*)   Well, this is important too. Get going!

POLLY   Oh, Mac! (*She is dragged away*)

MAC   Lucy, you were magnificent. Of course I felt sorry for her. That's why I couldn't treat the slut as she deserved. Just for a moment you thought there was some truth in what she said. Didn't you?

LUCY   Yes, my dear, so I did.

MAC   If there were any truth in it, her mother wouldn't have put me in this situation. Did you hear how she laid into me? A mother might treat a seducer like that, not a son-in-law.

LUCY   It makes me so happy to hear you say that from the

bottom of your heart. I love you so much I'd almost rather see you on the gallows than in the arms of another. Isn't that strange?

MAC   Lucy, I should like to owe you my life.

LUCY   It's wonderful the way you say that. Say it again.

MAC   Lucy, I should like to owe you my life.

LUCY   Shall I run away with you, dearest?

MAC   Well, but you see, if we run away together, it will be hard for us to hide. As soon as they stop looking, I'll send for you post haste, you know that!

LUCY   What can I do to help you?

MAC   Bring me my hat and cane.

(*Lucy comes back with his hat and cane and throws them into his cage*)

MAC   Lucy, the fruit of our love which you bear beneath your heart will hold us forever united.

(*Lucy goes out*)

SMITH   (*enters, goes into the cage, and says to Mac*)   Let's have that cane.

(*After a brief chase, in which Smith pursues Mac with a chair and a crowbar, Mac jumps over the bars. Constables run after him. Enter Brown*)

BROWN   (*off*)   Hey, Mac!—Mac, answer me, please. It's Jackie. Mac, please be a good boy, answer me, I can't stand it any longer. (*Goes in*) Mackie! What's this? He's gone, thank God! (*He sits down on the bed*)

(*Enter Peachum*)

PEACHUM   (*to Smith*)   My name is Peachum. I've come to collect the forty pounds reward for the capture of the bandit Macheath. (*Appears in front of the cage*) Excuse me! Is that Mr. Macheath? (*Brown is silent*) Oh. I suppose the other gentleman has gone for a stroll? I come here to visit a criminal, and who do I find sitting here but Mr. Brown! Tiger Brown is sitting here and his friend Macheath is not sitting here.

BROWN   (*groaning*)   Oh, Mr. Peachum, it wasn't my fault.

PEACHUM   Of course not. How could it be? You yourself would never . . . when you think of the situation it'll land you in . . . it's out of the question, Brown.

BROWN   Mr. Peachum, I'm beside myself.

PEACHUM   I believe you. You must be feeling terrible.

BROWN   Yes, it's this feeling of helplessness that gets a man down. Those fellows do just as they please. It's dreadful, dreadful.

PEACHUM   Wouldn't you care to lie down awhile? Just close your eyes and pretend nothing has happened. Imagine you're on a lovely green meadow with little white clouds overhead. The main thing is to forget all about those terrible things, those that are past, and most of all, those that are still to come.

BROWN (*alarmed*)   What do you mean by that?

PEACHUM   I'm amazed at your fortitude. In your position I should simply collapse, crawl into bed and drink hot tea. And above all, I'd find someone to lay a soothing hand on my forehead.

BROWN   Damn it all, it's not my fault if the fellow escapes. There's not much the police can do about it.

PEACHUM   I see. There's not much the police can do about it. You don't believe we'll see Mr. Macheath back here again? (*Brown shrugs his shoulders*) In that case, your fate will be hideously unjust. People are sure to say—they always do— that the police shouldn't have let him escape. No, I can't see that glittering Coronation procession just yet.

BROWN   What do you mean?

PEACHUM   Let me remind you of a historical incident which, despite having caused a great stir at the time, in the year 1400 B.C., is unknown to the public of today. On the death of the Egyptian king Ramses II, the police captain of Nineveh, or it may have been Cairo, committed some minor offense against the lower classes of the population. Even at that time the consequences were terrible. As the history books tell us, the coronation procession of Semiramis, the new queen, "developed into a series of catastrophes because of the unduly active participation of the lower orders." Historians still shudder at the cruel way Semiramis treated her police captain. I only remember dimly, but there was some talk of snakes that she fed on his bosom.

BROWN   Really?

PEACHUM   The Lord be with you, Brown. (*Goes out*)

BROWN   Now only the mailed fist can help. Sergeants! Report to me at the double!

(*Curtain. Macheath and Low-Dive Jenny step before the curtain and sing to song lighting*)

Second Threepenny Finale

What Keeps Mankind Alive?

I

MAC

You gentlemen who think you have a mission
To purge us of the seven deadly sins
Should first sort out the basic food position
Then start your preaching: that's where it begins.
You lot, who preach restraint and watch your waist as well
Should learn for all time how the world is run:
However much you twist, whatever lies you tell
Food is the first thing. Morals follow on.
So first make sure that those who now are starving
Get proper helpings when we all start carving.

VOICE (*off*)

What keeps mankind alive?

MAC

What keeps mankind alive? The fact that millions
Are daily tortured, stifled, punished, silenced, oppressed.
Mankind can keep alive thanks to its brilliance
In keeping its humanity repressed.

CHORUS

For once you must try not to shirk the facts:
Mankind is kept alive by bestial acts.

2

JENNY

You say that girls may strip with your permission.
You draw the lines dividing art from sin.
So first sort out the basic food position

Then start your preaching: that's where we begin.
You lot, who bank on your desires and our disgust
Should learn for all time how the world is run:
Whatever lies you tell, however much you twist
Food is the first thing. Morals follow on.
So first make sure that those who now are starving
Get proper helpings when we all start carving.

VOICE (*off*)

What keeps mankind alive?

JENNY

What keeps mankind alive? The fact that millions
Are daily tortured, stifled, punished, silenced, oppressed.
Mankind can keep alive thanks to its brilliance
In keeping its humanity repressed.

CHORUS

For once you must try not to shirk the facts:
Mankind is kept alive by bestial acts.

ACT THREE

7

That night Peachum prepares his campaign. He plans to disrupt the coronation procession by a demonstration of human misery.

Peachum's Outfitting Shop for Beggars

The beggars paint little signs with inscriptions such as "I gave my eye for my king," etc.

PEACHUM Gentlemen, at this moment, in our eleven branches from Drury Lane to Turnbridge, one thousand four hundred and thirty-two gentlemen are working on signs like these with a view to attending the Coronation of our Queen.

MRS. PEACHUM Get a move on! If you won't work, you can't beg. Call yourself a blind man and can't even make a proper K? That's supposed to be child's writing, anyone would take it for an old man's.

(*A drum roll*)

BEGGAR That's the Coronation guard presenting arms. Little do they suspect that today, the biggest day in their military careers, they'll have us to deal with.

FILCH (*enters and reports*) Mrs. Peachum, there's a dozen sleepy-looking hens traipsing in. They claim there's some money due them.

(*Enter the whores*)

JENNY Madam . . .

MRS. PEACHUM Hm, you look as if you'd fallen off your perches. I suppose you've come to collect the money for that

Macheath of yours? Well, you'll get nothing, do you understand, nothing.

JENNY   How are we to understand that, ma'am?

MRS. PEACHUM   Bursting in here in the middle of the night! Coming to a respectable house at three in the morning! With the work you do, I should think you'd want some sleep. You look like sicked-up milk.

JENNY   Then you won't give us the stipulated fee for turning in Mr. Macheath, ma'am?

MRS. PEACHUM   Exactly. No thirty pieces of silver for you.

JENNY   Why not, ma'am?

MRS. PEACHUM   Because your fine Mr. Macheath has scattered himself to the four winds. And now, ladies, get out of my parlor.

JENNY   This is too much. Just don't you try that on us. That's all I've got to say to you. Not on us.

MRS. PEACHUM   Filch, the ladies wish to be shown the door. (*Filch goes toward the ladies, Jenny pushes him away*)

JENNY   I'd advise you to hold your filthy tongue. If you don't, I'm likely to . . .

(*Enter Peachum*)

PEACHUM   What's going on, you haven't given them any money, I hope? Well, ladies, how about it? Is Mr. Macheath in jail, or isn't he?

JENNY   Don't talk to me about Mr. Macheath. You're not fit to black his boots. Last night I had to let a customer go because it made me cry into my pillow to think how I had sold that gentleman to you. Yes, ladies, and what do you think happened this morning? Less than an hour ago, just after I had cried myself to sleep, I heard somebody whistle, and out on the street stood the very gentleman I'd been crying about, asking me to throw down the key. He wanted to lie in my arms and make me forget the wrong I had done him. Ladies, he's the last gentleman left in London. And if our friend Suky Tawdry isn't here with us now, it's because he went on from me to her to comfort her too.

PEACHUM (*muttering to himself*)   Suky Tawdry . . .

JENNY   So now you know that you're not fit to black that gentleman's boots. You miserable stoolpigeon.

PEACHUM   Filch, run to the nearest police station, tell them Mr. Macheath is at Miss Suky Tawdry's place. (*Filch goes out*) But ladies, why are we arguing? The money will be paid out, that goes without saying. Celia dear, you'd do better to make the ladies some coffee instead of slanging them.

MRS. PEACHUM (*on her way out*)   Suky Tawdry! (*She sings the third stanza of the Ballade of Sexual Obsession*)

There stands a man. The gallows loom above him.
They've got the quicklime mixed in which to shove him.
They've put his neck just under where the noose is
And what's he thinking of, the idiot? Floozies.
They've all but hanged him, yet he can't ignore that call.
Sexual obsession has him in its thrall.
   She's sold him down the river heart and soul
   He's seen the dirty money in her hand
   And bit by bit begins to understand:
   The pit that covers him is woman's hole.
   Then he may rant and roar and curse his ruin—
   But soon as night falls he'll be up and doing.

PEACHUM   Get a move on, you'd all be rotting in the sewers of Turnbridge if in my sleepless nights I hadn't worked out how to squeeze a penny out of your poverty. I discovered that though the rich of this earth find no difficulty in creating misery, they can't bear to see it. Because they are weaklings and fools just like you. They may have enough to eat till the end of their days, they may be able to wax their floors with butter so that even the crumbs from their tables grow fat, but they can't look on unmoved while a man is collapsing from hunger, though of course that only applies so long as he collapses outside their own front door. (*Enter Mrs. Peachum with a tray full of coffee cups*)

MRS. PEACHUM   You can come by the shop tomorrow and pick up your money, but only when the Coronation's over.

JENNY   Mrs. Peachum, you leave me speechless.

PEACHUM   Fall in. We assemble in one hour outside Buckingham Palace. Quick march.

(*The beggars fall in*)

FILCH (*dashes in*)   Cops! I didn't even get to the police station. The police are here already.

PEACHUM   Hide, gentlemen! (*To Mrs. Peachum*) Call the band together. Shake a leg. And if you hear me say "harmless," do you understand, *harmless* . . .

MRS. PEACHUM   Harmless? I don't understand a thing.

PEACHUM   Naturally you don't understand. Well, if I say *harmless* . . . (*knocking at the door*) Thank God, this is the answer, *harmless*, then you play some kind of music. Get a move on!

(*Mrs. Peachum goes out with some beggars. The others except for the girl with the sign "A Victim of Military Tyranny," hide with their things upstage right behind the clothes rack. Enter Brown and constables*)

BROWN   Here we are. And now Mr. Beggar's Friend, drastic action will be taken. Put him in chains, Smith. Oh, here are some of those delightful signs. (*To the girl*) "A Victim of Military Tyranny"—is that you?

PEACHUM   Good morning, Brown, good morning. Sleep well?

BROWN   Huh?

PEACHUM   Morning, Brown.

BROWN   Is he saying that to me? Does he know one of you? I don't believe I have the pleasure of your acquaintance.

PEACHUM   Really? Morning, Brown.

BROWN   Knock his hat off.

(*Smith does so*)

PEACHUM   Look here, Brown, as long as you're *passing by*, passing, I say, Brown, I may as well ask you to put a certain Macheath under lock and key, it's high time.

BROWN   The man's mad. Don't laugh, Smith. Tell me, Smith, how is it possible that such a notorious criminal should be running around loose in London?

PEACHUM   Because he's your friend, Brown.

BROWN   Who?

PEACHUM   Mac the Knife. Not me. I'm no criminal. I'm a poor man, Brown. You can't abuse me, Brown, you've got the worst hour in your life ahead of you. Care for some coffee? (*To the whores*) Girls, give the chief of police a sip, that's no way to behave. Let's all be friends. We are all law-abiding people! The law was made for one thing alone, for the exploitation of those who don't understand it, or are prevented by naked misery from obeying it. And anyone who wants a crumb of this exploitation for himself must obey the law strictly.

BROWN   I see, then you believe our judges are corruptible?

PEACHUM   Not at all, sir, not at all! Our judges are absolutely incorruptible: It's more than money can do to make them give a fair verdict!

(*A second drum roll*)

PEACHUM   The troops are marching off to line the route. The poorest of the poor will move off in half an hour.

BROWN   That's right, Mr. Peachum. In half an hour the poorest of the poor will be marched off to winter quarters in the Old Bailey. (*To the constables*) All right, boys, round them all up, all the patriots you find here. (*To the beggars*) Have you fellows ever heard of Tiger Brown? Tonight, Peachum, I've hit on the solution and, I believe I may say, saved a friend from mortal peril. I'll simply smoke out your whole nest. And lock up the lot of you for—hm, for what? For begging on the street. You seem to have intimated your intention of embarrassing me and the Queen with these beggars. I'll just arrest the beggars. Let that be a lesson to you.

PEACHUM   Excellent, but—what beggars?

BROWN   These cripples here. Smith, we'll take these patriots along with us.

PEACHUM   I can save you from a hasty step; you can thank the Lord, Brown, that you came to me. You see, Brown, you can arrest these few, they're harmless, *harmless* . . .

(*Music starts up, playing a few measures of the "Song of the Insufficiency of Human Endeavor"*)

BROWN   What's that?

PEACHUM   Music. They play as well as they can. The Song of Insufficiency. You don't know it? Let this be a lesson to you.

(*Song lighting: golden glow. The organ is lit up. Three lamps are lowered from above on a pole and the signs say:*)

Song of the Insufficiency of Human Endeavor

1
Mankind lives by its head
Its head won't see it through
Inspect your own. What lives off that?
At most a louse or two.
   For this bleak existence
   Man is never sharp enough.
   Hence his weak resistance
   To its tricks and bluff.

2
Aye, make yourself a plan
They need you at the top!
Then make yourself a second plan
Then let the whole thing drop.
   For this bleak existence
   Man is never bad enough
   Though his sheer persistence
   Can be lovely stuff.

3
Aye, race for happiness
But don't you race too fast.
When all chase after happiness
Happiness comes in last.
   For this bleak existence
   Man is never undemanding enough.
   All his loud insistence
   Is a load of guff.

PEACHUM   Your plan, Brown, was brilliant, but hardly realistic. All you can arrest in this place is a few young fellows
celebrating their Queen's Coronation by arranging a little
fancy dress party. When the real paupers come along—
there aren't any here—there will be thousands of them.
That's the point: you've forgotten what an immense number
of poor people there are. When you see them standing out-

side the Abbey, it won't be a festive sight. You see, they
don't look good. Do you know what the rose is, Brown?
Yes, but how about a hundred thousand faces all flushed
with the rose: Our young Queen's path should be strewn
with roses not with the rose. And all those cripples at the
church door. That's something one wishes to avoid, Brown.
You'll probably say the police can handle us poor folk.
You don't believe that yourself. How will it look if six
hundred poor cripples have to be clubbed down at the
Coronation? It will look bad. It will look disgusting. Nause-
ating. I feel faint at the thought of it, Brown. A small chair,
if you please.

BROWN (*to Smith*) That's a threat. See here, you, that's
blackmail. We can't touch the man, in the interests of
public order we simply can't touch him. I've never seen the
like of it.

PEACHUM You're seeing it now. Let me tell you something:
You can behave as you please to the Queen of England. But
you can't tread on the toes of the poorest man in England,
or you'll be brought down, Mr. Brown.

BROWN So you're asking me to arrest Mac the Knife? Arrest
him? That's easy to say. You've got to find a man before
you can arrest him.

PEACHUM If you say that, I can't contradict you. So I'll find
your man for you; we'll see if there's any morality left.
Jenny, where is Mr. Macheath at this moment?

JENNY 21 Oxford Street, at Suky Tawdry's.

BROWN Smith, go at once to Suky Tawdry's place at 21
Oxford Street, arrest Macheath and take him to the Old
Bailey. In the meantime, I must put on my gala uniform.
On this day of all days I must wear my gala uniform.

PEACHUM Brown, if he's not on the gallows by six o'clock . . .

BROWN Oh, Mac, it was not to be. (*Goes out with constables*)

PEACHUM (*calling after him*) That was a lesson to you, eh,
Brown?

(*Third drum roll*)

PEACHUM Third drum roll. Change of direction. You will
head for the dungeons of the Old Bailey. March!

(*The beggars go out*)

PEACHUM (*sings the fourth stanza of the "Song of the In-sufficiency of Human Endeavor"*):
Man could be good instead
So slug him on the head
If you can slug him good and hard
He may stay good and dead.
 For this bleak existence
 Man's not good enough just yet.
 Don't wait for assistance.
 Slug him on the head.

(*Curtain. Jenny steps before the curtain with a hurdy-gurdy and sings the*)

Solomon Song

1

You saw sagacious Solomon
You know what came of him.
To him complexities seemed plain.
He cursed the hour that gave birth to him
And saw that everything was vain.
How great and wise was Solomon!
But now that time is getting late
The world can see what followed on.
It's wisdom that had brought him to this state—
How fortunate the man with none!

2

You saw the lovely Cleopatra
You know what she became.
Two emperors slaved to serve her lust.
She whored herself to death and fame
Then rotted down and turned to dust.
How beautiful was Babylon!
But now that time is getting late
The world can see what followed on.
It's beauty that had brought her to this state—
How fortunate the girl with none!

3
You saw the gallant Caesar next
You know what he became.
They deified him in his life
Then had him murdered just the same.
And as they raised the fatal knife
How loud he cried "You too, my son!"
But now that time is getting late
The world can see what followed on.
It's courage that had brought him to this state—
How fortunate the man with none!

4
You know the ever-curious Brecht
Whose songs you liked to hum.
He asked, too often for your peace
Where rich men get their riches from.
So then you drove him overseas.
How curious was my mother's son!
But now that time is getting late
The world can see what followed on.
Inquisitiveness brought him to this state—
How fortunate the man with none!

5
And now look at this man Macheath
The sands are running out.
If only he'd known where to stop
And stuck to crimes he knew all about
He surely would have reached the top.
Then suddenly his heart was won.
But now that time is getting late
The world can see what followed on.
His sexual urges brought him to this state—
How fortunate the man with none!

8

Property in Dispute[10]

A young girl's room in the Old Bailey.

Lucy.

SMITH (*enters*) Miss, Mrs. Polly Macheath wishes to speak with you.
LUCY Mrs. Macheath? Show her in.
(*Enter Polly*)
POLLY Good morning, madam. Madam, good morning!
LUCY What is it, please?
POLLY Do you recognize me?
LUCY Of course I know you.
POLLY I've come to beg your pardon for the way I behaved yesterday.
LUCY Very interesting.
POLLY I have no excuse to offer for my behavior, madam, but my misfortunes.
LUCY I see.
POLLY Madam, you must forgive me. I was stung by Mr. Macheath's behavior. He really ought not to have put us in such a situation, and you can tell him so when you see him.
LUCY I . . . I . . . shan't be seeing him.
POLLY Of course you will see him.
LUCY I shall not see him.
POLLY Forgive me.
LUCY But he's very fond of you.
POLLY Oh no, you're the only one he loves. I'm sure of that.
LUCY Very kind of you.
POLLY But, madam, a man is always afraid of a woman who loves him too much. And then he's bound to neglect and

avoid her. I could see at a glance that he is more devoted
to you than I could ever have guessed.

LUCY   Do you mean that sincerely?

POLLY   Of course, certainly, very sincerely, madam. Do believe me.

LUCY   Dear Miss Polly, both of us have loved him too much.

POLLY   Perhaps. (*Pause*) And now, madam, I want to tell you
how it all came about. Ten days ago I met Mr. Macheath
for the first time at the Cuttlefish Hotel. My mother was
there too. Five days later, about the day before yesterday,
we were married. Yesterday I found out that he was wanted
by the police for a variety of crimes. And today I don't
know what's going to happen. So you see, madam, twelve
days ago I couldn't have imagined ever losing my heart to
a man.
(*Pause*)

LUCY   I understand, Miss Peachum.

POLLY   Mrs. Macheath.

LUCY   Mrs. Macheath.

POLLY   To tell the truth, I've been thinking about this man
a good deal in the last few hours. It's not so simple. Because
you see, miss, I really can't help envying you for the way
he behaved to you the other day. When I left him, only
because my mother made me, he didn't show the slightest
sign of regret. Maybe he has no heart and nothing but a
stone in his breast. What do you think, Lucy?

LUCY   Well, my dear miss—I really don't know if Mr. Macheath is entirely to blame. You should have stuck to your
own class of people, dear miss.

POLLY   Mrs. Macheath.

LUCY   Mrs. Macheath.

POLLY   That's quite true—or at least, as my father always
advised me, I should have kept everything on a strictly
business footing.

LUCY   Definitely.

POLLY   (*weeping*) But he's my only possession in all the
world.

LUCY   My dear, such a misfortune can befall the most intelligent woman. But after all, you are his wife on paper.

That should be a comfort to you. Poor child, I can't bear to see you so depressed. Won't you have a little something?

POLLY   What?

LUCY   Something to eat.

POLLY   Oh yes, please, a little something to eat. (*Lucy goes out. Polly aside*) The hypocritical strumpet.

LUCY (*comes back with coffee and cake*)   Here. This ought to do it.

POLLY   You've really gone to too much trouble, madam. (*Pause. She eats*) That's a lovely picture of him you've got. When did he bring it?

LUCY   Bring it?

POLLY (*innocently*)   I mean when did he bring it up here to you?

LUCY   He didn't bring it.

POLLY   Did he give it to you right here in this room?

LUCY   He never was in this room.

POLLY   I see. But there wouldn't have been any harm in it. The paths of fate are so dreadfully crisscrossed.

LUCY   Must you keep talking such nonsense? You only came here to spy.

POLLY   Then you do know where he is?

LUCY   Me? Don't you know?

POLLY   Tell me this minute where he is.

LUCY   I have no idea.

POLLY   So you don't know where he is. Word of honor?

LUCY   No, I don't know. Hm, and you don't either?

POLLY   No. This is terrible. (*Polly laughs and Lucy weeps*) Now he has two commitments. And he's gone.

LUCY   I can't stand it any more. Oh, Polly, it's so dreadful.

POLLY (*gaily*)   I'm so happy to have found such a good friend at the end of this tragedy. That's something. Would you like a little more to eat? Some more cake?

LUCY   Just a bit! Oh, Polly, don't be so good to me. Really, I don't deserve it. Oh, Polly, men aren't worth it.

POLLY   Of course men aren't worth it, but what else can we do?

LUCY   No! Now I'm going to make a clean breast of it. Will you be very cross with me, Polly?

POLLY   About what?

LUCY   It's not real!

POLLY   What?

LUCY   This here! (*She indicates her belly*) And all for that criminal!

POLLY (*laughs*)   Oh, that's magnificent! Is it a cushion? Oh, you really are a hypocritical strumpet! Look—you want Mackie? I'll make you a present of him. If you find him you can keep him. (*Voices and steps are heard in the corridor*) What's that?

LUCY (*at the window*)   Mackie! They've caught him once more.

POLLY (*collapses*)   This is the end.

(*Enter Mrs. Peachum*)

MRS. PEACHUM   Ha, Polly, so this is where I find you. You must change your things, your husband is being hanged. I've brought your widow's weeds. (*Polly changes into the widow's dress*) You'll be a lovely widow. But you'll have to cheer up a little.

9

Five o'clock, Friday morning: Mac the Knife, who has been with the whores again, has again been betrayed by whores. He is about to be hanged.

Death cell.

The bells of Westminster ring. Constables bring Macheath shackled into the cell.

SMITH   Bring him in here. There go the bells of Westminster. Stand up straight, I'm not asking you why you look so worn out. I'd say you were ashamed. (*To the constables*) When the bells of Westminster ring for the third time, that will be at six, he's got to have been hanged. Make everything ready.

A CONSTABLE   For the last quarter of an hour all the streets around Newgate have been so jammed with people of every class you can't get through.

SMITH   Strange! Then they already know?

CONSTABLE   If this goes on, all London will know in another quarter of an hour. All the people who would otherwise have gone to the Coronation will come here. And the Queen will ride through empty streets.

SMITH   All the more reason for us to move fast. If we're through by six, that will give people time to get back to the Coronation by seven. So now, get going.

MAC   Hey, Smith, what time is it?

SMITH   Haven't you got eyes? Five-oh-four.

MAC   Five-oh-four.

(*Just as Smith is locking the cell door from outside, Brown enters*)

BROWN   (*his back to the cell, to Smith*)   Is he in there?

SMITH   You want to see him?

BROWN   No, no, no, for God's sake. I'll leave it all to you. (*Goes out*)

MAC   (*suddenly bursts into a soft unbroken flow of speech*) All right, Smith, I won't say a word, not a word about bribery, never fear. I know all about it. If you let yourself be bribed, you'd have to leave the country for a start. You certainly would. You'd need enough to live on for the rest of your life. A thousand pounds, eh? Don't say anything! In twenty minutes I'll tell you whether you can have your thousand pounds by noon. I'm not saying a word about feelings. Go outside and think it over carefully. Life is short and money is scarce. And I don't even know yet if I can raise any. But if anyone wants to see me, let them in.

SMITH   (*slowly*)   That's a lot of nonsense, Mr. Macheath. (*Goes out*)

MAC   (*sings softly and very fast the* "Call from the Grave":)
Hark to the voice that's calling you to weep.
Macheath lies here, not under open sky

Not under treetops, no, but good and deep.
Fate struck him down in outraged majesty.
God grant his dying words may reach a friend.
The thickest walls encompass him about.
Is none of you concerned to know his fate?
Once he is gone the bottles can come out
But do stand by him while it's not too late.
D'you want his punishment to have no end?[11]

(*Matthew and Jake appear in the corridor. They are on their way to see Macheath. Smith stops them*)

SMITH   Well, son. You look like a soused herring.

MATTHEW   Now the Captain's gone it's my job to get our girls in the family way, so when they're brought into court they can plead irresponsibility. It's a job for a horse. I've got to see the Captain.

(*Both continue toward Mac*)

MAC   Five twenty-five. You took your time.

JAKE   Yes, but, you see, we had to . . .[12]

MAC   You see, you see, I'm being hanged, man! But I've no time to waste arguing with you. Five twenty-eight. All right: How much can you people draw from your savings account right away?

MATTHEW   From our . . . what, at five o'clock in the morning?

JAKE   Has it really come to this?

MAC   Can you manage four hundred pounds?

JAKE   But what about us? That's all there is.

MAC   Who's being hanged, you or me?

MATTHEW   (*excitedly*)   Who was lying around with Suky Tawdry instead of clearing out? Who was lying around with Suky Tawdry, us or you?

MAC   Shut your trap. I'll soon be lying somewhere other than with that slut. Five-thirty.

JAKE   Matt, if that's how it is, we'll just have to do it.

SMITH   Mr. Brown wishes to know what you'd like for your . . . meal.

MAC   Don't bother me. (*To Matthew*) Well, will you or won't you? (*To Smith*) Asparagus.

MATTHEW   Don't you shout at me. I won't have it.

MAC   I'm not shouting at you. It's only that . . . Well Matthew, are you going to let me be hanged?

MATTHEW   Of course I'm not going to let you be hanged. Who said I was? But that's the lot. Four hundred pounds is all there is. No reason why I shouldn't say that, is there?

MAC   Five thirty-eight.

JAKE   We'll have to run, Matthew, or it'll be no good.

MATTHEW   If we can only get through. There's such a crowd. Scum of the earth! (*Both go out*)

MAC   If you're not here by five to six, you'll never see me again. (*Shouts*) You'll never see me again . . .

SMITH   They've gone. Well, what about it? (*Makes a gesture of counting money*)

MAC   Four hundred. (*Smith goes out shrugging his shoulders. Mac, calling after him*) I've got to speak to Brown.

SMITH   (*comes back with constables*): Got the soap?

CONSTABLE   Yes, but not the right kind.

SMITH   You can set the thing up in ten minutes.

CONSTABLE   But the trap doesn't work.

SMITH   It's got to work. The bells have gone a second time.

CONSTABLE   What a shambles!

MAC (*sings*)
Come here and see the shitty state he's in.
This really is what people mean by bust.
You who set up the dirty cash you win
As just about the only god you'll trust
Don't stand and watch him slipping round the bend!
Go to the Queen and say that her subjects need her
Go in a group and tell her of his trouble
Like pigs all following behind their leader.
Say that his teeth are wearing down to rubble.
D'you want his punishment to have no end?

SMITH   I can't possibly let you in. You're only number sixteen. Wait your turn.

POLLY   What do you mean, number sixteen? Don't be a bureaucrat. I'm his wife, I've got to see him.

SMITH   Not more than five minutes, then.

POLLY   Five minutes! That's perfectly ridiculous. Five minutes! How is one to say all one has to say? It's not so simple. This is good-bye forever. There's an exceptional amount of things for man and wife to talk about at such a moment . . . where is he?

SMITH   What, can't you see him?

POLLY   Yes, of course. Thank you.

MAC   Polly!

POLLY   Yes, Mackie, here I am.

MAC   Yes, of course!

POLLY   How are you? Are you quite worn out? It's hard!

MAC   But what will you do now? What will become of you?

POLLY   Don't worry, the business is doing very well. That's the least part of it. Are you very nervous, Mackie? . . . By the way, what was your father? There's so much you still haven't told me. I just don't understand. Your health has always been excellent.

MAC   Polly, can't you help me to get out?

POLLY   Oh yes, of course.

MAC   With money, of course. I've arranged with the warder . . .

POLLY   (*slowly*)   The money has gone off to Manchester.

MAC   And you've got none on you?

POLLY   No, I've got nothing on me. But you know, Mackie, I could talk to somebody, for instance . . . I might even ask the Queen in person. (*She breaks down*) Oh, Mackie!

SMITH   (*pulling Polly away*)   Well, have you raised those thousand pounds?

POLLY   All the best, Mackie, take care of yourself, and don't forget me! (*Goes out*)
(*Smith and a constable bring in a table with a dish of asparagus on it*)

SMITH   Is the asparagus tender?

CONSTABLE   Absolutely. (*Goes out*)

BROWN   (*appears and goes up to Smith*)   Smith, what does he want me for? It's good you didn't take the table in earlier. We'll take it right in with us, to show him how we feel about him. (*They enter the cell with the table. Smith goes out. Pause*) Hello, Mac. Here's your asparagus. Won't you have some?

MAC   Don't you bother, Mr. Brown. There are others to show me the last honors.[13]

BROWN   Oh, Mackie!

MAC   Would you be so good as to produce your accounts? You don't mind if I eat in the meantime, after all it is my last meal. (*He eats*)

BROWN   I hope you enjoy it. Oh, Mac, you're turning the knife in the wound.

MAC   The accounts, sir, if you please, the accounts. No sentimentality.

BROWN   (*with a sigh takes a small notebook from his pocket*) I've got them right here, Mac. The accounts for the past six months.

MAC   (*bitingly*)   Oh, so all you came for was to get your money before it's too late.

BROWN   You know that isn't so.

MAC   Don't worry, sir, nobody's going to cheat you. What do I owe you? But I want an itemized bill, if you don't mind. Life has made me distrustful . . . In your position, sir, you should be able to understand that.

BROWN   Mac, when you talk like that, I just can't think.
(*A loud pounding is heard rear*)

SMITH (*off*)   All right, that'll hold.

MAC   The accounts, Brown.

BROWN   Very well—if you insist. Well, first of all the rewards for murderers arrested thanks to you or your men. The government paid you a total of . . .

MAC   Three instances at forty pounds apiece, that makes a hundred and twenty pounds. One quarter for you comes to thirty pounds, so that's what we owe you.

BROWN   Yes—yes—but really, Mac, I don't think we ought to spend our last . . .

MAC   Kindly stop sniveling. Thirty pounds. And for the job in Dover eight pounds.

BROWN   Why only eight pounds, there was . . .

MAC   Do you believe me or don't you believe me? Your share

in the transactions of the last six months comes to thirty-eight pounds.

BROWN (*wailing*) For a whole lifetime . . . I could read . . .

BOTH Your every thought in your eyes.

MAC Three years in India—John was all present and Jim was all there—, five years in London, and this is the thanks I get. (*Indicating how he will look when hanged*)

Here hangs Macheath who never wronged a flea
A faithless friend has brought him to this pass.
And as he dangles from the gallowstree
His neck finds out how heavy is his arse.

BROWN If that's the way you feel about it, Mac . . . The man who impugns my honor, impugns me. (*Runs furiously out of the cage*)

MAC Your honor . . .

BROWN Yes, my honor. Time to begin, Smith! Let them all in! (*To Mac*) Excuse me, would you.

SMITH (*quickly to Macheath*) I can still get you out of here, in another minute I won't be able to. Have you got the money?

MAC Yes, as soon as the boys get back.

SMITH There's no sign of them. The deal is off.
(*People are admitted. Peachum, Mrs. Peachum, Polly, Lucy, the whores, the vicar, Matthew and Jake*)

JENNY They didn't want to let us in. But I said to them: If you don't get those pisspots you call heads out of my way, you'll hear from Low-Dive Jenny.

PEACHUM I am his father-in-law. I beg your pardon, which of the present company is Mr. Macheath?

MAC (*introduces himself*) I'm Macheath.

PEACHUM (*walks past the cage, and like all who follow him stations himself to the right of it*) Fate, Mr. Macheath, has decreed that though I don't know you, you should be my son-in-law. The occasion of this first meeting between us is a very sad one. Mr. Macheath. You once had white kid gloves, a cane with an ivory handle, and a scar on your neck, and you frequented the Cuttlefish Hotel. All that is left is your scar, no doubt the least valuable of your distinguishing marks. Today you frequent nothing but prison cells, and within the foreseeable future no place at all . . .

(*Polly passes the cage in tears and stations herself to the right*)

MAC   What a pretty dress you're wearing.

(*Matthew and Jake pass the cage and take up positions on the right*)

MATTHEW   We couldn't get through because of the terrible crush. We ran so hard I was afraid Jake was going to have a stroke. If you don't believe us . . .

MAC   What do my men say? Have they got good places?

MATTHEW   You see, Captain, we thought you'd understand. You see, a Coronation doesn't happen every day. They've got to make some money when there's a chance. They send you their best wishes.

JAKE   Their very best wishes.

MRS. PEACHUM (*steps up to the cell, takes up a position on the right*) Mr. Macheath, who would have expected this a week ago when we were dancing at a little hop at the Cuttlefish Hotel.

MAC   A little hop.

MRS. PEACHUM   But the ways of destiny are cruel here below.

BROWN (*at the rear to the vicar*)   And to think that I stood shoulder to shoulder with this man in Azerbaidjan under a hail of bullets.

JENNY (*approaches the cage*)   We Drury Lane girls are frantic. Nobody's gone to the Coronation. Everybody wants to see you. (*Stations herself on the right*)

MAC   To see me.

SMITH   All right. Let's go. Six o'clock. (*Lets him out of the cage*)

MAC   We mustn't keep them waiting. Ladies and gentlemen. You see before you a declining representative of a declining social group. We lower-middle-class artisans who work with humble jemmies on small shopkeepers' cash registers are being swallowed up by big corporations backed by the banks. What's a jemmy compared with a stock certificate? What's breaking into a bank compared with founding a bank? What's murdering a man compared with hiring a man? Fellow citizens, I hereby take my leave of you. I thank you for coming. Some of you were very close to me. That Jenny should have turned me in amazes me greatly. It is proof positive that the world never changes. A convergence of several unfortunate circumstances has brought about my fall. So be it—I fall.

(*Song lighting: golden glow. The organ is lit up. Three lamps are lowered on a pole, and the signs say:*)

Ballade in which Macheath begs all men for forgiveness

You fellow men who live on after us
Pray do not think you have to judge us harshly
And when you see us hoisted up and trussed
Don't laugh like fools behind your big mustaches
Or curse at us. It's true that we came crashing
But do not judge our downfall like the courts.
Not all of us can discipline our thoughts—
Dear fellows, your extravagance needs slashing
Dear fellows, we've shown how a crash begins.
Pray then to God that He forgive my sins.

The rain washes away and purifies.
Let it wash down the flesh we catered for
And we who saw so much, and wanted more—
The crows will come and peck away our eyes.
Perhaps ambition used too sharp a goad
It drove us to these heights from which we swing
Hacked at by greedy starlings on the wing
Like horses' droppings on a country road.
O brothers, learn from us how it begins
And pray to God that He forgive our sins.

The girls who flaunt their breasts as bait there
To catch some sucker who will love them
The youths who slyly stand and wait there
To grab their sinful earnings off them
The crooks, the tarts, the tarts' protectors

The models and the mannequins
The psychopaths, the unfrocked rectors
I pray that they forgive my sins.

Not so those filthy police employees
Who day by day would bait my anger
Devise new troubles to annoy me
And chuck me crusts to stop my hunger.
I'd call on God to come and choke them
And yet my need for respite wins:
I realize that it might provoke them
So pray that they forgive my sins.

Someone must take a huge iron crowbar
And stave their ugly faces in.
All I ask is to know it's over
Praying that they forgive my sins.

SMITH   If you don't mind, Mr. Macheath.

MRS. PEACHUM   Polly and Lucy, stand by your husband in his last hour.

MAC   Ladies, whatever there may have been between us . . .

SMITH (*leads him away*)   Get a move on!

Procession to the Gallows.

(*All go out through doors left. These doors are on projection screens. Then all reenter from the other side of the stage with shaded lanterns. When Macheath is standing at the top of the gallows steps Peachum speaks*)

PEACHUM
Dear audience, we now are coming to
The point where we must hang him by the neck
Because it is the Christian thing to do
Proving that men must pay for what they take.

But as we want to keep our fingers clean
And you are people we can't risk offending
We thought we'd better do without this scene
And substitute instead a different ending.

Since this is opera, not life, you'll see
Justice give way before Humanity.
So now, to throw our story right off course
Enter the royal official on his horse.

(*The signs read:*)

Third Threepenny Finale

Appearance of the messenger on horseback

CHORUS
Hark, who's here?
A royal official on horseback's here!

(*Enter Brown on horseback as the messenger*)

BROWN   I bring a special order from our beloved Queen to have Captain Macheath set at liberty forthwith (*all cheer*) since it's her Coronation, and raised to the hereditary peerage. (*Cheers*) The castle of Marmarel, likewise a pension of ten thousand pounds, to be his in usufruct until his death. To any bridal couples present Her Majesty bids me to convey her gracious good wishes.

MAC   Reprievéd! Reprievéd! I was sure of it.
When you're most despairing
The clouds may be clearing.

POLLY   Reprievéd, my dearest Macheath is reprievéd. I am so happy.

MRS. PEACHUM   So it all turned out nicely in the end. How nice everything would be if these saviors on horseback always appeared when they were needed.

PEACHUM   So please remain all standing in your places, and join in the hymn of the poorest of the poor, whose most arduous life you have seen portrayed here today, for in fact the fate they meet is bound to be grim. Saviors on horseback are seldom met with in practice once the man who's kicked about has kicked back. Which all means one shouldn't persecute wrongdoing too much.

ALL (*come forward, singing to the organ*)
    Don't punish our wrongdoing too much. Never
    Will it withstand the frost, for it is cold.
    Think of the darkness and the bitter weather
    The cries of pain that echo through this world.

Notes and Variants

A MAN'S A MAN

Texts by Brecht

The A Man's a Man song

1

Hey, Tom, have you joined up too, joined up too?
'Cos I've joined up just like you, just like you.
And when I sees you marching there
I know I'm back on the old barrack square.
Have you ever seen me in your life?
'Cos I've never seen you in my life.
   It ain't the plan
   For a man is a man
   Since time began.
   Tommy boy, let me tell you, it really ain't the plan
   For man is man!
   There's no other plan.
   The red sun of Kilkoa shines
   Upon our regimental lines
   Where seven thousand men can die
   And not a soul will bat an eye
   'Cos all the lot are better gone
   So who cares where Kilkoa's red sun shone?

2

Hey, Tom, was there rice in your Irish stew?
'Cos I had rice in my Irish stew
And when I found they'd left out the meat
The army didn't seem such a treat.
Hey, Tom, has it made you throw up yet?

'Cos I've not stopped throwing up as yet.
   It ain't the plan
   For a man is a man
   Since time began.
   Tommy boy, let me tell you, it really ain't the plan
   For man is man!
   There's no other plan.
   The red sun of Kilkoa shines
   Upon our regimental lines
   Where seven thousand men can die
   And not a soul will bat an eye
   'Cos all the lot are better gone
   So who cares where Kilkoa's red sun shone?

3

Hey, Tom, did you see Jenny Smith last night?
'Cos me I saw Jenny Smith last night.
And when I looks at that old bag
The army don't seem half such a drag.
Hey, Tom, have you also slept with her?
'Cos you know I've also slept with her.
   It ain't the plan
   For a man is a man
   Since time began.
   Tommy boy, let me tell you, it really ain't the plan
   For man is man!
   There's no other plan.
   The red sun of Kilkoa shines
   Upon our regimental lines
   Where seven thousand men can die
   And not a soul will bat an eye
   'Cos all the lot are better gone
   So who cares where Kilkoa's red sun shone?

4

Hey, Tom, have you got your kit packed up?
'Cos I have got my kit packed up.
And when I sees you with your kit
I feel the army's fighting fit.

But did you have bugger all to pack yours with?
'Cos I find I've bugged all to pack mine with.
 It ain't the plan
 For a man is a man
 Since time began.
 Tommy boy, let me tell you, it really ain't the plan
 For man is man!
 There's no other plan.
 The red sun of Kilkoa shines
 Upon our regimental lines
 Where seven thousand men can die
 And not a soul will bat an eye
 'Cos all the lot are better gone
 So who cares where Kilkoa's red sun shone?

5

Hey, Tom, are you quite ready to move off?
'Cos me I'm quite ready to move off.
And when I sees you march I guess
I'll march wherever the army says.
Have you got a clue where we're marching to?
'Cos I've not got a clue where we're marching to.
 It ain't the plan
 For a man is a man
 Since time began.
 Tommy boy, let me tell you, it really ain't the plan
 For man is man!
 There's no other plan.
 The red sun of Kilkoa shines
 Upon our regimental lines
 Where seven thousand men can die
 And not a soul will bat an eye
 'Cos all the lot are better gone
 So who cares where Kilkoa's red sun shone?

> ["Der Mann-ist-Mann-Song," from the 1927 edition of
> the play, republished in GW *Gedichte*, pp. 138 ff. The
> former edition gives Brecht's own tune, subsequently ar-
> ranged by Paul Dessau.]

Press Release

Disastrous prank by three privates of the Worchester Regiment stationed at Kankerdan, East India / Prank? Or crime? / J. Galgei, docker, takes himself for a soldier called Jerome Jip.

Saipong. All Hindustan is talking about the incredible case of J. Galgei,* a porter at the docks. Four private soldiers from Kankerdan, on detachment to Saipong, are alleged to have committed a hitherto baffling crime *in order to obtain whisky* (!!!), and to have been forced to abandon one of their number in the process. Realizing that the absence of the fourth man might have betrayed the crime in question they camouflaged it by exploiting the person of the docker J. Galgei. Moved in the first place *by mere sympathy*, the latter was twice persuaded to stand in at roll calls for the missing man, one Jerome Jip. However when he cited family reasons and refused to oblige them for an additional two days till the unit moved off they cast him as the leading player in *a comedy worthy of the silver screen.* Along with a canteen proprietress of most dubious character they conspired to give him an alleged British army elephant free gratis and for nothing to sell as he might wish. Due to the unbridled consumption of whisky then prevalent Galgei failed to detect the true character of this dangerous gift: a highly lifelike elephant constructed of nothing but some tarpaulins and his would-be benefactors the three privates. They thereupon arrested him for this "theft" at the "scene of the crime," and summarily shot him beneath the three sycamore trees of Saipong. They then revived this helplessly befuddled accomplice, who had fainted away well before his obviously faked execution, and told him he was to deliver a funeral oration on a certain Galgei who had just

* This was at a time when the three-day concentration of the Afghan Division provoked an enormous mêlée of soldiers and supply racketeers in Saipong, to say nothing of the less reputable camp followers associated with army units on the move.

been shot. Now highly confused, he complied with all their demands and offered virtually no resistance. The following day too inspired peculiar misgivings in the unfortunate docker, who by now had become unsure of his own personality. Using an army paybook the soldiers brought their cruel game to its climax. Galgei's attitude to his wife, who had managed to track him down in his military guise, showed that at this point he was already uncertain of his own identity. As soon as the "fun-loving" soldiers started making difficulties for him even with regard to his use of the name Jip, he so vehemently annexed that name that even the reappearance of the real Jip could not prise him away from it. Together with the simultaneous case of Sergeant P., who was so infuriated by the loss of self-control due to his unrestrained sexual urges as to castrate himself with his own hand, this entire episode shows how thin the veneer of individuality has become in our time.

["Für Zeitungen," from GW *Schriften zum Theater*, pp. 973 f. Prefaced to the 1925 typescript of the play.]

Epic Sequence of Events

The transformation of a live human being in the army camp of Kilkoa in the year nineteen hundred and twenty-five

1

then they all joined together to make a false elephant and led the man galy gay unto it and bade him sell it but the sergeant came as he was holding it by a rope and they were afraid saying: what will he do? for they could not stay with him because of the sergeant and they observed him over a wall when he was alone to see if he would examine the elephant and notice that it was unreal however they saw that the man never looked at it and from thenceforward they knew that there was one who believed what was good for him and would sooner know nothing therefore he ignored the elephant not seeing that it was unreal for he wished to sell it and the woman that was with him took the sergeant away

2

so the man sold the elephant that was not his and was unreal to boot but thereupon one of them approached him laid his hand on his shoulder and spake to him: what art thou doing? and because he could not justify himself they brought suit against him and they condemned him to death then he denied that he was the criminal galy gay but they acted as if they believed him not and did shoot deceivingly at him from seven rifle barrels and he fainted and fell

3

however when he awoke they put a box before him telling him that the man galy gay who had been shot lay within it thereupon his reason became utterly confused and he began to think that he was not galy gay who had been shot and lay within the box nor did he wish to be wherefore he stood up and spake about galy gay as though he were a stranger that they might believe that he was not he for he feared to die and they buried the box which was empty and he delivered the funeral speech

so they took him away with them that night

[“Epischer Verlauf.” Fragment from BBA 348/68.]

[Annex]

a man was traveling in a train from kilkoa to tibet and they laid a woman beside him that he might sleep with her and ask no questions for they had told him that he was one of their men and when he woke he found the woman beside him but he knew her not then they said to him: who is the woman with whom thou hast slept? and he did not know for he had not slept with the woman but did not know it when they saw that he knew her not they mocked him saying perchance thou knowest not thyself then he said i know myself but he lied they however tested him in all ways and he was downcast and sat apart and knew not who he was but then he heard a voice behind the partition and a man began to lament and say what a disgrace has overtaken me where is my name that once was great beyond the oceans where is the yesterday that has vanished even my raiment is gone that i wore

[Untitled. BBA 150/151.]

Two Notes

Execution

Galy Gay is led to the place of execution, but **since he is** being "inconspicuously" led by Jesse and Polly—"**the disgrace** for the regiment is too great; nothing of this must get out"— at first he is treated as a hero ("It's Jeraiah! Last-man-last-round Jip, the hero of Cochin Kula"). They all fête him; somebody asks him for a cigarette, hoping for reflected glory ("Happy to make your acquaintance. Wait till I tell them back home"). Then Uriah yells "It's a mistake!" and they all learn that he is a deserter. Throw things at him, spit at him.

Recruitment

Camp whores are sent ahead to admire his uniform. Two quarrel over him. He could sleep with three girls if it weren't for the discovery of some small outward lapse, an undone button or a missing shoulder strap, which leads to the suspicion that he is a swindler.

["Die Erschiessung" and "Die Werbung," from BBA 1080/75.]

Introductory Speech (For the Radio)

Look: our plays embrace part of the new things that came into the world long before the world war. This means at the same time that they no longer embrace a large part of the old things to which we are accustomed. Why don't they now embrace these old things which *were* once recognized and proper? I think I can tell you exactly. They no longer embrace these old things because the people to whom these things were important are today on the decline. But whenever a broad stratum of humanity is declining its vital utterances get weaker and weaker, its imagination becomes crippled, its appetites dwindle, its entire history has nothing more of note to offer, not even to itself. What a declining stratum like this does can no longer lead to any conclusions about men's doings. In the case of the arts this means that such people can no longer create or absorb art of any sort.

This stratum of humanity had its great period. It created monuments that have remained, but even these remaining monuments can no longer arouse enthusiasm. The great buildings of the city of New York and the great discoveries of electricity are not of themselves enough to swell mankind's sense of triumph. What matters most is that a *new human type* should now be evolving, at this very moment, and that the entire interest of the world should be concentrated on his development. The guns that are to hand and the guns that are still being manufactured are turned for him or against him. The houses that exist and are being built are built to oppress him or to shelter him. All live works created or applied in our time set out to discourage him or to put courage in him. And any work that has nothing to do with him is not alive and has nothing to do with anything. This new human type

will not be as the old type imagines. It is my belief that he will
not let himself be changed by machines but will himself change
the machine; and whatever he looks like he will above all look
human.

I would now like to turn briefly to the comedy *Mann ist
Mann* and explain why this introduction about the new human
type was necessary. Of course not all these problems are going
to arise and be solved in this particular play. They will be
solved somewhere quite different. But it struck me that all
sorts of things in *Mann ist Mann* will probably seem odd to
you at first—especially what the central figure, the porter
Galy Gay, does or does not do—and if so it's better that you
shouldn't think you are listening to an old acquaintance talking
or to yourself, as has hitherto nearly always been the rule in
the theater, but to a new sort of type, possibly an ancestor
of just that new human type I spoke of. It may be interesting
for you to look straight at him from this point of view, so as
to find out his attitude to things as precisely as possible. You
will see that among other things he is a great liar and an
incorrigible optimist; he can fit in with anything, almost without difficulty. He seems to be used to putting up with a great
deal. It is in fact very seldom that he can allow himself an
opinion of his own. For instance when (as you will hear) he
is offered an utterly spurious elephant which he can resell, he
will take care not to voice any opinion of it once he hears a
possible purchaser is there. I imagine also that you are used
to treating a man as a weakling if he can't say no, but this
Galy Gay is by no means a weakling; on the contrary he is
the strongest of all. That is to say he becomes the strongest
once he has ceased to be a private person; he only becomes
strong in the mass. And if the play finishes up with him con-
quering an entire fortress this is only because in doing so he is
apparently carrying out the determined wish of a great mass
of people who want to get through the narrow pass that the
fortress guards. No doubt you will go on to say that it's a
pity that a man should be tricked like this and simply forced
to surrender his precious ego, all he possesses (as it were);
but it isn't. It's a jolly business. For this Galy Gay comes to
no harm; he wins. And a man who adopts such an attitude is

bound to win. But possibly you will come to quite a different conclusion. To which I am the last person to object.

> ["Vorrede zu *Mann ist Mann*" from *Die Szene*, Berlin, April 1927, reprinted in GW *Schriften zum Theater*, pp. 976 ff. This was an introductory talk to the broadcast of the play by Berlin Radio on March 27, 1927. It also appears in a shortened and adapted form as a statement by Brecht in the opening program of Piscator's 1927–28 season. Part of another "introductory speech" is included in GW *Schriften zum Theater* as well, but discusses the theater in general rather than this particular play.]

Dialogue about Bert Brecht's Play *A Man's a Man*

—Where have you been to put you in such a bad mood and so foul a temper?

—I've been to Bert Brecht's play "A Man's a Man" and it's a bad play let me tell you and a waste of an evening.

—What makes you say that?

—Because it is a play that deals with ugly things such as are remote from me and the men in it are badly dressed and caked with the filth of their debased life such as is remote from me. And the plays I like are those in which moving or delightful things happen and clean well-dressed people perform.

—What's the good of being surrounded by moving or delightful things and clean well-dressed people if a red-hot lump of iron hits you and blots you out of life and the world?

—It is a play whose wit fails to make me laugh and its serious side to make me weep. And the plays I like are those in which the wit sparkles like fireworks or some sad occurrence moves my heart to compassion. For life is difficult and for a brief while I would fain be relieved of its burden.

—What's the good of enjoying wit like fireworks or having your heart moved at some sad occurrence if a red-hot lump of iron hits you and blots you out of life and the world?

—The plays I like are those that speak of the delights of nature, of the freshness of springtime and the rushing of the wind through the trees in summer, of the pale sky in April and the last blossoms in autumn.

—What's the good of the freshness of springtime and the rushing of the wind through the trees in summer, of the pale sky in April and the last blossoms in autumn, if a red-hot lump of iron hits you and blots you out of life and the world?

—I take pleasure in beautiful women and I love the desire that comes from the sight of them as they laugh and move in plays and seduce men and are taken by them. For then I feel that I am a man and mighty in sex.

—What's the good of feeling desire at the sight of beautiful women as they laugh and seduce men and are taken by them and feeling that you are a man and mighty in sex if a red-hot lump of iron hits you and blots you out of life and the world?

—But I loathe whatever is degrading and disparaging and I feel myself raised to a higher plane by the nobility immanent in the plays of the great masters; I love whatever is lofty and improving, such as makes me sense the might of a God and the existence of a just Power.

—What's the good of being raised to a higher plane by nobility and feeling the might of a God and the existence of a just Power if a red-hot lump of iron hits you and blots you out of life and the world?

—Why do you have to go on repeating the same words in answer to all I've been saying about the beautiful and elevating things in the plays of the great masters?

—Because you too can get caught up like that man in Bert Brecht's play so as to blot out your name and your self and your home and your wife and your memory, your laughter and your compassion, your desire for women and your elevation to God; because you too can be lined up like that man in a formation one hundred thousand strong, between man and man, dinner pail and dinner pail, just as millions of men have been lined up in the past and millions of men will be lined up in the future; because like that man you too can be hit by a red-hot lump of iron and blotted out of life and the world!!!

—*shouting*: Oh now I realize that it's a good play and its moral one to be taken to heart.

> ["Dialog zu Bert Brechts 'Mann ist Mann'" from GW *Schriften zum Theater*, pp. 978 ff. Date uncertain, but probably pre-1930.]

The Question of Criteria for Judging Acting

People interested in the ostensibly epic production of the play *Mann ist Mann* at the Staatstheater were of two opinions about the actor Lorre's performance in the leading part. Some thought his way of acting was perfectly right from the new point of view, exemplary even; others quite rejected it. I myself belong to the first group. Let me put the question in its proper perspective by saying that I saw all the rehearsals and that it was not at all due to shortcomings in the actor's technique that his performance so disappointed some of the spectators; those on the night who felt him to be lacking in "carrying-power" or "the gift of making his meaning clear" could have satisfied themselves about his gifts in this direction at the early rehearsals. If these hitherto accepted hallmarks of great acting faded away at the performance (only to be replaced, in my view, by other hallmarks, of a new style of acting) this was the result aimed at by the rehearsals and is accordingly the only issue for judgment: the one point where opinions can differ.

Here is a specific question: How far can a complete change in the theater's functions dislodge certain generally accepted criteria from their present domination of our judgment of the actor? We can simplify it by confining ourselves to two of the main objections to the actor Lorre mentioned above: his habit of not speaking his meaning clearly, and the suggestion that he acted nothing but episodes.

Presumably the objection to his way of speaking applied less in the first part of the play than in the second, with its long speeches. The speeches in question are his protest against the announcement of the verdict, his pleas before the wall when he is about to be shot, and the monologue on identity which he delivers over the coffin before its burial. In the first part it was not so obvious that his manner of speaking had been split up according to gests, but in these long summings-up the identical manner seemed monotonous and to hamper the sense. It hardly mattered in the first part that people couldn't at once recognize (feel the force of) its quality of bringing out the gest, but in the second the same failure of recognition completely destroyed the effect. For over and above the meaning of the individual sentences a quite specific basic gest was being brought out here which admittedly depended on knowing what the individual sentences meant but at the same time used this meaning only as a means to an end. The speeches' content was made up of contradictions, and the actor had not to make the spectator identify himself with individual sentences and so get caught up in contradictions, but to keep him out of them. Taken as a whole it had to be the most objective possible exposition of a contradictory internal process. Certain particularly significant sentences were therefore "highlighted," i.e. loudly declaimed, and their selection amounted to an intellectual achievement (though of course the same could also be the result of an artistic process). This was the case with the sentences "I demand a stop to all this." and "It did rain last night, didn't it?" By these means the sentences (sayings) were not brought home to the spectator but withdrawn from him; he was not led but left to make his own discoveries. The "objections to the verdict" were separated into stanzas by breaks as in a poem, so as to bring out their character of adducing one argument after another; at the same time the fact that the individual arguments never followed logically on one another had to be appreciated and even applied. The impression intended was of a man simply reading a case for the defense prepared at some quite different period, without understanding what it meant as he did so. And this was indeed the impression left on any of the audience who knew how to make such observations. At first sight, admittedly, it was possible to overlook the truly magnificent way in which the actor Lorre delivered his inventory. This may seem peculiar. For generally and quite rightly the art of not being overlooked is treated as vital; and here are we, suggesting that something is magnificent which needs to be hunted for and found. All the same, the epic theater has profound reasons for insisting on such a reversal of criteria. Part of the social transformation of the theater is that the spectator should not be worked on in the usual way. The theater is no longer the place where his interest is aroused but where he brings it to be satisfied. (Thus our ideas of tempo have to be revised for the epic theater. Mental processes, e.g., demand quite a different tempo from emotional ones, and cannot necessarily stand the same speeding-up.)

We made a short film of the performance, concentrating on the principal nodal points of the action and cutting it so as to bring out the gests in a very abbreviated way, and this most interesting experiment shows surprisingly well how exactly Lorre manages in these long speeches to mime the basic meaning underlying every (silent) sentence. As for the other objection, it may be that the epic theater, with its wholly different attitude to the individual, will simply do away with the notion of the actor who "carries the play"; for the play is no longer "carried" by him in the old sense. A certain capacity for coherent and unhurried development of a leading part such as distinguished the old kind of actor, now no longer matters so much. Against that, the epic actor may possibly need an even greater range than the old stars did, for he has to be able to show his character's coherence despite, or rather by means of, interruptions and jumps. Since everything depends on the development, on the flow, the various phases must be able to be clearly seen, and therefore separated; and yet this must not be achieved mechanically. It is a matter of establishing quite new rules for the art of acting (playing against the flow, letting one's characteristics be defined by one's fellow actors, etc.). The fact that at one point Lorre whitens his face (instead of allowing his acting to become more and more influenced by fear of death "from within himself") may at first sight seem to stamp him as an episodic actor, but it is really something quite different. To begin with, he is helping the playwright to make a point, though there is more to it than that of course. The character's development has been very carefully divided into four phases, for which four masks are employed—the docker's face, up to the trial; the "natural" face, up to his awakening after being shot; the "blank page," up to his reassembly after the funeral speech; finally the soldier's face. To give some idea of our way of working: opinions differed as to which phase, second or third, called for the face to be whitened. After long consideration Lorre plumped for the third, as being characterized, to his mind, by "the biggest decision and the biggest strain." Between fear of death and fear of life he chose to treat the latter as the more profound.

The epic actor's efforts to make particular incidents between human beings seem striking (to use human beings as a setting), may also cause him to be misrepresented as a short-range episodist by anybody who fails to allow for his way of knotting all the separate incidents together and absorbing them in the broad flow of his performance. As against the dramatic actor, who has his character established from the first and simply exposes it to the inclemencies of the world and the tragedy, the epic actor lets his character grow before the spectator's eyes out of the way in which he behaves. "This way of joining up," "this way of selling an elephant," "this way of conducting the case," do not altogether add up to a single unchangeable character but to one which changes all the time and becomes more and more clearly defined in course of "this way of changing." This hardly strikes the spectator who is used to something else. How many spectators can so far discard the need for tension as to see how, with this new sort of actor, the same gesture is used to summon him to the wall to change his clothes as is subsequently used to summon him there in order to be shot, and realize that the situation is similar but the behavior different? An attitude is here required of the spectator which roughly corresponds to the reader's habit of turning back in order to check a point. Completely different economies are needed by the epic actor and the dramatic. (The actor Chaplin, incidentally, would in many ways come closer to the epic than to the dramatic theater's requirements.)

It is possible that the epic theater may need a larger advance loan than the ordinary theater in order to become fully effective; this is a problem that needs attention. Perhaps the incidents portrayed by the epic actor need to be familiar ones, in which case historical incidents would be the most immediately suitable. Perhaps it may even be an advantage if an actor can be compared with other actors in the same part. If all this and a good deal more is needed to make the epic theater effective, then it will have to be organized.

> [Letter to the *Berliner Börsen-Courier*, March 8, 1931, published as part of the notes to the play in the Malik edition of 1938 and republished in GW *Schriften zum Theater*, pp. 982 ff.]

Scene 1 in English

The transformation of the porter Galy Gay in the barracks of Kilkoa in the year of 1925.

1

Kilkoa

Galy Gay and Galy Gay's wife

GALY GAY *sits one morning upon his chair and tells his wife:* Dear wife, I believe that it is within our means to buy a fish today. That should be allright for a porter, who drinks not at all, smokes very little and has almost no vices. Do you think, I should buy a big fish or do you need only a small one?

WIFE   A small one.

GALY GAY   That small fish, what kind shall it be?

WIFE   I would say, a good flounder. But please look out for the fish wifes. They are loose and you have a soft heart, Galy Gay.

GALY GAY   That's true but I hope they would not bother with a porter of such small means.

WIFE   You are like an elefant which is the most clumsy animal of the animal kingdom, but he runs like a freight train once he gets started. And there are those soldiers who are the most awful people in the world and who are said to be swarming at the station like bees. Sure they stand around at the market and you're lucky if they don't rob and kill you. You are only one and they are always four.

> [In Brecht's handwriting. BBA 1175/153–56, in folder of *Duchess of Malfi* material formerly belonging to Ruth Berlau.]

On Looking through My First Plays (v)

I turned to the comedy *A Man's a Man* with particular apprehension. Here again I had a socially negative hero who was by no means unsympathetically treated. The play's theme is the false, bad collectivity (the "gang") and its powers of attraction, the same collectivity that Hitler and his backers were even then in the process of recruiting by an exploitation of the petty-bourgeoisie's vague longing for the historically timely, genuinely social collectivity of the workers. Before me were two versions, the one performed at the Berlin Volksbühne in 1928 and the other at the Berlin Staatstheater in 1931. I decided to restore the earlier version, where Galy Gay captures the mountain fortress of Sir el-Djowr. In 1931 I had allowed the play to end with the great dismantling operation, having been unable to see any way of giving a negative character to the hero's growth within the collectivity. I decided instead to leave that growth undescribed.

But this growth into crime can certainly be shown, if only the performance is sufficiently alienating. I tried to further this by one or two insertions in the last scene.

> [From "Bei Durchsicht meiner ersten Stücke." GW *Schriften zum Theater*, p. 951. Written in March 1954 and originally forming part of the introduction of *Stücke I* and *II*.]

Editorial Notes

1. Evolution of the Play

The name Galy Gay and the basic idea of one man being forced to assume the personality of another both derive from the *Galgei* project which Brecht appears to have conceived as early as 1918 and begun developing in spring or early summer of 1920. "In the year of Our Lord . . . ," says a diary note of July 6, 1920,

> citizen Joseph Galgei fell into the hands of bad men who maltreated him, took away his name and left him lying skinless. Everyone should look to his own skin.

It was to be "simply the story of a man whom they break (they have to) and the sole problem is how long can he stand it. They [?] lop off his feet, chuck away his arms, saw a hole in his head till the whole starry heaven is shining into it: is he still Galgei? It's a sex murder story."

This play was to have been set in Augsburg, and its theme was how "Galgei replaces Pick the butter merchant for a single evening." An early scheme specifies eight scenes, thus:

1. In the countryside. Pick's death.
2. The Plärrer [i.e. the Augsburg fair]. Galgei's abduction.
3. The Shindy Club. Dagrobu [?meaning]. Pick's funeral. Galgei.
4. Ma Col's bedroom. Galgei half saved. The big row.
5. River. Murder of Galgei. His rescue.
6. Next morning at the club.
7. Galgei's house. Galgei's burial.
8. In the countryside. Pick's resurrection.

A fragmentary text of the first three scenes shows Pick going off in dudgeon; a splash is then heard. Scene 2 is described as *"Big swing-boats. Evening. Violet sky"* and opens with the news of Pick's death:

MATTHI   Who is going to pay Pick's taxes and emit Pick's farts?

Galgei, a fat man, is on the swings; by profession he is a carpenter. A bystander describes him:

> He is a most respectable man. Lives quietly and modestly with his wife. He's behaving very childishly today. It's the music. He's such a reliable worker.

Scene 3 at the Shindy Club's subterranean bar is subdivided into episodes. Ma Col (a proto-Begbick) is behind the bar polishing glasses. Enter Galgei with Ligarch, the club president, who was on the swings with him. Shaking hands, he says "I must remain what I am. But I'm in top form tonight . . . ," and there it breaks off. However, a slightly more detailed scheme than the first one takes it on:

> Galgei gatecrashes the Shindy Club. 1. He wants to ingratiate himself. 2. He takes part in the business. 3. He hasn't got a woman. 4. He takes over the butter business.

—while the remaining scenes are developed in a slightly different order thus:

4. Bedroom, white calico. Love.
   The screws are tightened. Galgei is caught.
   i.   He falls in love with Ma Col.
   ii.   He gets money. Hunger.
   iii. He falls out with Matthi.
   iv.   He goes to the butter business.
5. Bar. Brown. Beasts of prey. Schnaps.
   He is transformed. The big row in the club. Galgei feels that he is Pick.
   i.   He fights for Ma Col.
   ii.   He stands up for Salvarsan.
   iii. He abandons Lukas.
6. River meadows, green weeds, fat bodies.
   He turns nasty.
   i.   He murders Matti.
   ii.   He is overcome by doubt.
7. Bar.
   i.   He wakes up.
   ii.   He consoles Ma Col until he is at home.

A further sketch for scene 8 describes the setting as *"River. Dawn light. Distant sound of bells."* and has Ligarch saying to Galgei "Come. Today God is in Chicago. The sky is display-ing the *cruel* constellations."

Like Shlink in *In the Jungle*, a play which Brecht was to start planning only a year or more later, Galgei was supposed to lose his skin. He was fat and passive, so a note of May 1921 suggests, with

> a red wrinkled skin, particularly on the neck, close-cropped hair, watery eyes and thick soles. He seethes inwardly and cannot express himself. But the fact is that people look toward him.

This "lump of flesh" was to be like a jellyfish, an amorphous life-force flowing to fill whatever empty shape was offered it. It was like "a donkey living who is prepared to live like a pig. The question: Is he then living?

Answer: He is lived.

"What I'm not sure of," reflected Brecht, "is whether it is at all possible to convey the monstrous mixture of comedy and tragedy in Galgei, which lies in the fact of exposing a man who can be so manipulated and yet remain alive."

From then on the project seems to have stagnated, only to be revived in the summer of 1924 when Brecht was about to leave Bavaria for Berlin. The Augsburg context was now dis-carded, to be replaced by an Anglo-Indian setting derived from Brecht's interest in Kipling and first foreshadowed in a story and poem about "Larrys Mama," the "mummy" in question being the British (or Indian) army. The first version of the new scheme specifies no less than fifteen scenes as follows:

> 1. galgei goes to buy a fish. 2. soldiers lose fourth man. 3. buy galgei. 4. have to do without fourth man. 5. galgei plays jip. 6. jip's betrayal. 7. billiards. 8. elephant scene. 9. flight. 10. execution. 11. departure. 12. train on the move. 13. jip. 14. mime, niggerdance, boxing match. 15. general clean-up.

—also mentioning "Blody Five," a "Saipong Song" and such key phrases as "the gentleman who wishes not to be named,"

"1 = 0" ("one man is no man") and "there must be two souls in you," the old Faustian principle. Starting on his own, then later with Elisabeth Hauptmann's help, Brecht completed this to make the first full version of the play, an extremely long text which included the whole of *The Baby Elephant*, more or less as we now have it, as the penultimate scene. The characters at first included besides Galgei: John Cakewater (or Cake), Jesse Baker (or Bak), Uria Heep (presumably after Dickens) and Jerome Jip as the four soldiers, and Leokadja Snize as the canteen owner, with a daughter called Hiobya. In the course of the writing however these names gave way respectively to Galy Gay, Jesse Cakewater, Polly Baker, Uria Shelley, Jeraiah Jip, and Leokadja and Hiobya Begbick. The sergeant remained Blody Five throughout. Saipong, the original setting, became Kilkoa, and at some point in 1925 Brecht decided that the play's title would be *Galy Gay or Man = Man*.

Bound in with the script of this version is a good deal of miscellaneous material, which sets the tone thus:

the three knockabouts
the worst blokes in the indian army
the golden scum
knife between the teeth gents
you people stand in the corner when he comes in and smile
  horribly (this happens)

A discarded episode between Bak and Galgei goes:

bak: some people live like in a marriage ad, to put it scientif-
  ically their excrement is odorless but there are those who
  look life straight in the eye i don't know if you've ever
  felt the carnal pepper in you i'm talking about unchastity
galgei: i know what you mean
bak: have you ever handled a woman with paprika i'll never
  forget how a woman once bit me on the tit because i didn't
  beat her quite long enough
galgei: she liked your beating her did she
bak: that's not so uncommon but don't put on an act with
  me i bet you're just as ready to give your flesh its head in
  that sort of situation don't tell me a man with a face like

> yours isn't sensitive to the impressions one can pick up in gents' urinals say
> galgei: i must tell you that in the circumstances i find it difficult to put up with your remarks
> bak: take a good look at your innermost self do you feel any impulse say to hit me in the face?
> galgei: just a fleeting one
> bak: look the other way i get too excited when you look at me excuse me
>
> on another occasion someone describes a peculiarly bloody battle scene their hair stands on end as they sing like drunks he quivers like a rabbit
>
> the scum is bawling
>
> every spring blood has to flow
>
> jabyourknifeintohimjackhiphiphurrah

It ends with two significant phrases: "they bank on him entirely will go to the stake for him" and "he is ready to become a murderer, saint, merchant." A third—"He cannot say no"—comes in a slightly later scheme. There is also an unrealized idea for "Galgay [*sic*] choruses":

> All those who do far too much
> Have no time for sleeping
> Have no longer a cold hand
> For their best crimes
> Whatever happens
> Under the sun and under the moon
> Is as good as if
> Sun and moon were thoroughly used to it
> You'll see three soldiers in Kilkoa
> Commit an offense
> And when night came with its dangers
> You saw them go to bed
> But there are other criminals who
> Bear Cain's mark on their brows
> Before nightfall
> Seated at the bicycle races
> But these go to bed
> So do not lose heart
> For the moon goes on shining

> While they are provisionally asleep
> And next day they'll step with old
> Feet into new water
> For they are not always present
> But leave the wind blowing through the bushes for one
>   night
> And the moon shining for one night
> And next day look out on
> Changed world

The first published version is dated 1926 and bears the play's present title. It represents a reduced and somewhat subdued revision of its 1924–25 predecessor, with the penultimate scene now separated as an appendix under the title *The Baby Elephant or the Demonstrability of Any Conceivable Assertion*; the direction saying that it should be performed in the foyer only came later. This text, which doubtless bears a close relationship to that of the play's premières the same year, has been translated in full by Eric Bentley in the Grove Press *Seven Plays by Bertolt Brecht* (1961—to be distinguished from later Grove Press editions where the play has been adapted). The original Ullstein (Propyläen) edition also gives melody and piano accompaniment for the "A Man's a Man Song" which seems to have developed out of the "Saipong Song" mentioned earlier. An amended version of this text was used for Erich Engel's 1928 production at the Volksbühne, after which Arkadia (another offshoot of the Ullstein publishing empire) issued a mimeographed stage script. This in turn formed the basis of Brecht's own production with Peter Lorre at the Staatstheater in 1931. The major changes made up to this point included the elimination of Begbick's three daughters Hiobya, Bessie and Ann, who are described in the 1926 version as "half-castes who form a jazz band," and an extensive reshuffling of lines between the three soldiers. Our scenes 4 and 5 were run into one and scenes 6 and 7 were cut, while in our long scene 9 the soldiers were to sing the "Mandalay Song" (as in *Happy End*) and the "Cannon Song" (as in *The Threepenny Opera*) finishing up with the "A Man's a Man Song" and a very short final scene. For Brecht's production however Begbick's Interlude speech was shifted to form a prologue, its place being taken by Jesse's speech "I tell you, Widow Begbick" on pp. 38–39, which was to be delivered "before the portrait of Galy Gay as a docker." Blody Five was changed to *Blutiger Fünfer* (Bloody Five) throughout; it will be seen how as a character he diminishes. Both the "A Man's a Man Song" and the "Song of Widow Begbick's Rolling Bar" were thrown out, but a new "Song about the Flux of Things" (stylistically very close to the "Reader for Those who Live in Cities" poems) was brought in instead of the interpolated songs in scene 9. The play ended with the soldiers entraining as at the end of that scene. The program described it as a "parable."

This in turn formed the basis for the second published version, that of the Malik collected edition in 1938. Its text is the same as ours up to the end of Galy Gay's long verse speech in scene 9 (v), after which a slight shuffling of the dialogue, followed by a final brief speech from Galy Gay, allowed the play to end with that scene. In 1954, however, "on looking through his first plays" for Suhrkamp's new collected edition, Brecht decided to bring back scenes 10 and 11 from the 1926 version, modifying them slightly so as to include the final brief speech of 1938, which now occurs on p. 70. The result was the text which we now have. But of course Brecht never saw it staged in this form, and no doubt he would have modified it yet again. For of all his plays there was scarcely one that he found so difficult to let alone. All in all, he once wrote, "from what I learnt from the audiences that saw it, I rewrote *A Man's a Man* ten times." Looking at the material in the Brecht Archive one soon loses count. But it is easy to believe that he spoke the truth.

2. Notes on Individual Scenes

Scene numbers and titles are given as in our version of the play. Numbers in square brackets refer to those in whichever text is under discussion.

1. Kilkoa

The 1924–25 text describes the setting simply as "*road*." Otherwise this scene has remained unchanged apart from the wife's final line:

> Please don't wander around. I am going to bolt myself into the kitchen so you needn't be worried on account of all those idle soldiers.

This survived till 1931 and was then cut.

2. Street Outside the Pagoda of the Yellow God

The 1924–25 text has a version of this scene which finishes after "I'm hanging by my hair!" (p. 7) and appears to have been added after the writing of the following scene. In it Uriah refers to the army as "Mummy":

> the army whom we call mummy and who sends her sons to such towns half way across india pays them two and a half bottles of whisky per head.
> JESSE   nothing's stronger than mummy.

The opening stage direction specifies "*four soldiers and a machine-gun marching to their camp on whiskey*." The 1926 published version has them also singing the "A Man's a Man" Song, but in both texts the talk throughout is of whisky rather than beer. The 1926 version differs also from our text in (a) its omission of all Jesse's opening speech after "Kilkoa!" (p. 4); instead he continues with the words now given to Polly ("Just as our Queen's mighty tanks" etc., p. 4); (b) the wording of the first attempt to break into the temple; and (c) its omission of the paybook episode (pp. 7–8).

[2, amended to 3. in the huts, evening. cake, bak, heep, hiobja sneeze.]

This is in the 1924–25 version only and was later absorbed in our scenes 3 and 4. There are two alternatives for this short scene, the second of which is marked "Written by Hesse

Burri to dictation" (i.e. presumably Brecht's). In the first
Hiobja, who is also known as Hipsi, talks to the three soldiers
as the Wanted notice is being put up, and calls Blody Five
"the devil of saipong." His voice is then heard bawling out
the men:

> call those trousers? what? i'll have you scrubbing the
> shithouse with a toothbrush till your hair turns white
> you swine!

Rations are doled out and Jip's portion falls on the floor as
there is no one to take it. Blody asks "where's your fourth
man?" as at the top of p. 9. The three then agree that they
must find him before nightfall, and the text breaks off. A
page of notes follows with phrases like "the hell of kilkoa,"
"begbick the bloodsucker," "two cents a chair," "one full
whiskey," "our skins are at stake" and "the fragile rocking
chair," then a fresh start with

> *canteen. evening. hiobja begbick, soldiers*

The soldiers sing "In Widow Begbick's Rolling Bar," and one
Jack Townley (see the end of *The Baby Elephant*) complains
about the prices and says:

> i jack townley who unlike you footsloggers and gun-
> tuggers know such a metropolis as cairo like the back of
> my hand can only tell you i must have been in some 1500
> gin- rum- and alebars there with say between two and
> five ladies on each storey but so sinful an establishment
> as this is more than jack ever . . .

Enter then the three, who are asked by the others about their
missing fourth man. They buy drinks all round and are
charged two cents per chair, one of which breaks. The Wanted
notice goes up and the sergeant's voice is heard cursing the
men and announcing the Afghan campaign:

> i knew we'd be getting the scum of every regiment but
> now i come to look at you it's far worse than i thought
> it's my considered opinion that you're the most plague-
> ridden bunch of throwouts that ever wore its boots out in

the queen's service today i observed some individuals among the huts laughing in such a carefree way that it chilled me to the marrow i know who they are and let me tell you there will be one or two hairs in *their* christmas pudding

The rations are doled out; the sergeant asks about the missing fourth man, and the scene breaks off, all much as before.

3. Highway between Kilkoa and the Army Camp

In the 1924–25 text this is marked "brecht first version" and described as "deserted road. galgei carries leokadja begbick's cucumber basket for her." It starts with the entrance of Begbick and Galy Gay, much as on our p. 9, and has two alternative endings of which the second is close to our version. The 1926 version added the beginning of the scene somewhat as we now have it, taken from the abandoned canteen scene above. The rest of the scene was slightly revised and extended, leaving only a few lines to be added in the 1938 version to arrive at the present text.

4. The Widow Leocadia Begbick's Canteen

The 1924–25 scene 4 is set *"in the cantonment. night. leokadja. hiobja. roll call off."* The three soldiers are afraid as now that if it rains Jip's palanquin will be taken indoors, so they go off with Begbick's scissors, leaving her and Galy Gay to discuss whether he was or was not the man who carried her cucumbers. They make no serious approach as yet to Galy Gay.

The 1926 version starts as now, with material from the second part of the abandoned scene above. The opening song is accompanied by Begbick's three half-caste daughters, after which the dialogue (p. 13) is allocated rather differently from now, so that it is the soldiers who inquire about the missing man and say that the sergeant is "not nice," while it is Hiobja ("thou flower on the dusty path of the soldiery," as her mother calls her) who describes the sergeant's habits:

> They call him Blody Five, the Tiger of Kilkoa. His trademark is the Human Typhoon. His war cry on seeing a man ripe for the Johnny-are-you-dry wall is "Pack your suitcase, Johnny." He's got an unnatural sense of smell, he smells out crime. And each time he smells one he sings out "Pack your suitcase, Johnny."

—a reference, surely, to the line "Johnny Bowlegs, pack your kit and trek" in Kipling's "Song of the Banjo," which in turn derived from the South African song "Pack your kit and trek, Ferrera." The phrase recurs throughout this version of the play.

The appeal to Galy Gay which follows (pp. 14 ff.) is much as now except that it is all given to Polly and Galy Gay's speech on entering is omitted. The other soldiers do not exit, but remain to comment; Galy Gay is not undressed; and the bargaining over the uniform is somewhat shorter. Begbick's account of the effect of rain on the sergeant is the same as now from "On the contrary" (p. 17) to "kitten," but goes on to end

> For when it rains Blody Five turns into Blody Gent and for three days the bloody gent bothers only about girls.

On Galy Gay's departure after the announcement of the roll call there is no further bargaining (down to p. 18), nor are Polly's speech to Begbick and her seductive preparations included. Instead she tells Hiobja to put the tarpaulin over the wagon, after which Blody enters "*appallingly transformed*" and listens to the roll call outside:

BLODY   You're laughing. But let me tell you I'd like to see this all go up in flames, this Sodom with its bar and its rocking chair, and you who are a one-woman Gomorrah. Don't look at me so devouringly, you white-washed Babylon.

LEOKADJA   You know, Charlie, a woman likes to see a man being so passionate.

There is no verse speech by Begbick, and Blody goes on with his next speech as now, down to "mean business" (p. 19), after which the voice off summons the MG section, so that there is

no reference to Blody dressing in a bowler hat. The remainder
is much as now, except that there is no verse speech by Galy
Gay and no song by Begbick at the end, nor does Uriah provide beer and cigars. The song comes in the 1931 stage version,
where it is sung through a megaphone. In 1926 Polly says
"Drink a few cocktails and put them down to us," which
Galy Gay then proceeds to do. The scene ends with his
denying having carried Begbick's basket, and Begbick saying
"It's begun to rain."

5. Interior of the Pagoda of the Yellow God [misnumbered
   6 in the 1926 edition which specifies that the sacristan is
   Chinese. Cut in the Arkadia scripts of 1929–30.]

The 1924–25 version is close to our text, except that after
"doesn't seem to sleep very well" (p. 22) Uriah goes on to
say:

> i am sure you would be ashamed to tell a lie and here are
> 3 revolvers what's more made by everett & co each
> containing 6 bullets i am sure you would not wish to con-
> tain 6 bullets as you are not a revolver

—whereupon the sacristan aims a rifle at him. Wang shouts
"fire!" and the sacristan runs away.

The rest of the scene, with the drawing of the four men, is
virtually as now. In the Arkadia scripts this is the only part
to be retained; it is taken into the canteen scene when Wang
enters to order drink.

6. The Canteen [7 in the 1926 edition. Cut in the Arkadia
   scripts, but restored in modified form for the 1931 production.]

This scene remained unchanged since 1926 and would be almost the same in the 1924–25 version too but for the omission
of Jesse's and Polly's concluding remarks. It concludes with
Baker saying after "hanging by a hair" (p. 24):

> I shan't say anything more to him tonight.
> *Galgay yawns in his sleep and makes himself comfortable.*

7. Interior of the Pagoda of the Yellow God [8 in the 1926 edition. Cut in the Arkadia scripts.]

In the 1924–25 version this comes after the next canteen scene, but it is almost word for word as now apart from the substitution of beer for the original whisky. The 1926 text is even closer.

The 1931 text simply showed Jip outside the pagoda, surrounded by beer bottles and a large plate of meat, and had him deliver a verse speech paraphrasing his concluding speech here:

> What am I, Jeraiah Jip from Tipperary, to do
> When I'm told our entire army
> Twelve railway trains and four elephant parks
> Moved over the Punjab Mountains during the past month?
> Here however I can eat meat and drink beer
> My ten bottles a day, and in return have only to
> Look after the temple that there are no further incidents
> And get my food and get my beer and get my
> Orderly existence. True
> I ought to go and help them
> In their life's worst quandary, since I after all
> Am their fourth man. But why
> Does meat taste so good and
> Is beer so essential? True, Jesse will say "Jip's sure to
>   come"
> Once he's sober Jip will come.
> But this beefsteak suits me, good meat.
> Uriah may not wait quite so patiently since
> Uriah is a bad man.
> Jesse and Polly will say "Jip's sure to come." But
> Must a man abandon meat like this?
> Can he go away? If he's hungry?
> No, no. He mustn't if he cannot.

8. The Canteen

The 1924–25 version, like the 1926 published text, has Galy Gay half asleep while the three soldiers play billiards. The scene follows on scene 6 and starts with Polly's comment "He must be frozen stiff" (p. 28), then they wake Galy Gay up and continue approximately with the dialogue from "Dear sir" (p. 29) to where Galy Gay wants to leave (bottom of p. 30), Uriah's speech about the joys of army life being marked by Brecht "written by Hesse Burri in Augsburg." Next it appears that Galy Gay wants to rejoin his wife:

CAKE of course he needs a woman the fellow's like an elephant
URIAH he can get one with his next week's pay
BAK i'll go with him myself and pick one out so he doesn't go sick
CAKE meantime he can do it with begbick

Enter Blody Five, who brings in the wife (p. 33), after which the dialogue is roughly as now up to the wife's exit (p. 34), after which the soldiers congratulate themselves:

URIAH it's an honor for us to have a man like you in the unit
GALY GAY the honor's mine you people are so much sharper if i wasn't so uneducated i would never have become a docker that woman's a bit stupid and she's even more uneducated than me almost crude in some respects
POLLY is she at all faithful to you?
GALY GAY yes because i've got the money

Then they give him chewing gum:

GALY GAY this is the first time for me but i think it tastes nasty
POLLY that's just at first once you've got its inmost taste on your lips you'll find your tongue can't do without this sport any more than a boxer his punchball

As he polishes off his gum Polly tells him "your way of spitting out your gum is exactly like jip's except that it went to the left." The riddle (p. 32) appears to follow, though it is even more idiotic than now, being concerned with how many peas go in a pot. Then comes Wang's entry (p. 28) to buy drink. "I don't serve niggers or yellow men," says Begbick as he orders "seven bottles of good Old Tom Whisky for a white man"; and the scene ends with Uriah saying "Jip won't be back now."

[Scene: Bungalow/Late Afternoon]

The 1924–25 version therefore omits the reflections on "personality" (p. 29) and all the preliminaries to the elephant deal. However, they come into the outline sketch of a separate scene which follows the pagoda scene (our scene 7 above), in which *the three are packing their mg in grease galy gay is asleep on his chair.* This contains a first version of Uriah's speech about multiple opinions (p. 29), also an attack on personality; then when Galy Gay wakes up the soldiers pretend to be the voice of Buddha addressing him. Half awake, he knocks one of them flat and Blody 5 comes to see what the noise is about:

> URIAH   sorry sergeant we were just having a little game of golf

Bak (i.e. Polly) thereupon congratulates Galy Gay on his "phenomenal right hook" and reckons that he would make mincemeat of a "company of shiks" (i.e., presumably, Sikhs). He is applauded by "eleven soldiers of the worchester regiment stationed at kilkoa," with whom he then drinks toasts to the Queen, the Regiment and others. Once they have left he tries to go as in the middle of p. 30 and the text continues much as now up to Polly's inquiry about the elephant in the middle of p. 31, after which the episode concludes with a few changes.

In the 1926 published script all these elements are brought together to make scene 8 virtually as we have it. Wang orders "seven bottles of good old Victoria Whiskey"; Uriah's order and his remark about "tanking up on beer" are not included; nor is Polly's second speech about the peculiar attractions of military life in wartime (p. 30). The passage from Galy Gay's "But I believe" (p. 32) to "With me for a partner you can't go wrong" (p. 32), with its portrayal of him as a wrestler, is not included, so that Blody 5 appears almost at once after the riddle. Nor is Galy Gay's important remark about his wife's origin in a "province where almost all the people are friendly" (p. 33), a phrase presumably added in the 1950s, since it is not in the 1938 edition either. The 1926 scene ended without the Alabama lines but with Blody Five reappearing to shout "The army's moving off to Tibet!" After which

> *Exit, whistling "Johnny." Galy Gay picks up his clothes and tries to sneak away quietly. The three catch him and fling him into a chair.*

The mimeographed Arkadia script (1930 version) greatly economized by eliminating the second and third pagoda scenes (our scenes 5 and 7) and rolling scenes 4, 6 and 8 into one single canteen scene. It makes various cuts and changes: thus in scene 4 Blody 5 makes a pass at Hiobja, while at its end Galy Gay is seated in a rocking chair, denying that he carried Begbick's basket. Then Wang enters to order drinks as in scene 8 and does his demonstration with the drawing (our scene 5) in order to prove that his white servant cannot be the missing man. The soldiers have decided that they must get Galy Gay to go with them, when Blody reenters:

LEOKADJA   Cocktail or ale?
BLODY   Ale!

When Blody says he needs a woman, Begbick calls "Hiobja!" and he starts telling her about his pornographic pictures, much as in the 1924–25 version of scene 9. Begbick accuses him of abusing his uniform, saying that he should wear rubber shoes and a dinner jacket, after which the text is roughly as ours from Polly's "But how are we going to pull it off" (p. 28) to Galy Gay's "I believe I'm the right man" (p. 32). Blody's reappearance and the rest of the scene are approximately as in the 1926 version.

All this was altered in the 1931 production, where the latter part of scene 4 was much changed, with Galy Gay falling asleep after his denials and Begbick singing her verse offstage through a megaphone. A version of scene 6 followed under the title of "Return of the three soldiers the same night," after which the half-curtain was closed for Jip's verse monologue outside the pagoda (given on p. 258). It reopened on a version of scene 8 taken largely from the Arkadia script.

Interlude

This is not in the 1924–25 version. In the 1926 text it was to be spoken by Begbick "alongside a portrait of Mr. Bertolt Brecht." This was replaced in the Arkadia script by a "portrait of Galy Gay as a docker." In 1931 the portrait remained but the speech was shifted to make a prologue, being replaced by Jesse's long prose speech from pp. 38–39. In the 1938 Malik edition, as now, there was no mention of any portrait.

9. The Canteen [10 in the 1926 version]

The 1924–25 text was different from the present one, and a good deal longer. The setting to start with was "*canteen made of holow bamboos and grass matting,*" which Leokadja and Hiobja are busy dismantling. Galy Gay arrives all agog as Uriah and Polly are wondering what form their business deal should take; asking Leokadja to lend them her elephant's head they develop their plot from that. Enter Blody Five to show Hiobja his pictures:

> BLODY   hiobja i have a definite feeling that my sentiments for you have almost reached their peak scientifically speaking it's nothing for a girl to visit a man's room if he asks her only a swine would gossip about that my photographs are notable sights i have items you won't find in the british museum when you see them you may think them slightly too free but against that once you've seen them you never forget them
> HIOBJA   if they're truly scientific yes i'd like to see them but not in your room for a girl is a poor weak thing

Galy Gay takes a drink ("so that's gin it really does taste like a small fire") and the three soldiers assemble their elephant:

> KAKE   this tarpaulin makes so many folds in his belly that even leokadja begbick is blushing

Then Polly complains that he has to work the tail by hand:

> KAKE   polly when you look out of the back it isn't decent
> URIAH   the front and back legs must be coordinated somehow or it'll look bad

Meanwhile Hiobja is showing Blody's pictures to the troops. There is a poker game with Leokadja, Hiobja and Blody, who announces:

> better for them to be tied with a triple rope and dumped in an anthill than to be drunk this a.m. when we move off not even a sergeant could expect mercy in such an eventuality
>
> GALY GAY   that's order for you no matter whether it's a sergeant or an ordinary man he gets shoved in the hole

Among various disconnected snatches of dialogue here there is a Schweik-like reminiscence from Galy Gay:

> i had a friend a docker who in turn had a big red beard he could carry a hundredweight on his bare chest drank a pond dry daily and bashed the empire middleweight champion's eye flat for him this fellow had his beard removed one night because he'd seen a photo of the prince of wales and from then on he would run away from a chicken and couldn't lift more than 60lb he was so scared of ghosts at night that he married a widow fancy that

Meantime Leokadja attacks Blody and tells him he would look better in civilian clothes. Then the artificial elephant is ready.

At this stage there appears to be no formal subdivision of the scene into separate "numbers," nor is there an interspersed song. Galy Gay flings himself into the deal with "Another swig" as in our text, while Uriah introduces Billy Humph as now. Galy Gay is by no means shocked at the latter's appearance:

> right billy you and i are going to get on splendidly as long as you're with me you can behave just like at home

Inside Billy, Bak (i.e. Polly) exclaims "himmel arsch und wolkenbruch," prompting Galy Gay to ask "did you say something billy." Since Billy is "a little memento of my grandfather" Galy Gay much regrets having to auction him:

> for instance i ride billy humph myself round the fortifications whenever i feel like it i may add i nurtured him at my bosom he was breast-fed like you and me so every-

body sing when he comes up for auction since this is a
moment i shall always remember for after it's over my
heart may well break
all sing "it's a long way to tipperary" including billy

The auction follows, much as in our sub-scene II, though with
some additions, for instance:

SOLDIERS   billy what do you think of women?
BILLY   *shits*
URIAH   that isn't nice of you billy you have a dirty mind

Galy Gay calls for bids, but is arrested. Blody 5 enters in
civilian garb and Galy Gay chases the elephant out, shouting
"stop thief, stop thief!"

The next installment, marked by Brecht *"blody's k.o.,"*
corresponds to our sub-scene IVa. Blody invites Hiobja to
"a few cocktails" and reads the newspaper, making a hole in
it to spy on the soldiers, who are drinking cocktails too. Uriah
pops the bowler hat on him and asks "where did you get this
personality from, mister?" But Leokadja sings his praises:

eleven days after the battle of lake chad river (mind how
you dismantle the bamboos up there) 50 blokes from the
42nd who'd seen the devil face to face sneaked into a
bungalow drank paraffin and shot crazily at everyone who
passed by then a man arrived riding an elephant and addressed them for five minutes on his own and decided
they ought to be shot after which 50 men came out and
let themselves be mown down in a heap like young sick
lamas the name of this man was blody five the batik man

They invite him to show his skill with a revolver, as on p. oo,
but using a cigar instead of an egg; then after he misses it the
text goes on (as also in 1926) with Blody cursing them as
"piss containers" and telling them how he won the name Blody
Five by shooting five "Shiks" at the battle of "Dschadseefluss,"
literally lake Chad river. In both versions the soldiers then
comment on his military virtues: "and at the same time you're
such a nice person. Kindly too, come to think of it." In the
1924–25 text they have a sack race with him, after which he

takes Hiobja on his knee, is photographed by flashlight, and has to pay up.

The next sub-scene, marked by Brecht "*hongkong,*" has the three soldiers entering with Galy Gay and telling him that "four hundred shiks, an entire battalion, are looking for you." So they take the billiard table and use it as a boat in which to escape to Hong Kong. They sing "Nearer, my God, to Thee," as on the doomed *Titanic*, while Uriah cites a line from Brecht's early poem "Tahiti" (which was also to be incorporated in a similar episode in *Mahagonny*, scene 16). What looks like another version has Heep (i.e. Uriah) saying:

> raise your eyes jerome jip d'you see the widows on the shores of bombay see them waving their petticoats they're crying their eyes out and on sumatra your orphans will soon be oppressed by usurers
>
> KAKE   it's just gray fields on the coastline and the wind whipping them set the topsail there's going to be a storm tonight
>
> BAK   hold tight jenny this gunboat is rocking dreadfully
>
> KAKE   it's the atlantic rollers continually heaving up and down
>
> GALGEI   hey you must go faster
>
> HEEP   can you see a sail on the horizon behind us?
>
> KAKE   no not yet
>
> GALGEI   is it dangerous here where have we got to?
>
> KAKE   seven degrees east of ssw
>
> BAK   if night doesn't fall too soon we can still make gibraltar
>
> HEEP   the best thing would be to sing stormy the night to keep up our spirits have you any biscuits left?
>
> KAKE   stormy the night is a fine thing when your spirits are getting low
>
> GALY GAY [*sic*]   anyway let's just sing through it
>   *they sing "asleep in the deep"*
>
> HEEP   now pipe down and best pray by yourselves for i think that's the island of tahiti the most charming island of them all where as many ships have gone aground as there are fish in the arctic sea
>
> BAK   take off your hat you lout
>
> HEEP   hear the wind whistling in the rigging?

GALY GAY   go quicker and go carefully for i tell you the wind's rising hour by hour

KAKE   yes and now we must strike the foresail who knows what will become of us if the storm keeps getting so much worse?

A *"flight to hongkong"* sub-scene follows, starting with a soldier asking the four "Who are you?"

BAK   oh just tourists

SOLDIER   we know them and where's your luggage?

BAK   yes galgay where's the luggage?

URIAH   bak's got a straw hat

SOLDIER   which of you is galgay?

URIAH   oh nobody

SOLDIER   someone just mentioned the name galgay

URIAH   really did you hear that name?

SOLDIER   you know perfectly well it's the name of a no-torious criminal

URIAH   anyhow my name isn't galgay and i wouldn't wish it to be

SOLDIER   is your name galgay?

GALGAY   me? certainly not

BAK   ah?

SOLDIER   did you say something?

BAK   not a word sir

SOLDIER   what's your name supposed to be sir?

GALGAY   jip jerome jip

SOLDIER   what are you?

GALGAY   docker sir

SOLDIER   what?

GALGAY   soldier i mean a thousand apologies

SOLDIER   no nonsense from you now that stolen elephant is written all over your face

KAKE   sir i object to your way of addressing our friend jerome jip i can answer for him personally

GALGAY   there you are

KAKE   indeed yes let us through this is our jip and these are my fists

SOLDIER   all right so long as you answer for him very well

BAK   that went off all right d'you want to look round hong-kong galgei?

GALGAY   kindly don't call me galgei they seem to know

everything in this place and i don't want to look at
hongkong but to hide

BAK all right then wait on the pier a moment till we've
gone

GALGAY no no don't leave now it's terribly risky

URIAH yes but we must get our paybooks stamped you'll
have to wait here

GALGAY i'll have to come along

BAK out of the question it'd look as if you were scared
just wait here a moment and keep an eye on my straw hat

GALGAY where is it?

BAK if you hold out you'll be allowed to see it good-bye

SOLDIER got your paybook on you?

GALGAY yes here sir

an elephant appears at the back galgay sees him

GALGAY would you come over here sir i've got my paybook

SOLDIER where are you off to stay where you are

GALGAY you can see my paybook very well over here sir

SOLDIER you what's that?

GALGAY for god's sake what do you mean sir?

SOLDIER don't tell me there's anything wrong with your
eyesight just look where i'm pointing

GALGAY an elephant

SOLDIER emphatically an elephant very quick of you to
spot it and who would you say that elephant belonged
to eh?

Galy Gay wakes up and asks "is this honkong?" then is told
by a soldier that it certainly isn't: it is Saipong. Then Blody
Five appears and the episode ends with Galy Gay's protests
as the soldiers threaten that he will be shot "under the three
ash trees of saipong." "oh uriah, ka, bak," he cries, "help me!"

The *"trial"* sub-scene [numbered 5 by Brecht] corresponds
to our III and is close to it as far as "Yes, in Kankerdan I was
with you" on p. 46, after which it goes on as in the 1926
version to where Galy Gay appeals to Uriah. Uriah then
"turns away," and as Galy Gay is marched off to be shot he
sees Bak (i.e. Polly) dressed as himself and exclaims "there
he is."

GALY GAY he was standing there all the time and i didn't
see him

In the *"execution"* sub-scene they march Galy Gay off and on again to the sound of a drum, much as in the 1926 IV, which this resembles down to where Galy Gay is blindfolded. "this galy gay in him has got to be shot," says Uriah. Bak bursts out laughing, but they shoot and he falls. Then Leokadja: "what a noise you are making really you're pushing him too far now he really believes he is dead he's just lying there but finish dismantling my walls first it's two a.m." In a fragmentary passage she goes on:

> without generals my sweet child you can make a war but without the widow begbick my dear boy you would just burst into tears as soon as things got hot and where there's a bar there'll be a urinal too that'll probably apply as long as the world lasts
>
> SOLDIERS widow begbick you can count on our acting accordingly
>
> BEGBICK ah yes it's a pleasant life i shan't be coming back here there are all kinds of places for widow begbick and as long as the army eats and drinks widow begbick won't grow old today was a fine day so tomorrow we'll be traveling north in those rumbling trains i've always been fond of cigars and words like afghanistan

The last sub-scene in the 1924–25 version is marked "6. *breaking camp.*" As in the 1926 version it starts with the soldiers carrying in the box—Begbick's piano apparently in this case—and singing Chopin's "Funeral March" to the words "Never again will the whiskey pass his lips" (twice). After Galy Gay has been told that he is to deliver the funeral oration (p. 54) there are snatches of our present text, followed by the greater part of the oration ("Lift up this crate" etc., p. 58), then some dialogue where, as in the 1926 version, the soldiers fit him out with equipment, finishing up with the Anglo-German cry "drei cheers für unseren cäpten." Elements of Galy Gay's verse speech (pp. 56–57) are appended.

In 1926 all this scene 9 material was pulled pretty well into its present shape. The scene was divided into six music-hall "numbers," most of them followed by a verse of the "A Man's a Man Song" and formally introduced by Uriah who blows a whistle and announces the titles. Only IVa [5], the episode with Blody Five, is termed a "subsidiary number." The introductory section differs both from the 1924–25 version and from our present text, but includes parts of the latter, notably the concept of the "man who doesn't wish to be named" (p. 41). Blody is not on till [2], the auction episode, though his voice off is audible in [1] saying "Johnny, pack your kit"; the display of dirty photographs, much shortened, takes place in [5]. In [1], which is close to our version, Galy Gay is disturbed by the elephant's ramshackle appearance, only cheering up in [2] when it becomes clear that Begbick will none the less buy it ("An elephant is an elephant, especially if someone is buying him") (p. 40). After Galy Gay has been bound (p. 42) [2] continues with a dialogue between Leokadja and Blody, who desires her daughters but is at this point told to present himself in a dinner jacket and bowler hat. After that Blody's "subsidiary number," minus the flashlight photo episode and all the passages of the 1924–25 version already cited, was shifted to follow the trial and execution, while the two Hongkong sub-scenes were cut.

[3], the Trial, is close to our text as far as "in Kankerdan I was with you" (p. 46), but continues with Uriah's announcement of the verdict which is now in our IV (p. 47) as far as "a man's going to be shot" (p. 48), followed by a verse of the song. [4], the Execution, then follows on from there, starting with Begbick's next speech, and is virtually the same as our IV till Uriah's "so that he can hear that he's dead" on p. 000. This is where Blody enters in a dinner jacket and has his bowler hat rammed down by Uriah with the cry "Shut up, you civilian!"; verse 4 of the song follows. [5] then corresponds to our IVa, and starts with the dirty photographs, continuing with Uriah's "My dear Fairchild, give us a sample" (p. 51) and the shooting demonstration, done this time with an egg. The story about the five Shiks follows (cf. p. 51) leading straight into the Soldier's entrance as at the end of our version (p. 53). After this Blody wants to dance and calls for Hiobja, then makes do with her mother, saying "A woman's a woman."

[6], corresponding to our V, is announced by Uriah as at the bottom of p. 53. The crate this time is Begbick's nickelodeon; the Chopin march is sung as before; then comes an

approximate version of our text as far as the long verse speech, with Begbick's speech about the move ("The army," p. 57) brought forward to where the train whistles are now heard (p. 57). The verse speech itself is shorter than now, but the rest of the sub-scene is much the same, with the addition at the end of the loading of the bundled-up Human Typhoon and the singing of the last verse of the song.

In the Arkadia script of 1930 there was no "A Man's a Man Song," and the numbers were announced by projections. Blody's entry in civilian clothes, seeking Hiobja, took place at the beginning of 1, which had the soldiers singing "Widow Begbick's Brothel in Mandalay" with the refrain "Quick, Blody, he," etc. He did not appear in 2, which ended with Galy Gay bound and the singing of the "Cannon Song." Number 3 was slightly shortened and 4 only began with the soliders' complaints about the bad light (p. 49), then continued roughly as now to its ending. Next Blody appeared and the projector started showing the time, starting with two o'clock. There was no number corresponding to our IVa. At 2:00 the soldiers decide to feed Galy Gay, and Begbick tells them to take the nickelodeon case and chalk his name on it, with a cross against it. At 2:01 he eats and the soldiers bring in the case, singing the Chopin march. At 2:03 Galy Gay starts practicing his military movements (p. 54) and Begbick offers him castor oil. At 2:05 the trains start whistling and Begbick makes her speech about the move. Galy Gay washes as instructed by her (p. 57) and asks how many are going to Tibet (as in scene 11 of the 1926 version of our scene 10, p. 64) and so on to "Everybody the same" (p. 64).

> GALY GAY   You know, Widow Begbick, one man is no man. So let me tell you there's not all that much difference between yes and no, and so I'm getting rid of what I didn't like about myself, and I'll be agreeable.

At 2:07 the cars roll in with Begbick's Beer Wagon hitched up to them, and the troops entrain. A projection says "Burial and Funeral Oration of Galy Gay, the Last Personality in the Year 1928" and leads into the oration and the ensuing dialogue down to "three cheers." At 2:10 Polly delivers a harangue, ending up with an N.C.O.-like "one-two-three-four" repeated four times; then

> one-two-three . . .
> GALY GAY   Four! *Steps into the gap and marches radiantly behind the other three into the car, singing the "A Man's a Man Song." The car rolls off.*

A projection then announces the title of our scene 11 and goes on: "The scum capture it [i.e. the fortress] on behalf of Royal Shell. Private Jeraiah Jip is one of them. You have seen how he can be used for any desired purpose. In our day he is used to make war." A brief ending to the play follows.

For the 1931 production Begbick's poem of the "Flux of Things" was included. The scene [9] began with a Voice as now; then number 0 followed, finishing with Galy Gay's "For you I may have one" (p. 38), which led straight into 1. This was shortened, with a new bridge into 2, which added a new ending to the Arkadia version. No. 3 followed this version as far as Galy Gay's "You must be mistaking me for someone else" (p. 45), after which new material led into the next installment of the song. In 4 there was a cut of about a page; in 4a of about a page and a half. No. 5 followed the Arkadia version as far as "Everybody the same," then came "All aboard!" (p. 58) and the funeral oration, leading to the following ending of the play (which is also that of the 1938 Malik edition):

> GALY GAY   Well, why haven't I got a pack? [p. 58]
> POLLY   A complete uniform for our fourth man! [p. 15]
> *The soldiers bring in the things and make a ring round Galy Gay so as to hide him from the audience. Meanwhile the band plays the war march and Begbick comes to the center of the stage and speaks.*
> BEGBICK   The army is on the move to the northern frontier. The fire-belching cannon of the northern battlefields are waiting for it. The army is athirst to restore order in the populous cities of the north.
> *The ring of soldiers opens. Galy Gay, Uriah, Jesse and Polly line up, with Galy Gay in the middle bristling with assorted weapons. They mark time to the music.*

GALY GAY *loudly*   Who is the enemy?

URIAH *loudly*   Up to now we have not been told which country we are invading.

POLLY *loudly*   But it looks more and more like Tibet.

JESSE *loudly*   But we have been told that it is a pure war of defense.

Then Galy Gay speaks the concluding verses on p. 70, after which Begbick comes downstage and says "Quod erat demonstrandum." With the exception of this ending the Malik text of the scene is almost exactly the same as ours.

10. In the Moving Train [11 in 1926 version]

Like our scene 11 this was omitted from the Arkadia scripts, the 1931 production and the 1938 Malik edition, all of which ended with scene 9. In the 1950s Brecht restored it, using the 1926 text with small modifications of which the most significant was the insertion of the passage from "sir" to "she says" in Galy Gay's speech on the Tibetan War (p. 61), with its indication that they are about to invade his wife's home.

The 1924–25 script contains two versions of the scene. In the first, which Brecht labeled *"old train scene"* the setting is as now, but it opens with the three developing a photograph (presumably that of Blody and Hiobja). The dialogue approximates ours as far as Galy Gay's "If the train doesn't stop" (p. 60) after which Blody wakes up, sees the three defaulters and tells them to arouse Galy Gay:

> he's got too good a conscience 'hey wake that man up i want to get a bit better acquainted with him man to man

he tells the three to hand over their revolvers, but is scared off when Uriah dons his (Blody's) bowler hat. Galy Gay then asks what has been going on, to which Kake (Jesse) replies:

> yesterday you got mixed up in some affair of a docker trying to sell an army elephant and being shot for it then you were taken ill and didn't want to be who you were
> GALY GAY   who was i then?
> KAKE   you're no better i see you were private jip but for quite a time you didn't know it and kept talking about a

grass hut and a wife and stuff like that and you'd entirely
forgotten all about being a soldier

They continue to confuse him about his identity, talking about
his paybook and its description of him, the tattooing on his
arms etc. Polly puts his head out of the window and is guillo-
tined, then he does the same to Galy Gay and suggests that
they all sing "the bilbao men's song," whose text however is
not given. The soldiers go off to play cards, and Galy Gay
asks "what's shaking so?" (p. 59), after which the scene continues very roughly as now, but omitting the whole Fairchild
episode and ending slightly differently, with the troops all
singing "Tipperary."

The second version is headed "*2 train scene*" and is close
to our text as far as Galy Gay's speech on the Tibetan War.
Then Blody Five appears with a long monologue version of
the self-castration episode (pp. 63–64), after which the rest
is much as above.

[*outside the camp signs of an army on the move*]

In this discarded scene from the 1924–25 script Jip appears to
the tune of "Tipperary" in search of the other three.

> BEGBICK   you're in luck they've announced a big theater
> performance for this evening to fish people's money out
> of their pockets one of them is actually going to act a
> baby elephant which is a piece of pure malice on their
> part as he's already been brought to his senses once by
> the sale of a phony elephant the man's called jerome jip
> you probably know him
> *jip hurries on*

When Blody appears, full of threats, Begbick roars with
laughter and pushes her cart past him. Fragments then suggest that prior to the writing of the second train scene (above)
this was to have been the self-castration scene. In one Blody
delivers his monologue carrying "*a lamp a length of catgut
and a breadknife*"; another gives a shorter version as follows:

> BLODY   there's nothing can be done to stop this sensuality
> which simply prevents you doing your duty the enemy is

in your own house but the army which has so far earned
nothing but glory cannot have its best men attacked by
rot but even if there is no way of making your conduct
sheet white once more at least a terrible example should
be instituted

since a strong unchastity originating in the womb
hung my breadbasket ever higher and failed to
respond to hard beds and unseasoned fare
but often and repeatedly dragged me down among the
    animals
i shall utterly etch away this excess and herewith
shoot off my cock
goes into the undergrowth

[*theater a plank stage beneath a few rubber trees with chairs
facing it*]

This scene, only found in the 1924–25 script, is the performance subsequently detached to form *The Baby Elephant*. As
far as the "Grieving Mother Soliloquy" (p. 79) the text is
almost word for word as now, except that it is Bobby Pall,
not Jackie. Then Bak (Polly) says:

you may even be able to move them to tears it's the most
moving bit if this goes over well perhaps i'll stay in the
theater for life *curtain rises* the baby elephant has had to
leave because it feels unwell after those great proofs the
criminal will be even deeper in the toils so tell me o baby
elephant's mother something about thy son come deliver
the grieving mother soliloquy

—which is differently worded. Then after the soldiers applaud and Uriah has told "Jip" to get "out on that stage!"
(p. 80):

*galy gay trots along the footlights eyes the three and
hums it's a long way as the soldiers cheer*
URIAH   oh for christ sake drop that nonsense
BAK   he's waking up he's breaking through this damned
notion of acting a singing elephant

Then Polly makes his speech asking if he thinks "that this
woman is your mother?" (p. 80).

GALY GAY   it's a long way *cheers*

URIAH   you've misappropriated army funds

BAK   that's the disease you suffer from *aloud* the baby elephant has been overcome by the confusions of a guilty conscience

GALY GAY   get on with the play bak

The ending, after the Soldiers' "That's a rank injustice" (p. 80), is almost exactly as in our text except that the final song is omitted and two further pages are included after "common sense" (p. 83). The closing stage direction adds "*to the singing of yes we have no bananas.*"

11. Deep in Remote Tibet Lies the Mountain Fortress of Sir El-Djowr [misnumbered 10 in the 1926 edition, which adds the direction "*Columns of troops are marching along singing the 'A Man's a Man Song'* "].

Like scene 10, this was omitted after the 1926 edition and reintroduced by Brecht in the 1950s. He then replaced the MG by a cannon, cut Blody 5's entry (with his old catchphrase "Johnny, pack your kit") and substituted Galy Gay's speech starting "I want to shoot first" (p. 66). After Galy Gay's call through the megaphone, too, the ending was different; the reference to the "friendly people" from Sikkim once again dates from the 1950s. The verse comes from the conclusion of the Malik version of 1938, the final roll call from that of 1926, which however ended with the four marching off to the "A Man's a Man Song" and Polly calling back to the audience "He'll be the death of us all yet."

In the 1924–25 script there were several versions of this scene. One is virtually as in the 1926 edition. Another, called "new last scene" is set in "*a dugout in tibet during an artillery bombardment.*" Enter the three soldiers asking if they can "play a spot of pokker here?" [*sic*]. Blody, now quite subdued, is there and when Galy Gay enters they all stand up. He complains about the noise:

if all this warfare doesn't stop soon i'm going to smash the place up *explosion* pokker demands total concentra-

tion above all how is one to bring off a decent royal
flush with a din like this going on stop chewing your
mustache sergeant

BLODY   i'm very sorry i'm afraid i forgot

In what seems the earliest version, marked by Elisabeth
Hauptmann "Summer 1925, Augsburg," the setting is *"canteen
packing up toward morning signs of an impending move,"*
with Blody making all the troops except the machine-gunners
do knee-bends. Jip arrives and is greeted, and a version of the
first two-thirds of the present scene follows, as far as his exit
(p. 68). Then there is a fragmentary *"long thin subdued
conversation in the cool half-light"* between Galy Gay and
Begbick, who thinks of selling her canteen and coming to
Tibet with him. There is a long discussion with Hiobja, then
Blody summons Galy Gay and the scene breaks off.

The version marked "second ending" starts with Jip arriving
as in the discarded "outside the camp" scene above. The three
enter, and Blody hobbles out of the undergrowth to introduce
the real Jip, who is promptly knocked down by a hook to the
chin from Galy Gay. Then comes *"Widow Begbick's canteen
in the gray half-light. Noises outside of packing up and moving
off."* Confronting his friends much as on pp. 67–68, Jip curses
them and is given Galy Gay's old papers. Then Blody appears and marches the three off to the "Johnny-keep-your-
pants-dry-wall" where they are shoved into an anthill. Left
alone with Begbick, Galy Gay orders "a few cocktails and a
cigar," and her approach to him (p. 68) follows. They are
thinking of going to Tibet together as business partners; however, Blody summons him. Hiobja tells him she knows something discreditable about Blody, which makes Galy Gay slap
Begbick's bottom and say they will get to Tibet all right.
Blody then appears *"laughing horribly"* and asks Galy Gay
who he is:

GALY GAY   A man. Named Jeraiah Jip. And a man's a man,
my lad. But no man is no man.

With that he gives Blody a stare, opens the window and asks
the world what makes Lionel Fairchild, a sergeant in the
Indian Army, speak so softly and prance like a stilt-walker.

Suppose that in a rice-field near the Tibetan frontier, unobserved by other men but observed by a young girl, a man tears out his legendary sensuality by the roots with the aid of a penknife. Suppose he bellows like a donkey bellowing. Sergeant Blody Five, Human Typhoon, what's it like when you bellow?

SOLDIERS *laugh louder* Go on, Typhoon, bellow!

BLODY FIVE *bellows* A man's a man. But Blody Five is Blody—*his voice goes into a shrill falsetto*—Five.

SOLDIERS *roaring with laughter* He's chopped off his manhood! He's castrated himself!

Galy Gay bares his teeth in a smile and sits down. The laughter spreads backward until it is as though the whole Indian Army were laughing. Exit Blody Five, swept away by the laughter. A soldier in the window points at him.

SOLDIER That was the Human Typhoon. And here—*indicating Galy Gay*—sits Jeraiah Jip who blasted him into Abraham's bosom as you might say. He'll be the death of us all yet.

Dance. Military music. It's a long way to Tipperary.

RISE AND FALL OF
THE CITY OF MAHAGONNY

Text by Brecht

Notes to the Opera *Rise and Fall of the City of Mahagonny*

OPERA—

Our existing opera is a culinary opera. It was a means of pleasure long before it turned into merchandise. It furthers pleasure even where it requires, or promotes, a certain degree of education, for the education in question is an education of taste. To every object it adopts a hedonistic approach. It "experiences," and it ranks as an "experience."

Why is *Mahagonny* an opera? Because its basic attitude is that of an opera: that is to say culinary. Does *Mahagonny* adopt a hedonistic approach? It does. Is *Mahagonny* an experience? It is an experience. For—Mahagonny is a piece of fun.

The opera Mahagonny pays conscious tribute to the irrationality of the operatic form. The irrationality of opera lies in the fact that rational elements are employed, solid reality is aimed at, but at the same time it is all washed out by the music. A dying man is real. If at the same time he sings, we are translated to the sphere of the irrational. (If the audience sang at the sight of him the case would be different.)

The more unclear and unreal the music can make the reality—though there is of course a third, highly complex and in itself quite real element which can have quite real effects but is utterly remote from the reality of which it treats—the more pleasurable the whole process becomes: the pleasure grows in proportion to the degree of unreality.

The concept of opera—far be it from us to profane it—leads in *Mahagonny*'s case to all the rest. The intention was that a certain unreality, irrationality and lack of seriousness should be introduced at the right moment, so as at once to transcend itself and wash itself out.* The irrationality which makes its appearance here is appropriate only to the point at which it does so.

Such an approach is purely hedonistic.

As for the content of this opera, *its content is pleasure*. Fun, in other words, not only as form but as object. At least, enjoyment was meant to be the object of the inquiry even if the inquiry was intended to be an object of enjoyment. Enjoyment appears here in its current historical rôle: as a commodity.**

It is undeniable that this content is bound at present to have a provocative effect. In the thirteenth section, for instance, where the glutton stuffs himself to death, he does so because there is general starvation. Although we never even hinted that others were starving while he stuffed, the effect was provocative. Not everyone who is in a position to stuff himself

---

* These narrow limitations do not prevent the introduction of an element of instruction and directness or the basing of the whole arrangement on gests. The eye that reduces everything to its gestic aspect is morality. I.e. the depiction of mores. But from a subjective point of view . . .

Let's have another drink
Then we won't go home tonight
Then we'll have another drink
Then we'll have a break.

The people who sing like this are subjective moralists. They are describing themselves.

** Romanticism likewise is a commodity. It figures only as content, not as form.

dies of it, yet many are dying of hunger because he dies from stuffing himself. His pleasure is provocative because it implies so much.† Opera as a means of pleasure is generally provocative in contexts like this today. Not of course so far as the handful of opera-goers are concerned. In its power to provoke we can see reality reintroduced. *Mahagonny* may not taste all that good; it may even (thanks to guilty conscience) make a point of not doing so; but it is culinary through and through.

Mahagonny is nothing more or less than an opera.

—WITH INNOVATIONS!

When the epic theater's methods begin to penetrate the opera the first result is a radical *separation of the elements*. The great struggle for supremacy between words, music and production—which always brings up the question "which is the pretext for what?": is the music the pretext for the events on the stage, or are these the pretext for the music? etc.—can simply be bypassed by radically separating the elements. So long as the expression "Gesamtkunstwerk" (or "integrated work of art") means that the integration is a macédoine, so long as the arts are supposed to be "fused" together, the various elements will all be equally degraded and each will act as a mere "feed" to the rest. The process of fusion extends to the spectator, who gets thrown into the melting pot too and becomes a passive (suffering) part of the total work of art. Witchcraft of this sort must of course be fought against.

---

† "A dignified gentleman with an empurpled face had fished out a bunch of keys and was making a strident demonstration against the Epic Theater. His wife stood by him in this decisive moment. She stuck two fingers in her mouth, screwed up her eyes and blew out her cheeks. Her whistle made more noise than the key of his cash-box." (Alfred Polgar, describing the Leipzig première of *Mahagonny*.)

Whatever is intended to produce hypnosis, is likely to induce improper intoxication, or creates fog, has got to be given up.

Words, music and setting must become more independent of one another.

(a) *Music*

For the music, the change of emphasis proved to be as follows:

Dramatic Opera	Epic Opera
The music dishes up	The music communicates
Music which heightens the text	Music which sets forth the text
Music which proclaims the text	Music which takes the text for granted
Music which illustrates	Which takes up a position
Music which depicts the psychological situation	Which conveys the attitude
Music plays the chief part in our thesis.*	

(b) *Text*

We had to make something instructive and direct of our piece of fun if it was not to be merely irrational. The form that suggested itself was that of the moral tableau. The tableau is depicted by the characters in the play. The text had to be neither moralizing nor sentimental, but to put morality and sentimentality on view. The spoken word was no more important than the written word (of the titles). Reading seems to encourage the audience to adopt the most relaxed attitude toward the work.

---

* The large number of craftsmen in the average opera orchestra allows of nothing but associative music (one flood of sound leading to another), and so the orchestral apparatus needs to be cut down to thirty specialists or less. The singer becomes a reporter, whose private feelings must remain a private affair.

(c) *Image*

Showing independent works of art as part of a theatrical performance is a new departure. Neher's projections adopt an attitude toward the events on the stage; as when the real glutton sits in front of the glutton whom Neher has drawn. Each scene repeats in fluid form what is fixed in the image. These projections of Neher's are quite as much an independent component of the opera as are Weill's music and the text. They provide its visual aids.

Of course such innovations also demand a new attitude on the part of the audiences who frequent opera houses.

[...]

Perhaps Mahagonny is as culinary as ever—just as culinary as an opera ought to be—but one of its functions is to change society; it brings the culinary principle under discussion, it attacks the society that needs operas of such a sort; it still perches happily on the old limb, perhaps, but at least it has started (out of absent-mindedness or bad conscience) to saw it through. . . . All this is the effect of the innovations.

Real innovations attack the roots.

> [From "Anmerkungen zur Oper 'Aufstieg und Fall der Stadt Mahagonny'" in GW *Schriften zum Theater*, pp. 1004 ff.; originally published over the names of Brecht and (Peter) Suhrkamp in *Versuche 2*, 1931. These notes, which are given complete in *Brecht on Theatre* under the title "The Modern Theater is the Epic Theatre," have here been shorn of those passages which are not primarily relevant to the present work. This has meant the omission of all section 1, the long table contrasting epic and dramatic theater in section 3, all but the last two paragraphs of section 4 and the whole of section 5. The full essay is perhaps the most important pre-1933 statement of Brecht's ideas about the theater in general.]

On Texts by Weill

On Kurt Weill's Notes to *Mahagonny*

Slightly more than a year before the Leipzig première of the full opera, Weill and Neher seem to have prepared a *Regiebuch* or promptbook for supplying to prospective directors of this work. The main body of this is in the archives of Universal-Edition, and has never to our knowledge been published. Its Foreword, however, was published in that firm's magazine *Anbruch* at the beginning of 1930 (*Anbruch*, Vienna, Jan. 1930, Jg. 12, Nr. 1, p. 5), along with a note by the editors to say that the promptbook was being worked on by all three collaborators including Brecht. Whether or not this was ever the case, Brecht's notes were in the event written independently, as we have seen, and only published in 1931. The Foreword, which Weill alone signed but intended to precede the prompt-book notes, has been reprinted in his *Ausgewählte Schriften*, ed. David Drew, Suhrkamp, Frankfurt 1975, pp. 57 ff. Besides this there is also a much shorter "Notes" by Weill which appeared in *Die Musik*, Stuttgart, for March 1930 (Jg. 22, Nr. 6, p. 29) and is likewise reprinted in *Ausgewählte Schriften*, pp. 56–57. All three will be resumed in what follows. Page references have been amended to correspond to our text; originally they were to the 1929 piano score.

In his Foreword Weill takes up his analysis of the operatic form very much where he left it in his note on *The Three-penny Opera* (see p. 333). *The Threepenny Opera*, by this account, when back to the first principles of music theater. It was a "dialogue opera," a cross between opera and play, where the story progressed between the musical "numbers," with the latter acting as interruptions to its development. The epic form of theater—an expression which Weill had presumably picked up from Brecht—consisted in his view in a "step-by-step juxtaposition of situations," in other words very much what Brecht meant by "each scene for itself." In *Mahagonny* this structural principle was no longer independent of the music and to some extent in conflict with it but was based on musical units rather than on scenes. For self-contained musical forms, so Weill now argued, each expressed a situation and could therefore be strung together on the same epic thread to make not merely a "chronicle" but at the same time "that heightened form of musical theater," an opera. The criteria were accordingly in the first place musical, and Brecht's libretto had been written with such a musical sequence in view. This, though not stated specifically in the Foreword, was made very clear in the shorter "Notes," where Weill described the work as a succession of twenty-one self-contained musical forms. The libretto was "a linear sequence of situations" which added up to a dramatic work only as their musical expression unreeled. The music was not designed to move the story forward; instead, as each step forward was taken, a new musical situation was created. Such was the principle on which the opera was built.

The "situations" of the libretto were so many *Sittenschilderungen*. Here Weill was using the same term that Brecht employed for the whole work: a "genre painting" like those Victorian canvases entitled *The Last Day in the Old Home* etc., a "depiction of mores." It was, in other words, a loose succession of tableaux, and these were concerned primarily with The City. In the brief summary of the story given in Weill's Foreword it is significant that there is no specific mention of America, or Alaska, or Florida; merely of "the city" and "the gold coast." For, as he points out, this story "is a parable of modern life." The city itself is a reflection of human needs, and it is these needs that cause it to boom and collapse. It has accordingly to be defined simply in terms of its human implications: of its origins in people's attitudes and its reciprocal effect on them. "All the songs in this opera are accordingly expressions of the masses" even when it is only a single soloist that actually sings them. What counts is the attitude of the group: the group of newcomers to Mahagonny confronting the group of founders; the group of objectors to the new rule of "anything goes" as against the group who support it. Individual fates, says Weill, are portrayed only incidentally, and then only when they typify in some way the fate of the city as a whole. The essential framework of the story is thus much simpler than might be supposed, and nothing outside it is meant to be significant. The name "Mahagonny" itself is just an arbitrary one for the concept of a city. The American allusions are not to be taken seriously, for "the city's geographical location is not relevant."

As for the style of performance, this too is specified by Weill as extremely simple. It should, he says, be determined by the style of the music and follow the development of the musical forms. Hence it needs to be quite free from exaggeration and stylization, avoiding the grotesque, the ironic and the balletic alike. For the music is neither symbolic nor illustrative, but merely expressive of the human attitudes involved in the story. The actor-singers therefore are not called on to underline this, but rather to give an almost concert-like performance and allow the music to speak for itself. In this connection it is interesting that Weill called for the actors to restrict themselves to "the simplest and most natural gests"—the concept of "gestic" acting being one that Brecht had not yet introduced in his theoretical notes.

For *Mahagonny* he demands "the utmost economy of scenic means" and also of the actors' means of expression. The director's guiding principle must be the same as determined the structure of the work: the fact "that one is dealing with *self-contained musical forms*" (Weill's italics). Nonetheless there is one such means that must not be dispensed with, and that is the projections devised by Neher, which in Weill's view are so essential a part of the opera that they ought to be supplied to prospective producers along with the score and the orchestral parts. These "visual aids," as Weill terms them, not only function as a further illustration of the situations portrayed but serve above all to achieve the required economy. All that is needed then is a number of good projectors and "an adroit arrangement of surfaces" such as will allow Neher's images and (even more important) his written texts to be clearly seen from every part of the audience. Given this, the actor can perform in front of the projections with a minimum of props, and only the lightest type of set is needed, one "capable of transfer from the theater to any old platform." Once again, it looks as if Weill has in mind the possibility of staging this work outside the conventional opera houses, and he seems to emphasize this by his final recommendations. For here he proposes putting the orchestra on a level with the audience instead of in the normal pit, and extending the stage into the orchestra by building out a kind of rostrum. The solos are then to be staged as close as possible to the audience.

This is where the promptbook proper begins, and its much more specific instructions are clear evidence of Neher's cooperation. They go into considerable detail, scene by scene, and we will accordingly summarize the relevant points in so far as they are not already embodied in our text. First however there is a brief description of the kind of stage which Weill has already outlined. It is to have a semicircular apron built out into the orchestra and fringed by small footlights which can be switched on whenever a scene is played there. A gangway connects this apron with the stage proper. Instead of a backdrop there is to be a big screen, preferably movable, made of canvas or wood. There is also to be a typical Brechtian half-curtain about seven feet high. At the same time a further warning is given against creating too "American" an atmosphere by means of the costumes and the set. There must be no element of "Wild West or cowboy romanticism" such as had been hitherto associated (though the collaborators of course do not say so) with Brecht's work. After that come the detailed notes:

Act 1

Scene 1. Fatty's dialogue with Moses must be "sluggish and lazy" and always trailing away into nothingness.

Scene 5. Is to be played partly on the apron, partly well forward on the main stage. At the outset the four men are on the apron and the gangway becomes a gangplank leading to the boats from which they have supposedly come. It is signposted accordingly. Another signpost with the sign "To Mahagonny" is shaped rather like a gallows. There is a blackboard headed "Prices in the City of Mahagonny" waiting to be chalked on by Begbick. In front of this are hung the pictures of girls (p. 94), which are drawn in the Japanese style and are initially rolled up so that the audience cannot see them. At the end of the scene the half-curtain closes, and Jim and Jenny are left alone on the apron.

Scene 7. A makeshift bar inscribed "At the Sign of the Rich Man" (p. 89) has been created from the back of the first scene. The reaction of Fatty and Moses to Begbick's agitated remarks is to remain "maliciously relaxed" so as to arouse her even further. Their comments are accompanied by broad grins, suggesting (it must be assumed) that they are deliberately provoking her.

Scene 9. "At the Sign of the Rich Man" once more, but showing enough improvements to that establishment to suggest that Mahagonny is expanding. When Jim "jumps up" (p. 105) and the quarrel with Begbick and her supporters begins, the men of the chorus are to appear comparatively uninvolved: they are simply objecting to the disturbance. As the disturbance progresses however they get increasingly angry with Jim, until something approaching a public riot develops.

Scene 10. There are to be no noise effects during the typhoon: no wind, rain and so forth. At the outset of the scene everybody stops moving, then at number 138 in the introductory music (piano score p. 119) a projection shows a crowd in flight. This is followed by actual members of the chorus fleeing across the stage with handcarts, luggage, children, animals and so forth. Just at the end of the introduction everybody moves downstage. At the conclusion of the scene Jenny, Begbick, Bill, Jim and Joe remain downstage lying on their faces as the remainder disperse. A wind then gets up, driving scraps of paper and leaves across the stage.

Scene 11. The posters saying "It is prohibited" etc. are to be put up during the scene.

Act 2

Scenes 12 and 13. Between these scenes three projections are shown silently. They are supposed to show how Mahagonny has developed from its somewhat ramshackle origins to become a modern city. The words "Anything Goes" are shown above each of them.

Scene 15. At the end of the duet between Jim and Joe (p. 120, piano score number 63), the two men pose together in friendship and are photographed for the newspapers. At the appearance of the referee, Moses and Joe are weighed on a big weighing machine, starting with the former.

Scene 17. For Jim's solo scene as a prisoner he is to stand in a wooden box on a small platform. The box covers all the middle part of him, from the neck to the knee. During the orchestral passages one or two people walk past looking at him; he has been put on public exhibition. Otherwise he is alone. It is night time and the only light is a lantern near the footlights.

Act 3

Scene 18. The "three tiers of benches" are to take the form of a symmetrical stand facing the audience, with a central portion and two wings running at an angle downstage. Each tier is about nineteen inches above the next. Right behind, at the top, there is a beer cask. The table stands in the center and is a plain wooden one. When Moses goes into his routine speech for the prosecution (starting with the case of Tobby Higgins) he must deliver it "like a universally familiar song which a tedious formality demands." The spectators pay no attention because they are all much more interested in the silent by-play of the bribery negotiations; and Moses himself knows that this is what really matters. During the first case therefore they continue as at the outset, reading their papers, smoking and drinking beer (gum-chewing not being mentioned). They only begin to wake up when Moses announces the opening of the case against Jim MacIntyre.

Scene 19 [20 in piano score]. The initial stage direction is as in our text, except that there is a makeshift gallows in lieu of the electric chair. As Jim sings "Don't let false hopes blind you" (p. 110; see also Editorial Notes p. 302) a succession of preoccupied-looking men enter right, walk briskly past and enter the new revolving door of "At the Sign of the Rich Man," which has become an extremely elegant establishment. Jim concludes "You die and you are gone," and the half-curtain then closes. Moses's voice is heard behind it calling "Ready!"; the lights flicker and go out; then the lights on the apron are lit. Begbick walks up to her blackboard to chalk up the new price of whisky: $100 a bottle. She has bottles of whisky with her and sells one each to Bill and Tobby. Jenny and Bill enter through the half-curtain.

Ditto |21 in piano score]. Begbick sits under her blackboard with her two $100 notes, saying nothing as the four men start to sing "God in Mahagonny." Moses then makes his entrance as God, stepping through the half-curtain in a long black coat, with his hat pulled over his eyes. The other men are highly surprised by this and somewhat thrown out, right up to the point where they decide to assert themselves with "Cause we've been in hell for years already." At the start of the *Furioso* passage in the orchestra (piano score p. 306) they are then to follow this up by smashing the chairs and the blackboard, seizing chair legs and any other available weapons and dashing off through the half-curtain.

Scene 20 [the Finale]. The initial stage direction is as in our text except that it is specified that each group should consist of between five and seven people. After the ending of the last chorus it is intended that the main projection screen should divide to show a further large crowd which advances downstage between the leading columns. The whole mob is then to spread right across the stage and advance on the audience like a mass demonstration, before the main theater curtain falls to cut them off.

Aside from the points already mentioned, Weill's brief "Notes" of March 1930 add nothing further to this analysis. They are however important for their account of the work's origins, which they trace back to his first meeting with Brecht in the spring of 1927. According to Weill the two men were talking about the opera medium when the word "Mahagonny" was mentioned (clearly by Brecht, though he does not say so) and with it "the notion of a 'paradise city.'" This, he says, fired him to experiment with a setting of five of Brecht's existing "Mahagonny Songs" for the Baden-Baden festival that summer. The ensuing *Songspiel* version was "nothing but a stylistic exercise for the opera proper," on which, he says, they had already started work. The *Song* form adopted for Baden-Baden was to be followed up in *The Threepenny Opera*, the *Berlin Requiem* of 1929 and finally *Happy End*, but naturally proved "inadequate for a full-length opera," which called for larger-scale musical forms even while sticking as close as possible to the ballad style. Brecht and he therefore went back to the opera project as soon as the Baden-Baden performance was over, and "worked on its libretto for almost a year." From this, as also from the first surviving libretto discussed below, it is clear that Brecht constructed his text very much in consultation with Weill and bearing the musical requirements in view. The score itself was finished, according to the same "Notes," in November 1929.

Editorial Notes

1. *Songs, Songspiel, Opera*

Possibly the first of Brecht's writings about his mythical city was a fragmentary scene with two whores headed "AUF NACH MAHAGONNY," which seems to bear no relation at all to the subsequent opera. Already before leaving Bavaria however he had begun writing the "Mahagonny Songs," of which three were included in his 1924 plan for his first collection of poems, the *Devotions for the Home*. There were four in all, each with a strongly American flavor (whiskey, poker, Jack Dempsey, the moon of Alabama and so on), and in Berlin he added two more songs which his new collaborator Elisabeth Hauptmann actually wrote for him in English. These are almost the only tangible evidence of the kind of theme discussed by Brecht and Kurt Weill when they first met nearly three years later, shortly after the publication of the *Devotions*, which now included all six songs, with Brecht's own tunes. What they at once envisaged, it seems, was a large-scale opera in which Mahagonny would emerge as a contemporary Sodom or Gomorrah. But the immediate task which presented itself in May 1927 was the provision of a small-scale "scenic cantata" for the forthcoming Baden-Baden music festival, and they decided to base this on the Mahagonny Songs. Weill accordingly set Songs 1 to 3 (omitting the still unpublished no. 4) and the two English-language parodies, while Brecht wrote a new poem to serve as a finale under the title "Aber dieses ganze Mahagonny." The six songs were then alternated with orchestral interludes on the following pattern: Mahagonny Song no. 1/Little March/Alabama Song/Vivace/Mahagonny Song no. 2/Vivace assai/Benares Song/Sostenuto (Choral)/Mahagonny Song no. 3/Vivace assai/Finale "Aber dieses ganze Mahagonny." There was no dialogue, but the characters were given suitably Anglo-Saxon names: Jessie, Bessie, Charlie, Billy,

Bobby and Jimmy. This was the work performed on July 17, after which it was shelved for the next thirty years.

A "first sketch" for the opera, published in the magazine *Das neue Forum* in 1957–58, would appear to list the texts for Caspar Neher's projected scene titles in the Songspiel, as the Baden-Baden version was termed. They run:

> 1. The great cities in our day are full of people who do not like it there. 2. So get away to Mahagonny, the gold town situated on the shores of consolation far from the rush of the world. 3. Here in Mahagonny life is lovely. 4. But even in Mahagonny there are moments of nausea, helplessness and despair. 5. The men of Mahagonny are heard replying to God's inquiries as to the cause of their sinful life. 6. Lovely Mahagonny crumbles to nothing before your eyes.

Although we have none of Brecht's characteristic notes and schemes other than this to show how the opera was planned, the basis of the work is fairly clear. On the one hand there were the songs taken over from the Songspiel version, together with part of Mahagonny Song no. 4 and seven other pre-existing poems, which the collaborators now changed and threaded together to make the backbone of the opera. On the other hand there was this new framework with its apocalyptic message deriving apparently from Brecht's discarded plan for *The Flood* or *Collapse of the Paradise City Miami*, which originally had nothing directly to do with the Mahagonny myth. The result was the libretto script which is now in the archives of Universal-Edition, Weill's publishers. This antedates not only the version which Brecht published in the *Versuche* in 1931, which is the basis for the GW text which we reproduce, but also the piano score of 1929. It is entitled simply *Mahagonny*, "opera in 3 acts by Kurt Weill. Text by Bert Brecht."

This script gives the characters as Widow Leokadja Begbick, Fatty der Prokurist, Trinity Moses (identified as a bass), Jimmy Mahonney, Fresserjack (or Guzzlerjack), Sparbüchsenbilly (Piggybank Billy), Alaskawolfjoe and Jenny Smith. Of these only Jimmy and Billy are taken over from the Songspiel, though the name Jenny occurs in a rough draft of a "Mahagoni" song in one of Brecht's notebooks of 1922–23. The piano score of 1929 amends Jimmy to Jim Mahoney (with the normal single "n"), drops Jenny's surname and adds Tobby Higgins, noting that he can be doubled with Jack. Just about that time, however, Weill decided that "the use of American names . . . risks establishing a wholly false idea of Americanism, Wild West or suchlike," so that with Brecht's concurrence a note was added to the full score saying:

> In view of the fact that those amusements of man which can be had for money are always and everywhere the same, and since the amusement town of Mahagonny is thus international in the broadest sense, the names of the leading characters can be changed into the customary [i.e. local] forms at any given time. The following names are therefore recommended for German performances: Willy (for Fatty), Johann Ackermann (for Jim), Jakob Schmidt (for Jack O'Brien [actually the name of one of the world middleweight champions about whom Brecht wrote a poem in 1927]), Sparbüchsenheinrich (for Bill), Josef Lettner (for Joe).

These German names are to be found in *Versuche 2*, the final text, where the work is described as "an attempt at epic opera, a depiction of mores." However, Brecht for some unknown reason made Ackermann Paul, not Johann, though he is always the latter in performance.

The various incorporated poems, including the Mahagonny songs, will be given in full in the volume of *Songs and Poems from Plays* currently being prepared. They are, in brief:

Alabama Song (scene 2)
On the Cities (scene 3)
Mahagonny Song no. 4 (scene 3, refrain only)
Mahagonny Song no. 1 (scene 4)
The Johnny-doesn't-want-to-be-human Song (scene 8)
Against Being Deceived (scene 11 in our text, scene 20 in piano score)
Blasphemy (scene 11)
The Lovers (scene 14)
Mahagonny Song no. 2 (scene 16)
Tahiti (scene 16)

Jenny's Song (scene 16)
Benares Song (scene 19 of piano score, later cut)
Mahagonny Song no. 3 (scene 19)
Poem on a Dead Man (scene 20)

There was also a discarded "Chewing-gum Song." How all these were manipulated and worked into the opera will be discussed in the notes on individual scenes which follow. These are based on a comparison of the typescript libretto (which incidentally bears no corrections or marks by Brecht), the piano score (1929) and the final *Versuche* text of 1931 from which our own derives. We have changed the name Mahoney to MacIntyre to correspond with our translation.

2. The Opera: Notes on Individual Scenes

Scene 1

Typescript and piano score specify that the Wanted notice for Begbick, Moses and Fatty should be projected on the half-curtain, giving their photographs, accusing them of procuring and fraudulent bankruptcy, and ending up "ALL THREE ARE FUGITIVES." Both give slightly more detailed stage directions than our text, and indicate that the scene titles are to be projected on the half-curtain in red handwriting.

Instead of "At the Sign of the Rich Man" (p. 89) both have "Die hier-darfst-du-Schenke—" "The Just-do-it Saloon." This solo by Begbick is termed "Aria" in the script, starting at "It will be like a web" (p. 88). The six final lines come from the Songspiel finale.

Scene 2

Is to be played before the half-curtain, according to the piano score. It consists of the Alabama Song originally written by

Elisabeth Hauptmann. The piano score omits the second verse, which originally had "girl" rather than "boy" throughout. This reading was followed by the script and Weill's manuscript score, both of which were however amended to read "boy."

Scene 3

In the typescript there was to be an opening projection "showing a view of the city of New York and also the photographs of a lot of men." In the piano score the former was amended to "a city of millions." The initial four-line chorus was published as a poem in *Simplicissimus* for September 6, 1927, under the title "On the Cities"; later Brecht wanted to take it into the *Devotions*. The duet by Fatty and Moses which follows, according to the Weill-Neher "Suggestions," was to be sung into a microphone. With "But once you sit" (p. 91) it takes up the refrain of Mahagonny Song no. 4.

Scene 4

Is again performed before the half-curtain, and consists of Mahagonny Song no. 1.

Scene 5

In the script Trinity Moses puts up pictures of nudes, not just of girls. Jenny's Arietta (to use the script's term) "Won't you bear in mind" (p. 96) is slightly differently worded in the script, while in the verse starting "Jenny Smith from Oklahoma" (p. 96) the third line is "I have been in the cold cities." Then the solo and chorus following straight on from there, starting "I know those Jimmys, Jimmys, Jimmys from Alaska's snow" is separated off and headed "Song," with the six girls joining in after "to Mahagon they go." All this is given its present wording in the piano score, which has a different setting of the Arietta from that now used, Weill having rewritten it for Lotte Lenya in the Berlin production of 1931.

Scene 6

Script and piano score specify that this is to be played before the half-curtain, on which is projected a plan of the city.

Scene 7

The hotel is again the "Hier-darfst-du-Schenke" in script and piano score. According to Drew the name was changed a few weeks before the Leipzig première. The script describes Begbick as "rushing in wearing white make-up." Her opening speech is broken into verse lines and ends after "I've seen them" (p. 99) with "They're taking their money off with them!" In her cantabile solo starting "I too once tarried" (p. 100) Begbick's "And our great passion to talk of" is "And all the future to talk of."

Scene 8

In script and piano score this starts with the same projection as scene 5. Jim's solo "I think that I just might eat my hat" (p. 103) is headed "Song" on the script and derives from an earlier "Johnny Is Sick of Being Human Song" which evidently antedates the naming of the characters. It is said by Werner Otto to derive from an unidentified record of a song in English. It had a melody by Brecht, a middle verse which went

I think I'd just better get rid of my woman
I think she and I are through
Tell me why should I be stuck with my woman
When I'm stuck for money too?

—and a longer refrain, which takes in the present text right down to "Oh, fellas, I'm sick of being human " (p. 104), whence presumably the song's name. This follows each of the two verses in the script, which has a concluding remark by Joe.

Scene 9

The script has this introduced by a title in "giant flaming letters" saying "SENSATION!" The scene is again the "Hier-darfst-du-Schenke" in the script and on the piano score, which has Jack commenting "That's what I call real Art" after the glutinous introductory piano solo, taken apparently from "The Maiden's Prayer." This version has Jim calling Begbick a "just-do-it bitch."

After "The river frozen every day" (p. 105) and Jim's three lines following, the script has a different version of the rest of the scene, as follows:

BEGBICK
    If only those stupid idiots
    Would stay put in Alaska
    For all they want is to disturb
    Our quiet, our friendship.

JENNY
    Jimmy, listen to me
    And put the knife away.

BEGBICK
    What is it you want?
    Catch a fish and be happy
    Smoke a cigar and forget
    Your crappy Alaska.

THE GIRLS
    Leave the switchblade in your pocket!

CHORUS OF MEN
    Quiet! Quiet!

JACK, JOE, BILL
> Jimmy, put the knife away!
> Come along and please behave!

JIM
> Hold me back
> Or something nasty'll happen!

CHORUS *mocking*
> Those are the Jimmys, Jimmys, Jimmys from Alaska's
>   snows
> The dead don't have it half so bad as they did
> That's how they made their dough! That's how they made
>   their dough!

JIM *shouting*
> It's just too dull here!

CHORUS *general tumult*
> Go throw him out!

At this point the stage lights go out. Sudden deathly hush. On the background in big writing "Hurricane over Florida!!" If possible to be followed by 160 feet of film with shots of typhoons.

SINGLE VOICES
> A hurricane!!
> A typhoon!!!
> A hurricane over Florida moving toward Mahagonny!!!!!!
> *The darkness lightens somewhat.*

CHORUS *bursting forth*
> How frightful! A disaster!
> The town of pleasure will be doomed
> On the mountain's peaks the hurricanes hover
> Sudden death rises up out of the sea.
> Where is there a wall that will keep me safe?
> Where is there a cavern to protect me?
> *Chorus rushes out. Begbick, Moses, Fatty and Jim remain.*

MOSES
> Lock the doors!
> Take the money to the cellar.

BEGBICK
    Oh, don't bother
    It doesn't matter.

JIM
    laughs.

Scene 10

The script accordingly makes our scene 10 the concluding part of the previous scene. The piano score separates it off exactly as now, except that there is a note soon after the second projection, saying "Thereafter typhoon scenes can be shown, using stage or film aids: storms, water, collapsing buildings, men and animals fleeing etc."

Scene 11 [*10 in script*]

Script locates this "Inside the Hier-darfst-du-Schenke" as in scene 7. It omits Jenny's repeat of "Oh Moon of Alabama" (p. 108) which is now sung over the top of Jack's solo, gives this solo to the trio Jack-Joe-Bill, and shortens it, omitting the last line. Then after Begbick's "Then you think it was wrong of me to forbid anything?!" (p. 112) Jim's answer (in verse) is:

    Sure. Because when I feel like it
    I'd sooner smash up your chairs
    And your lamp
    And kick over your glasses.
    He does so.
    Just like the hurricane does.
    That's how I do it.
    You can make money out of it.
    Have some.

Begbick's answer was then addressed to him only and to be sung on top of a repeat of "We do not need a hurricane" etc. (p. 110) by the other three men. The script also provides a different ending to the scene after Jim's four lines starting "So I say what I said before" (p. 113), cutting straight from "because they've forbidden it" to his repeat of "Your life in this world's what you make it" six lines later. There is then no chorus, and Jenny says:

> Be quiet, boys
> If they hear us we'll be lynched.

JIM   No. we're going to stop being quiet from now on. *He smashes the boards announcing prohibitions.*

> *Lights dim down. Projection at the back: Mahagonny on the point of destruction, illuminated with blood-red rays. From the darkness we hear the chorus of Mahagonnyites, interrupted by the subversive songs of Jimmy and his friends: so do whatever you enjoy, etc. The "Your life in this world" song becomes increasingly dominant, and is eventually taken up by the entire chorus. The singing stops, the projection disappears, till all that can be seen in the background is a geographical sketch with an arrow slowly approaching Mahagonny, showing the hurricane's path.*

The piano score has the scene as now, except that it puts Jim's solo "Don't let false hopes blind you" (p. 110) in the last scene but one, just before his execution. The present placing of the song seems to have been decided without Weill's agreement.

This song comes from a poem of about 1920 which had been included in the *Devotions* under the title "Against Deception" but was earlier called "Lucifer's Evening Song." Jim's other solo which succeeds this in our text ("If you're short of cash" p. 111) forms part of the "A Reader for Those who Live in Cities" cycle of 1926–27, and was published as such in 1960 under the title "Blasphemy."

Scene 12 [11 in script]

This opens the second act in script and piano score. In the former the stage directions begin as now, but the first place mentioned is Miami, not "Atsena." The second announcement then is "Hurricane already in Miami. Miami in ruins"; the third "Hurricane going straight for Mahagonny. Three minutes away." Then:

> *The music stops, and now, one minute from Mahagonny, the arrow suddenly comes to a halt, the chorus bursts out in a scream of terror, then the arrow makes a quick semi-circle round Mahagonny and goes on.*

After which there is the chorus as now, less the repeat for the last line. The piano score follows this, but substituting "Atsena," as far as "Three minutes away," then finishes as now with "*All stare horrified*" etc.

Scene 13 [12 in script]

The script puts the opening chorus as part of the preceding scene, but introduces it by the same projected titles as now. It is however not sung by the chorus proper but by the four friends, in front of the half-curtain. The piano score has it as now, but with the wording bowdlerized to read "Love is the next thing on the list," rhyming with "Fourth, in drinking you must persist." The two musicians of Brecht's stage direction are there to play zither and bandoneon, a type of accordion, in the accompaniment to Jack's solo.

At the end of the scene the script makes the friends appear without Jack to sing this refrain. From now on however the order of the lines rotates. Thus it is now sexual act first, followed by boxing, drinking and "Fourth, don't forget the joys of eating"; then at the end of the next scene it is boxing, drinking, eating, and sexual act; then at the end of the boxing scene, when only Jim and Bill are left to sing it, drinking, eating, sexual act and boxing, in that order; then finally when Jim is arrested at the end of the next scene it is back to normal, with the whole chorus singing "Back once again to the joys of eating" and so on.

Scene 14 [13 in script]

The script shows that this was originally to be considerably tighter and more realistic. Its opening stage direction is:

> *The word* LOVE *in huge letters on a background with, in front of it, right the Mandlay* [sic] *Brothel with a line of men forming. The three friends join the line. Erotic pictures are immediately shown on a canvas screen. Meanwhile Begbick's voice is heard off.*

Begbick's and the men's opening lines are as now, but the stage directions differ: the men *"murmur after her"* and instead of the room getting dark *"The men are getting impatient"* before their "Quick, fellas, hey!" etc. From there on the rest of the scene is different. First Trinity Moses

> *steps out in front of the brothel.*
> We thank all you gents for the patience you've been
>   showing.
> I'm told that another three gents can shortly go in.
> Experience will tell you: to savor love at its best
> Every client needs a moment of rest.

> *Moses ushers out three gentlemen and lets three in. The rest go on waiting. The three who have been ushered out rejoin the line. Further pictures are shown, and Begbick's voice is again heard.*

BEGBICK
> Let the tips of your fingers
> Stroke the tips of her breasts
> And wait for the quivering of her flesh.
THE MEN *murmur after her:*

[the same words, then] *"the men become impatient"* once more and repeat their "Mandalay" chorus. Moses *"reemerges from the brothel"* and again sings his four lines. Then

> *Moses ushers out the three gentlemen just admitted and lets in Jim, Bill and Joe, who have jostled their way to the front. The remainder are once again shown pictures.*

BEGBICK'S VOICE
> Introducto pene frontem in fronte ponens requiescat.

THE MEN *in frantic impatience:*
>   Will the moon shine every night over you,
>   Fellas, move faster, for the green moon's setting.
>   *The three friends are ushered out and step in front of the half-curtain, which closes.*

They close the scene by singing the next round of the refrain.

This version of the scene, which omits the "Crane Duet" (p. 117), was originally set by Weill as shown in the revised 1969 edition of the piano score which David Drew has edited for Universal Edition. An alternative version however is appended to the script and marked in pencil "For the libretto." This starts more or less as in our text, except that in the opening stage direction the men are not standing in line but "*sitting on a long bench*," with the change of lighting in the room, etc., leading after The Men's single line "Will the moon shine every night over you, Mandalay?" to the introduction of the "Crane Duet," thus:

> *This scene is closed off by an inner curtain. The background music dies away.*
> *Before this inner curtain, which still displays the word "LOVE," Jim and Jenny are sitting on two chairs at some distance from each other. He is smoking, she is applying make-up.*

JENNY   See those two cranes in a great circle wheeling!

etc. as in the manuscript of the new version. This manuscript appears not to have survived, but in the 1929 piano score the "Crane Duet" has been set and everything before it marked as an optional cut. In addition, all Moses' lines, the stage directions of the script and Begbick's Latin sentence have been omitted, so that there are purely orchestral passages where Moses originally sang. The new duet is thought by Drew to derive from one of Brecht's love sonnets, though no such poem is known; if so, then it could hardly be earlier than 1925 (as it would stylistically seem to be). It was published in his *A Hundred Poems* in 1951 as a poem under the title "The Lovers." Weill's setting dates from October 1929.

For the 1931 Berlin production the first part of the scene, as now bowdlerized, was restored and the duet cut. At some later point Weill decided that it would go best in the last act, but he never prescribed a place for it and there is no evidence that Brecht was consulted. The revised piano score suggests putting it in scene 19 in lieu of the spoken dialogue from Jim's "you're even wearing a white dress" (p. 137) to Jenny's "Kiss me, Jimmy" p. 137).

Scene 15 [14 in script]

Apart from the rotation of lines in the final refrain, and the effects of the musical setting, this scene has scarcely changed since the first script.

Scene 16 [15 in script]

In the script the stage direction omits all mention of playing pool. Where our text has "THE MEN" it has JIM AND THE MEN," which is also how the song was set in the piano score. The song is "Mahagonny Song No. 2," which the script gives them to sing as printed in the Devotions, but without verse 2 and its refrain. In the piano score and our text verse 2 and refrain follow verse 1 (the piano score gives them to Jim and a trio of Fatty, Bill and Moses), while the refrain of verse 3 ("You won't need five bucks a day") concludes the scene. For the Leipzig production however there was a cut from the first "Still they all felt satisfied" (p. 123) as far as Begbick's "Time to pay up now" (p. 124), and this was accepted by the composer from then on.

Script and piano score have Jim "*drunkenly bawling*" the song "We poured all our whiskey straight down the toilet" (p. 124) which uses verses 1, 3 and 2 (in that order) of the poem "Tahiti" which Brecht wrote about 1921. "Stormy the Night," of which one quatrain is sung on p. 125, was first cited in In the Jungle (see Plays 1, p. 437) and comes from that old favorite of Brecht's, the nineteenth-century ballad "Das See-mannslos" (or "Asleep on the Deep").

In the script Jenny's solo "Gents, when I was young"

(p. 127) is headed "Jenny's Song." Besides some minor verbal differences it has a third verse, which goes:

> I can't go with you in future, Jimmy
> Yes, Jimmy, it's sad for me.
> You'll still be my favorite all right, but
> You're a waste of my time, you see.
> I must use the little time that's left me
> Jimmy
> Or I'll lose my grip on it.
> You're only young once, and that's
> Not enough.
> I tell you, Jimmy
> That I'm shit.
> Oh, Jimmy, you know what my mother told me

—and so on as before. Thereafter the scene ends almost immediately, thus:

BEGBICK
    Again I say:
    Pay!
JIM *says nothing.*
BEGBICK
    Then let the police take him away!

—followed by Moses's lines (bottom of p. 128) and then the refrain, this time by all the men, starting "Back once again to the joys of eating." This was cut by Weill (see the 1969 revised piano score).

A version of Jenny's song, starting "When I put on my wedding dress," is included in a fragmentary *Threepenny Opera* scene set in Polly's room. It has a melody in Brecht's notation.

Scene 17 [*16 in script*]

The script has Jim sitting shackled in a little cage, past which the chorus of the previous scene pass as they leave the stage. His solo is headed "Jimmy's Aria." In the piano score he is *"lying in a forest, tied to a tree by the leg."* For the Kassel production of March 12, 1930, the aria was shifted to the next scene, its place being taken by "Don't let false hopes blind you" (now in our scene 11) from the penultimate scene. Weill found this made a more effective ending to the second act, but for the Berlin production he reduced it to one verse only and reset it for chorus (or male chorus) leaving it in full in the penultimate scene.

Scene 18 [17 in script]

According to script and piano score this starts the third act. The former specifies a projected title saying "Like the rest of the world's law courts, that of Mahagonny convicts people if they are poor." The first defendant then is Joe (not Tobby) Higgins, who is charged, in Moses's words

> With premeditated murder of five men
> For the purpose of trying out an old revolver
> Defendant, you have
> Cut off five human lives in their prime.

Then "Till today" etc., as now. Jim's offense however, as announced again by Moses (p. 130), is:

> Second, the case of Jimmy MacIntyre
> Charged with failure
> To pay for three bottles of whiskey
> And a curtain rod.

When he repeats this to Jim (as on p. 132) his last two lines are omitted. Against Begbick's speech which follows (p. 132) a penciled note says "The warrant for Begbick can be projected at this point." Then after Bill's appeal at the top of p. 134, the Men say nothing, but merely *"cheer and boo."* It is Moses, not Fatty, who calls "Your Honor, what is the verdict?" (p. 134), and Begbick's first two lines following, when she pronounces judgment, are omitted; moreover she gives him four years in prison, rather than probation, for the seduction of a girl (not named). Otherwise the scene is virtually as now.

[*Scene 19 in piano score only.*]

This was not in the script, and was cut in the original Leipzig production. It consisted of the "Benares Song," played before the half-curtain by Jenny, Begbick, Fatty, Bill, Moses and Tobby Higgins. A projected title said

> *In those days Mahagonny was already full of people in search of another, better city: Benares. But Benares was visited by an earthquake.*

The five singers then "*sit on high barstools drinking iced water. The men read papers,*" and go into the song. The text is slightly different from that published in the *Devotions*, and goes:

JENNY
    There is no whiskey in this town.
BEGBICK
    There is no bar to sit us down.
FATTY, BILL, MOSES
    Oh—
JENNY
    Where is the telephone?
FATTY, BILL, MOSES
    Oh—
BEGBICK
    Is here no telephone?
MOSES
    Oh Sir, God damn me, no.
FATTY, BILL, MOSES, TOBBY HIGGINS
    Oh—
JENNY AND BEGBICK
    Let's go to Benares
    Where the sun is shining.
    Let's go to Benares
    Johnny, let us go.

JENNY
    There is no money in this land.
BEGBICK
    There is no boy to shake with hands.
FATTY, BILL, MOSES
    Oh—
JENNY
    Where is the telephone? [etc.]
JENNY
    There is not much fun on this star.
BEGBICK
    There is no door that is ajar.
FATTY, BILL, MOSES
    Oh—
JENNY
    Where is the telephone? [etc.]
ALL
    Worst of all, Benares
    Is said to have been perished by an earthquake.
    Oh my good Benares!
    Oh where shall we go?
JENNY
    Where shall we go?
BEGBICK
    Where shall we go?

Scene 19 [18 in the script, 20 in the piano score]

The script has the opening stage direction as now, except that instead of an electric chair being made ready, "*On the right stands a makeshift gallows.*" The "white dress" (p. 137) was black. Jim's speech recommending Jenny to Bill (bottom of p. 137) has an extra line, "For *he* can live without fun." Moses says "Ready!" before "*They walk to the execution site*" (p. 138), and then after the "First, don't forget" refrain, Moses asks

    Have you a last request?
JIM
    Yes.

I would like once again
To hear the girls sing
The song of the moon
Of Alabama.
The girls sing the Alabama Song as Jim mounts the gallows.
MOSES
Have you anything else to say?
JIM
Yes.
I would like
You all not to let my horrible death
Put you off living the way that suits you, carefree.
For I too
Am not sorry
That I did
What I wanted.
Listen to my advice.
He climbs on a bucket, and as they fasten the noose round his neck he sings:

—all four verses of "Don't let false hopes blind you" (as in our scene 11), after which Moses says "Ready" again, and there is a blackout. Then the half-curtain closes, and Jenny, Fatty, Moses and two unnamed men come out and sing "Mahagonny Song No. 3" ("God in Mahagonny"). It is arranged as in our text, except for the omission of verse 2 ("Mary Weeman" etc.), and in the script it concludes the scene.

In the piano score there is no repeat of the "Alabama Song," so that Jim's speech "Yes. I would like" etc., now printed as prose, follows straight on Moses's "Have you a last request?" Then *"He stands in front of the electric chair and, as they prepare him for execution, sings* "Don't let false hopes blind you," with Jenny joining in the last verse, now softened to say "You stand" rather than "You die." When it is over Jim

> *sits on the electric chair. They put the helmet over his head*

—and Moses says "Ready!" Blackout. End of scene. Our text from Jim's "Yes. Do you really want" (p. 138) to "in that electric chair" (p. 138) is accordingly omitted, and the "God in Mahagonny" setting made into the beginning of the next scene, where it is sung before the half-curtain by Jenny, Fatty, Bill, Moses and a fourth man.

Jim's final speech of remorse in our text relates to a letter of Weill's to his publisher dated March 25, 1930, i.e. just after the Leipzig première, saying that such a speech was needed "for the understanding of the whole thing." This presumably led to the cutting of his previous "Yes, I would like" speech before his song. When or why Brect decided to remove the song from this scene is not known, though it must have been before *Versuche 2* went to press.

Scene 20 [*19 in script, 21 in piano score*]

In the script this is preceded by a projected inscription saying

NEXT DAY THE WHOLE OF MAHAGONNY WAS ON FIRE. THE BURIAL OF J. MACINTYRE THE LUMBERJACK BECAME A TURN-ING-POINT IN THE CITY'S HISTORY. DO NOT BE RESENTFUL BUT OBSERVE THIS VAST DEMONSTRATION, WHICH IS STAGED IN THE PUBLIC INTEREST.

Then the half-curtain opens, showing the projection of Mahagonny in flames and the people of the city gathering upstage with "*placards, signs and banners.*" The only words here are those of the chorus "Still, we're only building Mahagonny" as at the end of our scene 1, which is taken from the finale of the Songspiel. After this a stage direction says:

> *After the song the crowd starts moving in small squads, each carrying its placards etc. and marching in a big semi-circle from back left down past the footlights to back right. The placards say roughly:*
> 1. For the natural order of things.
> 2. For the natural disorder of things.
> 3. For the corruptibility of our courts.
> 4. For the incorruptibility of our courts.
> 5. For freedom for the rich.
> 6. For freedom for everybody.
> 7. For the unjust distribution of worldly goods.

8. For the just distribution of unworldly goods.
9. For the general meanness of the human race.
10. (A giant placard) *Against the human race.*
*In the middle of the procession comes a squad carrying
Jim's coffin. The play ends with huge songs as the demonstrators continue incessantly marching.*

Curtain.

End of the opera.

In the piano score, after the singing of "God in Mahagonny,"
there is a projection saying

> *At that time huge demonstrations took place in Mahag-
> onny against the steep rise in the cost of living. The par-
> ticipants carried Jim MacIntyre's coffin with them.*

The half-curtain opens on the projection of Mahagonny burning while Begbick, Fatty and Moses stand downstage and sing
"Still, we're only building Mahagonny" as before, in place of
the lines now given to the First Column. Then the demonstra-
tions begin, starting with a group of men *"carrying Jim's hat
and stick on a satin cushion"* and singing the quatrain which
our text gives to the Second Column. Meanwhile a second
group enters carrying his *"ring, watch, revolver and checkbook,"* singing "Your life in this world's what you make it"
like our Third Column. The three soloists repeat "Still, we're
only building Mahagonny," and *"A group of girls appears,
including Jenny. They are carrying Jim's shirt,"* and sing
"Oh, moon of Alabama." Then comes Bill *"at the head of a
column of men"* and sings "You can wet his mouth," or
"Poem on a Dead Man," in which he is joined by the other
soloists in succession and the chorus. It is arranged thus: Bill
sings verse 1 as a solo, with his column of men repeating the
last line. Then a stage direction describes the demonstrators'
placards, which are six in number, comprising those numbered
1, 2, and 5–8 in the script (above). Moses then sings verse 2
"at the head of a fresh column," who join the first in singing
its last line. Then Begbick "appears with a third column."
They are carrying Jim's body, and she sings verse 3 ("You

can press cash") with all three columns joining in the last line. Finally Fatty enters with the fourth column and an enormous placard saying "For the continuation of the Golden Age," and sings verse 4, with the insertion of a third line "You can put a clean shirt on his body." The full chorus, singing the last line as we have it, concludes the scene and the work.

This "Poem on a Dead Man" also previously formed part of Weill's *Berliner Requiem*, which was first performed in the summer of 1929; the poem had been written by Brecht some five years earlier. Its fourth verse went originally

> You can reminisce about his shining hour
> You can let his shining hour be forgotten
> Can live worse than he did, can live better
> Nothing you can do will help a dead man.

—without the fifth and final line. According to Werner Otto this is another poem that derives from a gramophone record in English. It has not been identified.

THE THREEPENNY OPERA

Texts by Brecht

Additional songs from *The Bruise*

SECOND PART

After Mr. Peachum and his friend Macheath have left, Mr. Brown sings these stanzas to the "Mac the Knife" tune:

Oh, they're such delightful people
As long as no one interferes
While they battle for the loot which
Doesn't happen to be theirs.

When the poor man's lamb gets butchered
If two butchers are involved
Then the fight between those butchers
By the police must be resolved.

THIRD PART

As they drive up in four or five automobiles the gang sing:

Song to Inaugurate the National Deposit Bank

Don't you think a bank's foundation
Gives good cause for jubilation?
Those who hadn't a rich mother
Must raise cash somehow or other.
To that end stocks serve much better
Than your swordstick or Biretta
But what lands you in the cart

Is getting capital to start.
If you've got none, why reveal it?
All you need to do is steal it.
Don't all banks get started thanks to
Doing as the other banks do?
How did all that money come there?—
They'll have taken it from somewhere.

*And Mr. Macheath walks with a light step in the direction of
the West India Dock . . . humming a few new verses to an
instantly obsolete ballad:*

How's mankind to get some money?
In his office, cold like snow
Sits the banker Mac the Knife, but he
Isn't asked, and ought to know.

In Hyde Park behold a ruined
Man reclining in the sun
(While down Piccadilly, hat and cane, let this be a lesson to
    you)
Strolls the banker Mac the Knife, and
God alone knows what he's done.

FOURTH PART

Closing verses of the ballad

So we reach our happy ending.
Rich and poor can now embrace.
Once the cash is not a problem
Happy endings can take place.

Smith says Jones should be indicted
Since his business isn't straight.
Over luncheon, reunited
See them clear the poor man's plate.

Some in light and some in darkness
That's the kind of world we mean.
Those you see are in the light part.
Those in darkness don't get seen.

[From "Die Buele" in Brecht, *Versuche*, re-edition 1959, pp. 229 ff., and GW *Texte für Film* pp. 329 ff. This was Brecht's proposed treatment for Pabst's *Threepenny Opera* film, for which see the introduction (p. xxv). In the Second Part the police also sing the "Whitewash Song" subsequently used in the Berliner Ensemble production of *Arturo Ui*, for which see *Plays*, Volume 6, p. 466. Excepting the re-use of the Mac the Knife ballad, there were no settings to these songs by Weill. Three of them also occur in *The Threepenny Novel*.]

Appendix

New closing verses to the Ballad of Mac the Knife

And the fish keep disappearing
And the Law's perturbed to hear
When at last the shark's arrested
That the shark has no idea.

And there's nothing he remembers
And there's nothing to be done
For a shark is not a shark if
Nobody can prove he's one.

The New Cannon Song

1

Fritz joined the Party and Karl the S.A.
And Albert was up for selection
Then they were told they must put all that away
And they drove off in every direction.
  Müller from Prussia
  Requires White Russia
  Paris will meet Schmidt's needs.
  Moving from place to place
  Avoiding face to face
  Contact with foreign forces
  Equipped with tanks or horses

Why, Meier from Berlin is bound to
End up in Leeds.

2

Müller found the desert too hot
And Schmidt didn't like the Atlantic.
Will they ever see home? That's the problem they've got
And it's making them perfectly frantic.
　　To get from Russia
　　Back home to Prussia
　　From Tunis to Landshut:
　　Moving from place to place
　　Once they come face to face
　　With nasty foreign forces
　　Equipped with tanks or horses
　　Their leader gives no lead because he's
　　Left them for good.

3

Müller was killed, and the Germans didn't win
And the rats ran around in the rubble.
All the same, in the ruins of Berlin
They're expecting a *third* lot of trouble.
　　Cologne is dying
　　Hamburg is crying
　　And Dresden's past all hope.
　　But once the U.S.A.
　　Sees Russia's in its way
　　With a bit of luck that ought to
　　Set off a new bout of slaughter
　　And Meier, back in uniform, might
　　Get the whole globe!

Ballad of the good living of Hitler's minions

1

That drug-crazed Reich Marshal, who killed and jested
You saw half Europe scoured by him for plunder

Then watched him sweat at Nuremberg—and no wonder—
Outbulging those by whom he'd been arrested.
And when they asked him what he did it for
The man replied: for Germany alone.
So that can make a man weigh twenty stone?
Don't pull my leg; I've heard that one before.
No, what made him a Nazi was just this:
One must live well to know what living is.

2

Then Schacht, the Doctor who cut out your money—
The sheer length of his neck still has me baffled—
As banker once he fed on milk and honey
As bankrupter he's sure to dodge the scaffold.
He knows he won't be tortured, anyway
But ask Schacht, now he's finally been floored
Just why he joined the others in their fraud
He'll say ambition made him go astray.
But we know what pushed him to the abyss:
One must live well to know what living is.

3

And Keitel, who left the Ukraine all smoking
And licked the Führer's boots clean with his spittle
Because he'd built the Wehrmacht up a little—
Ask that tank expert why, he'll think you're joking.
Sipping, he'll say: I followed Duty's call!
So Duty made his casualties so great?
No question of acquiring an estate?
That kind of thing we don't discuss at all.
We get one. "How?" 's a question we dismiss.
One must live well to know what living is.

4

They all have great ideas in untold numbers
And lay claim to the loftiest of wishes
And none of them mentions the list of dishes
But each of them has demons plague his slumbers.

Each saw himself no doubt as Lohengrin
Or Parsifal; so how was he to fail?
Behind Moscow they sought the Holy Grail
And just Valhalla crumbled, not Berlin.
Their private problems all boiled down to this:
One must live well to know what living is.

New Version of the Ballad in which Macheath Begs Forgiveness

You fellow men who like to live, like us
Pray do not think you have to judge us harshly
And when you see us hoisted up and trussed
Don't laugh like fools behind your big mustaches.
Oh, you who've never crashed as we came crashing
Don't castigate our downfall like the courts:
Not all of us can discipline our thoughts—
Dear fellows, your extravagance needs slashing
Dear fellows, we've shown how a crash begins.
Pray then to God that he forgive our sins.

The rain washes away and purifies.
Let it wash down the flesh we catered for.
And we who saw so much, and wanted more—
The crows will come and peck away our eyes.
Perhaps ambition used too sharp a goad
It drove us to these heights from which we swing
Hacked at by greedy starlings on the wing
Like horses' droppings on a country road.
Oh, brothers, learn from us how it begins
I pray that you kindly forgive our sins.

The men who break into your houses
Because they have no place to sleep in
The gossipper, the man who grouses
And likes to curse instead of weeping;
The women stealing your bread ration
Could be your mothers for two pins.
They're acting in too mild a fashion—
I pray you to forgive their sins.

Show understanding for their trouble
But none for those who, from high places
Led you to war and worse disgraces
And make you sleep on bloodstained rubble.
They plunged you into bloody robbery
And now they beg you to forgive.
So choke their mouths with the poor débris
That's left of where you used to live!

And those who think the whole thing's over
Saying "Let them expiate their sins"
Are asking for a great iron crowbar
To stave their ugly faces in.

New Chorale

Don't punish small wrong-doings too much. Never
Will they withstand the frost, for they are cold.
Think of the darkness and the bitter weather
The cries of pain that echo round this world.

But tackle the big crooks now, all together
And chop them down before you're all too old:
Who caused the darkness and the bitter weather
And brought the pain that echoes round this world.

> ["Anhang" to *The Threepenny Opera*, in GW *Stücke* 2,
> pp. 491 ff., excluding the "Neufassung der Ballade vom
> angenehmen Leben," which differs only marginally from
> that in our text, and the closing verses from the film
> version, which we have given above(p. 315). These dates
> indicate that the first and fourth of these songs were
> written in 1948, and the other two in 1946.]

On *The Threepenny Opera*

Under the title *The Beggar's Opera*, *The Threepenny Opera*
has been performed for the past two hundred years in theaters
throughout England. It gives us an introduction to the life of

London's criminal districts, Soho and Whitechapel, which are still the refuge of the poorest and least easily understood strata of English society just as they were two centuries ago.

Mr. Jonathan Peachum has an ingenious way of capitalizing on human misery by artificially equipping healthy individuals as cripples and sending them out to beg, thereby earning his profits from the compassion of the well-to-do. This activity in no sense results from inborn wickedness. "My position in the world is one of self-defense" is Peachum's principle, and this stimulates him to the greatest decisiveness in all his dealings. He has but one serious adversary in the London criminal community, a gentlemanly young man called Macheath, whom the girls find divine. Macheath has abducted Peachum's daughter Polly and married her in highly eccentric fashion in a stable. On learning of his daughter's marriage—which offends him more on social grounds than on moral ones—Peachum launches an all-out war against Macheath and his gang of rogues; and it is the vicissitudes of this war that form the content of *The Threepenny Opera*. However, it ends with Macheath being saved literally from the gallows, and a grand, if somewhat parodistic operatic finale satisfactorily rounds it all off.

The *Beggar's Opera* was first performed in 1728 at the Lincoln's Inn Theatre. Contrary to what a number of German translators have supposed, its title does not signify an opera featuring beggars but "the beggar's opera," in other words an opera for beggars. Written in response to a suggestion by the great Jonathan Swift, *The Beggar's Opera* was a parody of Handel, and it is said to have had a splendid result in that Handel's theater became ruined. Since there is nowadays no target for parody on the scale of Handel's theater all attempt at parody has been abandoned: the musical score is entirely modern. We still however have the same *sociological* situation. Just like two hundred years ago we have a social order in which virtually all levels, even if in a wide variety of ways, pay respect to moral principles not by leading a moral life but by living off morality. Where its form is concerned, the *Threepenny Opera* represents a basic type of opera. It contains elements of opera and elements of the drama.

["Über die Dreigroschenoper—1" from GW *Schriften zum Theater*, p. 987. Dated January 9, 1929, when it appeared as an article in the *Augsburger Neueste Nachrichten* to introduce the production in Brecht's home town.]

A Statement

A Berlin paper has noticed, a bit late in the day, that the Kiepenheuer edition of the Songs to *The Threepenny Opera* gives Villon's name but fails to give that of his German translator Ammer: this in spite of the fact that 25 of my 625 verses are indeed identical with his excellent translation. A statement is called for. Accordingly I truthfully state that, alas, I forgot to mention Ammer's name. This in turn I attribute to my fundamental lack of rigor in matters of intellectual property.

["Eine Erklärung," from GW *Schriften zur Literatur und Kunst* 1, p. 100, originally published in the *Berliner Börsen-Courier* on May 6, 1929, in response to an exposure by Alfred Kerr. The theater's program too had mentioned "additional ballads by François Villon" without giving Ammer's name. Brecht in fact borrowed rather more than twenty-five lines, this being only the amount he left unaltered. Thereafter he paid Ammer (real name Karl Klammer) a small royalty, and also wrote the sonnet which prefaced Kiepenheuer's republication of his Villon translation in 1930 (see *Poems 1913–1956*, pp. 180, 549). Karl Kraus's comment was that "the little finger of the hand with which Brecht took 25 verses of Ammer's Villon translation is more original than the man Kerr who caught him out."]

Notes to *The Threepenny Opera*

THE READING OF PLAYS

There is no reason why John Gay's motto for his *Beggar's Opera*—nos haec novimus esse nihil—should be changed for the *Threepenny Opera*. Its publication represents little more than the prompt-book of a play wholly surrendered to theaters, and thus is directed at the expert rather than at the consumer. This doesn't mean that the conversion of the maximum number of readers or spectators into experts is not thoroughly desirable; indeed it is under way.

The *Threepenny Opera* is concerned with bourgeois conceptions not only as content, by representing them, but also through the manner in which it does so. It is a kind of report on life as any member of the audience would like to see it. Since at the same time, however, he sees a good deal that he has no wish to see; since therefore he sees his wishes not merely fulfilled but also criticized (sees himself not as the subject but as the object), he is theoretically in a position to appoint a new function for the theater. But the theater itself resists any alteration of its function, and so it seems desirable that the spectator should read plays whose aim is not merely to be performed in the theater but to change it: out of mistrust of the theater. Today we see the theater being given absolute priority over the actual plays. The theater apparatus' priority is a priority of means of production. This apparatus resists all conversion to other purposes, by taking any play which it encounters and immediately changing it so that it no longer represents a foreign body within the apparatus—except at those points where it neutralizes itself. The necessity to stage the new drama correctly—which matters more for the theater's sake than for the drama's—is modified by the fact that the theater can stage anything: it theaters it all down. Of course this priority has economic reasons.

THE PRINCIPAL CHARACTERS

The character of *Jonathan Peachum* is not to be resumed in the stereotyped formula "miser." He has no regard for money. Mistrusting as he does anything that might inspire hope, he sees money as just one more wholly ineffective weapon of defense. Certainly he is a rascal, a theatrical rascal of the old school. His crime lies in his conception of the world. Though it is a conception worthy in its ghastliness to stand alongside the achievements of any of the other great criminals, in making a commodity of human misery he is merely following the trend of the times. To give a practical example, when Peachum takes Filch's money in scene 1 he does not think of locking it in a cashbox but merely shoves it in his pocket: neither this nor any other money is going to save him. It is pure conscientiousness on his part, and a proof of his general despondency, if he does not just throw it away: he cannot throw away the least trifle. His attitude to a million shillings would be exactly the same. In his view neither his money (or all the money in the world) nor his head (or all the heads in the world) will see him through. And this is the reason why he never works but just wanders round his shop with his hat on his head and his hands in his pockets, checking that nothing is going astray. No truly worried man ever works. It is not meanness on his part if he has his Bible chained to his desk because he is scared someone might steal it. He never looks at his son-in-law before he has got him on the gallows, since no conceivable personal values of any kind could influence him to adopt a different approach to a man who deprives him of his daughter. Mac the Knife's other crimes concern him only in so far as they provide a means of getting rid of him. As for Peachum's daughter, she is like the Bible, just a potential aid. This is not so much repellent as disturbing, once you consider what depths of desperation are implied when nothing in the world is of any use except that minute portion which could help to save a drowning man.

The actress playing *Polly Peachum* should study the foregoing description of Mr. Peachum. She is his daughter.

The *bandit Macheath* must be played as a bourgeois phenomenon. The bourgeoisie's fascination with bandits rests on a misconception: that a bandit is not a bourgeois. This misconception is the child of another misconception: that a bourgeois is not a bandit. Does this mean that they are identical? No: occasionally a bandit is not a coward. The qualification "peaceable" normally attributed to the bourgeois by our theater is here achieved by Macheath's dislike, as a good businessman, for the shedding of blood except where strictly necessary—for the sake of the business. This reduction of bloodshed to a minimum, this economizing, is a business principle; at a pinch Mr. Macheath can wield an exceptionally agile blade. He is aware what is due to his legend: a certain romantic aura can further the economies in question if enough care is taken to spread it around. He is punctilious in ensuring that all hazardous, or at any rate bloodcurdling actions by his subordinates get ascribed to himself, and is just as reluctant as any professor to see his assistants put their name to a job. He impresses women less as a handsome man than as a well situated one. There are English drawings of the *Beggar's Opera* which show a short, stocky man of about forty with a head like a radish, a bit bald but not lacking dignity. He is emphatically staid, is without the least sense of humor, while his solid qualities can be gauged from the fact that he thinks more of exploiting his employees than of robbing strangers. With the forces of law and order he is on good terms; his commonsense tells him that his own security is closely bound up with that of society. To Mr. Macheath the kind of affront to public order with which Peachum menaces the police would be profoundly disturbing. Certainly his relations with the ladies of Turnbridge strike him as demanding justification, but this justification is adequately provided by the special nature of his business. Occasionally he has made use of their purely business relationship to cheer himself up, as any bachelor is entitled to do in moderation; but what he appreciates about this more private aspect is the fact that his regular and pedantically punctual visits to a certain Turnbridge coffee house are *habits*, whose cultivation and proliferation is perhaps the main objective of his correspondingly bourgeois life.

In any case the actor playing Macheath must definitely not base his interpretation of the part on this frequenting of a disorderly house. It is one of the not uncommon but none the less incomprehensible instances of bourgeois demonism.

As for Macheath's true sexual needs, he naturally would rather satisfy them where he can get certain domestic comforts thrown in, in other words with women who are not entirely without means. He sees his marriage as an insurance for his business. His profession necessitates temporary absences from the capital, distasteful as they may be, and his subordinates are highly unreliable. When he pictures his future he never for one moment sees himself on the gallows; just quietly fishing the stream on a property of his own.

Brown the police commissioner is a very modern phenomenon. He is a twofold personality: his private and official natures differ completely. He lives not in spite of this fission but through it. And along with him the whole of society is living through his fission. As a private individual he would never dream of lending himself to what he considers his duty as an official. As a private individual he would not (and must not) hurt a fly. . . . In short, his affection for Macheath is entirely genuine; the fact that it brings certain business advantages does not render it suspect; too bad that life is always throwing mud at everything. . . .

HINTS FOR ACTORS

As for the communication of this material, the spectator must not be made to adopt the empathetic approach. There must be a process of exchange between spectator and actor, with the latter at bottom addressing himself directly to the spectator despite all the strangeness and detachment. The actor then has to tell the spectator more about his character "than lies in the part." He must naturally adopt the attitude which allows the episode to develop easily. At the same time he must also set up relationships with episodes other than those of the story, not just be the story's servant. In a love scene with Macheath, for instance, Polly is not only Macheath's beloved but also Peachum's daughter; and not only his daughter but also his employee. Her relations with the spectator must embrace her criticisms of the accepted notions concerning bandits' women and shopkeepers' daughters.

1.* [p. 157] The actors should refrain from depicting these bandits as a collection of those depressing individuals with red neckerchiefs who frequent places of entertainment and with whom no decent person would drink a glass of beer. They are naturally sedate persons, some of them portly and all without exception good mixers when off duty.

* [These figures refer to the superscript numbers in our text.]

2. [p. 157] This is where the actors can demonstrate the practical use of bourgeois virtues and the close relationship between dishonesty and sentiment.

3. [p. 158] It must be made clear how much brutality a man needs to create a situation in which a decent attitude (that of a bridegroom) is possible.

4. [p. 161] What has to be shown here is the displaying of the bride and her fleshliness, at the moment of their final allocation. At the very instant when supply must cease, demand has once again to be stimulated to its peak. The bride is desired all round; the bridegroom then sweeps the board. It is, in other words, a thoroughly theatrical event. At the same time it has to be shown that the bride is hardly eating. How often one sees the daintiest creatures wolfing down entire chickens and fishes! Not so brides.

5. [p. 174] In showing such matters as Peachum's business the actors do not need to bother too much about the normal *development of the plot*. It is however important that they should present a development rather than an ambience. The actor playing one of the beggars should aim to show the selection of an appropriately effective wooden leg (trying on one, laying it aside, trying another, then going back to the first) in such a way that people decide to see the play a second time at the right moment to catch this turn; nor is there anything to prevent the theater featuring it on the screens in the background.

6. [p. 182] It is absolutely essential that the spectator should see Miss Polly Peachum as a virtuous and agreeable girl. Having given evidence of her uncalculating love in the second scene, she now demonstrates that practical-mindedness which saves it from being mere ordinary frivolity.

7. [p. 186] These ladies are in undisturbed posession of their means of production. Just for this reason they must give no impression that they are free. Democracy for them does not

represent the same freedom as it does for those whose means of production can be taken away from them.

8. [p. 189] There is where those Macheaths who seem least inhibited from portraying his death agony commonly balk at singing the third verse. They would obviously not reject the sexual theme if a tragedy had been made of it. But in our day and age sexual themes undoubtedly belong in the realm of comedy; for sex life and social life conflict, and the resulting contradiction is comic because it can only be resolved historically, i.e. under a different social order. So the actor must be able to put across a ballad like this in a comic way. It is very important how sexual life is represented on stage, if only because a certain primitive materialism always enters into it. The artificiality and transitoriness of all social superstructures becomes visible.

9. [p. 192] Like other ballads in the *Threepenny Opera* this one contains a few lines from Francois Villon in the German version by K. L. Ammer. The actor will find that it pays to read Ammer's translation, as it shows the differences between a ballade to be sung and a ballade to be read.

10. [p. 212] This scene is an optional one designed for those Pollys who have a gift for comedy.

11. [p. 217] As he paces round his cage the actor playing Macheath can at this point recapitulate all the ways of walking which he has so far shown the audience. The seducer's insolent way, the hunted man's nervous way, the arrogant way, the experienced way and so on. In the course of this brief stroll he can once again show every attitude adopted by Macheath in the course of these few days.

12. [p. 217] This is where the actor of the epic theater is careful not to let his efforts to stress Macheath's fear of death and make it dominate the whole message of the act, lead him to throw away the depiction of *true* friendship which follows. (True friendship is only true if it is kept within limits. The moral

victory scored by Macheath's two truest friends is barely diminished by these two gentlemen's subsequent moral defeat, when they are not quick *enough* to hand over their means of existence in order to save their friend.)

13. [p. 220] Perhaps the actor can find some way of showing the following: Macheath quite rightly feels that in his case there has been a gruesome miscarriage of justice. And true enough, if the judicial system were to bring about the apprehension of more bandits than it does at present it would lose what little reputation it has.

ABOUT THE SINGING OF THE SONGS

When an actor sings he undergoes a change of function. Nothing is more revolting than when the actor pretends not to notice that he has left the level of plain speech and started to sing. The three levels—plain speech, heightened speech and singing— must always remain distinct, and in no case should heightened speech represent an intensification of plain speech, or singing of heightened speech. In no case therefore should singing take place where words are prevented by excess of feeling. The actor must not only sing but show a man singing. His aim is not so much to bring out the emotional content of his song (has one the right to offer others a dish that one has already eaten oneself?) but to show gestures that are so to speak the habits and usage of the body. To this end he would be best advised not to use the actual words of the text when rehearsing, but common everyday phrases which express the same thing in the crude language of ordinary life. As for the melody, he must not follow it blindly: there is a kind of speaking-against-the-music which can have strong effects, the results of a stubborn, incorruptible sobriety which is independent of music and rhythm. If he drops into the melody it must be an event; the actor can emphasize it by plainly showing the pleasure which the melody gives him. It helps the actor if the musicians are visible during his performance and also if he is allowed to make visible preparation for it (by straightening a chair perhaps or making himself up, etc.). Particularly in the songs it is important that "he who is showing should himself be shown."

WHY DOES THE MOUNTED MESSENGER
HAVE TO BE MOUNTED?

The *Threepenny Opera* provides a picture of bourgeois society, not just of "elements of the Lumpenproletariat." This society has in turn produced a bourgeois structure of the world, and thereby a specific view of the world without which it could scarcely hope to survive. There is no avoiding the sudden appearance of the Royal Mounted Messenger if the bourgeoisie is to see its own world depicted. Nor has Mr. Peachum any other concern in exploiting society's bad conscience for gain. Workers in the theater should reflect just why it is so particularly stupid to deprive the messenger of his *mount*, as nearly every modernistic director of the play has done. After all, if a judicial murder is to be shown, there is surely no better way of paying due tribute to the theater's rôle in bourgeois society than to have the journalist who establishes the murdered man's innocence towed into court by a swan. Is it not a piece of self-evident tactlessness if people persuade the audience to laugh at itself by making something comic of the mounted messenger's sudden appearance? Depriving bourgeois literature of the sudden appearance of some form of mounted messenger would reduce it to a mere depiction of conditions. The mounted messenger guarantees you a truly undisturbed appreciation of even the most intolerable conditions, so it is a sine qua non for a literature whose sine qua non is that it leads nowhere.

It goes without saying that the third finale must be played with total seriousness and utter dignity.

> ["Anmerkungen zur 'Dreigroschenoper,'" from GW *Schriften zum Theater*, pp. 991 ff. and Stücke pp. 487 ff., omitting paragraphs 2 ("Titles and screens") and 6 ("Why does Macheath have to be arrested twice over?"), which refer to Brecht's theater as a whole rather than to this particular play. For these see *Brecht on Theatre*.]

Stage Design for *The Threepenny Opera*

In the *Threepenny Opera* the more different the set's appearance for playing and for songs, the better its design. For the

Berlin production (1928) a great fairground organ was placed at the back of the stage, with steps on which the jazz band was lodged, together with colored lamps that lit up when the orchestra was playing. Right and left of the organ were two big screens for the projection of Neher's drawings, framed in red satin. Each time there was a song its title was projected on them in big letters, and lights were lowered from the grid. So as to achieve the right blend of patina and newness, shabbiness and opulence, the curtain was a small, none too clean piece of calico running on metal wires. The Paris production (1937) moved the opulence and patina downstage. There was a real satin drapery with gold fringes, above and to the side of which were suspended big fairground lamps which were lit during the songs. The curtain had two figures of beggars painted on it, more than life size, who pointed to the title "The Threepenny Opera." Screens with further painted figures of beggars were placed downstage right and left.

PEACHUM'S BEGGARS' OUTFITTING SHOP

Peachum's shop must be so equipped that the audience is able to grasp the nature of this curious concern. The Paris production had two shop windows in the background containing dummies in beggars' outfits. Inside the shop was a stand from which garments and special headgear were suspended, all marked with white labels and numbers. A small low rack contained a few worn-out shoes, likewise numbered, as if on display in a museum showcase. The Kamerny Theater in Moscow showed Mr. Peachum's clients entering the dressing booths as normal human beings, then leaving them as horrible wrecks.

> ["Aufbau der 'Dreigroschenoper'-Bühne," from GW *Schriften zum Theater*, pp. 1000 ff. Dated c. 1937. Tairoff's production at the Kamerny Theater in Moscow took place in 1930. The designer for Aufricht's Paris production of 1937, directed by Francesco de Mendelsohn, was Eugène Berman.]

On a Text by Weill

On Kurt Weill's Open Letter

Before the end of 1928 Kurt Weill had been asked by his publishers Universal-Edition if he would write a few words about the implications of *The Threepenny Opera* for their journal *Anbruch*, one of the two leading music magazines of the time. In the editors' view Brecht and Weill had succeeded remarkably in reflecting the social and artistic conditions of their age, so that what struck them most was its sociological significance: an expression which seems to echo Brecht's concern in his debate with Fritz Sternberg the previous year (see "Shouldn't we Abolish Aesthetics?" in *Brecht on Theatre*, p. 20 ff.) with "capturing the theater for a *different* audience." Weill responded with an open letter to the editors very much along these lines, claiming that he and his collaborator had created a new genre for which the public had evidently been waiting. It was not so much that future works in the wake of *The Threepenny Opera*—for he made it clear that this first success was to be followed up—would rehabilitate the operetta, or traditional musical comedy, though clearly this was something which had been preoccupying the critics. What he and Brecht had done rather, in his view, was to get a foothold in what he termed "a consumer industry hitherto reserved for a very different category of writer and musician." In other words, here were two artists of exceptional skill and sophistication who had succeeded in appealing to a far less narrow audience than normally went to the opera and the symphony concert. They had breached the barrier between highbrow and low-.

Weill did not claim to be the only composer to have explored in this direction. Without mentioning Hindemith by name he made it clear how much pioneer work had been done thanks to that composer's initiatives at the Donaueschingen and

Baden-Baden music festivals over the previous seven years. As he pointed out, a whole movement had been set on foot for harnessing modern music to pedagogic and utilitarian ends— film music, music for youth orchestras and the like—and in the process its means of expression had been greatly simplified, so that "modern" no longer necessarily meant inaccessible and difficult to perform. This in turn was only part of a larger trend affecting all the arts in Weimar Germany and Soviet Russia at the time: a trend towards impersonal, collective works of art with a social as well as a "purely" artistic objective. Hitherto grand opera had remained outside this, addressing itself to a distinctive audience of opera-goers which had little to do with the ordinary theater audience. The achievement of *The Threepenny Opera*, in Weill's view, was to break down the medium's "splendid isolation."

For opera by tradition was an aristocratic art form, depen- dent on a particular social order. And this tradition still per- sisted, leading even the most modern opera composers to pick on themes, literary texts and principles of construction such as no theater of the day would tolerate. In the theater proper plays with a social message or at least a topical theme now pre- dominated—the so-called "Zeittheater" or "theater of the times." Not so in the opera, where the whole framework of the medium needed first to be demolished and rebuilt from scratch. This is where *The Threepenny Opera* was making its special contribution, by going right back and tackling such basic questions as "what on earth can music, and particularly singing, be doing in the theater?" Weill's method, he said, was to work against Brecht's plot (which he for some reason termed "realistic"), interrupting it by music or joining in at those points where "there was nothing else for it but to sing." It was a help too that "opera" itself was part of the theme: that the evening had to be presented as an opera for beggars, while the Third Act Finale, far from being a mere parody, used operatic convention as the only possible way of bringing the story to its happy ending: in short that the more preposterous aspects of the opera medium now became functional. This had to be achieved without reliance on virtuoso singers, by "writing a kind of music that would be singable by actors." The tunes had to be catchy ones, and the result was an entirely new category of musical theater.

[For the original text of Weill's letter see Kurt Weill: *Ausgewählte Schriften*, ed. David Drew, Suhrkamp, Frankfurt 1975, pp. 54 ff. Originally published in *Anbruch*, Vienna, January 1929, Jg. 11. Nr. 1, p. 24.]

Transcript

Conversation between Brecht and Giorgio Strehler on October 25, 1955, with regard to the forthcoming Milan production. (Taken down by Hans-Joachim Bunge.)

Strehler had prepared twenty-seven precisely formulated questions for Brecht about the production of *The Threepenny Opera*. He began by asking its relation to the original *Beggar's Opera* and the extent of Elisabeth Hauptmann's and Kurt Weill's collaboration.

Brecht and Hauptmann told him that a play had been needed to open the Theater am Schiffbauerdamm under Fischer and Aufricht's direction on August 28, 1928. Brecht was engaged on *The Threepenny Opera*. It was based on a translation made by Elisabeth Hauptmann. The ensuing work with Weill and Elisabeth Hauptmann was a true collaboration and proceeded step by step. Erich Engel agreed to take over the direction. He had directed Brecht's early plays and Brecht had attended many of his rehearsals; he was the best man for an experiment like this. Perhaps the hardest thing was choosing the actors. Brecht went primarily for cabaret and revue performers, who had the advantage of being artistically interested and socially aggressive. During the summer Caspar Neher prepared his designs. According to Brecht he idea underlying *The Threepenny Opera* was: "criminals are bourgeois: are bourgeois criminals?"

Strehler asked whether there was any material about the first performance. He was convinced that a "Model" was useful and wanted to use it for his production. The sort of thing that would be of practical interest to him was to know the style of the production and the historical setting of the first performance. He asked if he was right in assuming that Brecht had shifted *The Threepenny Opera* to the Victorian era because of the latter's essentially bourgeois character, which meant that London rather than, say, Paris or Berlin provided the best setting. Brecht replied that from the outset he had wanted, primarily because of the shortage of time, to change the original as little as possible. Transporting it to Paris or some other city would have meant extensive changes in the portrayal of the setting, which in turn would have entailed much additional research. But even the best of principles couldn't be maintained in the long run, and working on the play had led to the realization that the original date could usefully be advanced a hundred years. A good deal was known about the Victorian age, which at the same time was remote enough to be judged with critical detachment, thus permitting the audience to pick out what was relevant to them. Set in that period the play would be more easily transported to Berlin than if set in that in which Gay had (of necessity) had to locate it.

Strehler observed that the music which Weill wrote in 1928 was of its own time and therefore evidently in deliberate contrast with the period of the play. Brecht said this was a gain for the theater. The underlying thought was: beggars are poor people. They want to make a grand opera, but lack money and have to make do as best they can. How to show this? By a splendidly entertaining performance (which at the same time, of course, must lay bare the conditions prevailing at that period) and simultaneously by making evident all that which failed to achieve the object intended, frequently indeed producing results actually opposed to it. For instance the beggar actors are quite unable to portray respectability (such as ought to be particularly easy in a Victorian setting), so that there are continual lapses, particularly in the songs. The grand manner at which they are aiming goes wrong, and suddenly it all turns into a dirty joke. This isn't what the beggar actors want, but the audience loves it and applauds, with the result that it all keeps slipping further into the gutter. They are alarmed by this, but all the same it works. Their plan to create a grand theater proves impossible to realize. Because of their restricted means it only half comes off. (Here again the Victorian age gives the right picture.) In such a beggar's opera decency would be no inducement to the audience to stay in its seats; its preferences are accordingly respected. Only the finale has once again been carefully rehearsed, so that the level originally aimed at can at least be achieved here. Yet even this is a failure, for it succeeds only as parody. In short there is a perpetual effort to present something grandiose, but each time it is a fiasco. All the same a whole series of truths emerge.

Brecht gave an instance: unemployed actors trying to portray the Geneva Conference. Unfortunately they have a quite wrong idea of it, and so with the best will in the world all their crocodile-like efforts to present Mr. Dulles, for instance, as a Christian martyr are a failure, because they have no proper notion either of Mr. Dulles or of a Christian martyr. Whatever they do is successful only in making people laugh. But to laugh is to criticize.

Strehler suggested that the *Beggar's Opera* was originally aristocratic in both form and content, a skit on Handel's operas for instance. Brecht had kept its form and its sense. All this was still valid in 1928. Capitalist society was still on its feet then, as was grand opera. Meantime there had been a war, but the problems had remained in many ways generally the same. Today however there were distinctions that must be made. Its relevance would still apply as forcefully in Italy and similar capitalist countries.

Brecht agreed. He thought the play ought to have the same power of attack in contemporary Italy as it had had at the time in Berlin.

Strehler asked how far was *The Threepenny Opera* an epic play and how epic ought the production to be.

Brecht emphasized that both considerations to a great extent applied. The socially critical stance must not be abandoned for a moment. The main prop here was the music, which kept on destroying the illusion; the latter however had first to be created, since an atmosphere could never be destroyed until it had been built up.

Strehler expressed regret that so many *Threepenny Opera* productions had been prettified. Not that its socially critical aspects could be entirely camouflaged, but it had remained a nice theatrical revolution which failed to get across the foot-lights, not unlike those lions that can be safely visited in zoos, where you are protected from attacks by iron bars. The average director made concessions to his audience and it wasn't going to pay 2,000 lire to have filth thrown at it. The way *The Threepenny Opera* was normally performed, like an elegant Parisian opera, everybody found it "nice."

Brecht explained that when *The Threepenny Opera* was originally staged in Germany in 1928 it had a strong political and aesthetic impact. Among its successful results were:

1. The fact that young proletarians suddenly came to the theater, in some cases for the first time, and then quite often came back.
2. The fact that the top stratum of the bourgeoisie was made to laugh at its own absurdity. Having once laughed at certain attitudes, it would never again be possible for these particular representatives of the bourgeoisie to adopt them.

The Threepenny Opera can still fulfill the same function in capitalist countries today so long as people understand how to provide entertainment and, at the same time, a bite instead of mere cosy absurdity. The important point now being: look, beggars are being fitted out. Every beggar is a monstrosity. The audience must be appalled at its own complicity in such poverty and wretchedness.

Strehler asked if Brecht could suggest any ways of ensuring that *The Threepenny Opera* should be as artistically effective and topically relevant in 1955 as in 1928. Brecht replied that he would heighten the crooks' make-up and render it more unpleasant. The romantic songs must be sung as beautifully as possible, but the falsity of this "attempt at a romantic island where everything in the garden is lovely" needed to be strongly underlined.

Strehler was anxious to get material about the set, but what his Milan production most needed was some suggestions about costumes, since he felt that the 1928 costumes, which so far as he knew were based wholly on the Victorian era, would no longer be of use to him. Brecht corrected him, saying that far from being Victorian the 1928 costumes had been gathered from the costumiers and were a complete mixture. He would not think of abandoning the use of rhyme as in the *Beggar's Opera*, nor, with it, the "jazzed up Victorianism" of the Berlin production. In the Moscow production Tairoff had entirely modernized the costumes so as to conjure up the (by Moscow standards) exotic appeal of Paris fashions.

Brecht said that Strehler had the right picture: up went the curtain on a brothel, but it was an utterly bourgeois brothel. In the brothel there were whores, but there was no mystique about them, they were utterly bourgeois whores. Everything is done to make things proper and lawful.

Strehler asked how far *The Threepenny Opera* was a satire on grand opera, to which Brecht replied: only in so far as grand opera still persists, but that this had never been so important in Germany as in Italy. The starting point must always be a poor theater trying to do its best.

Strehler asked what did Brecht think about adaptation to bring it up to date. Brecht thought such a procedure acceptable.

Strehler's question sprang from the fact that it would be impossible, for instance, to stage *The·Threepenny Opera* in Naples using Kurt Weill's music. However in Milan there were parallels with the reign of Umberto I which would be brought out. To this extent Milan was comparable with London, while the popular note struck by the music would have the same reception as in Berlin. The bourgeoisie was the same. But Strehler wondered if the need to Italianize the names might not eliminate the necessary critical detachment: for "one must bare one's teeth for the truth."

Brecht wondered if it might not be possible to set *The Threepenny Opera* in the Italian quarter of New York, around 1900 perhaps. The music would be right too. He had not gone into the question as yet but at the moment he thought it a possible transposition. The New York Italians had brought everything, including their emotions, from back home, but it had all got commercialized. There would be a brothel, but one like at home, to which they'd go because they felt it was "like being back at mama's."

Strehler took this idea further and asked if it wouldn't mean adding a prologue. Here again Brecht agreed, in so far as some explanation would be needed. It would have to be established that the New York beggar actors were a group of Italians, that it was all like in Milan but a long way off. The first sky-scrapers could have been built, but the group must be wretchedly poor. All they want to do is to stage something "like back home."

Strehler had a suggestion for the prologue. A film of Milan could be shown, leading the actors to want to perform some-thing recalling that city, whereupon the curtain would rise and the play begin.

Another reservation of Strehler's concerned the Italian actor's penchant for improvisation. "You send someone off to choose a costume and he comes back with fifty." There was also the problem of "the epic style of portrayal." According to Strehler it is not easy for the Italian actor to play on more than one level at a time, i.e. roughly to the effect that "I am acting a man trying to act this character." He asked if it was at all possible to perform Brecht's plays—e.g. *Die Mutter*, which he described as the "stronghold of the epic theater"— except in an epic manner, and where if anywhere they could be performed if one had no actors or directors who had been trained for them. "What is the result of acting them in the wrong way?" Brecht: "They can certainly be performed, but what emerges is normal theater, and three-quarters of the fun is lost."

Strehler wanted some advice about what to do with actors who knew nothing about epic theater. He asked if it was possible to perform a Brecht play given only *one* actor familiar with the epic theater, and he inquired about methods for teaching the epic way of acting.

Brecht told Strehler not to worry and that our own acting too was only partly epic. It always worked best in comedies, since they anyway entail a measure of alienation. The epic style of portrayal was more easily achieved there, so that it was a good idea generally to stage plays more or less as com-edies. He suggested using an aid which he had tried himself: having the actors intersperse what he called "bridge verses," thus turning their speech into a report in indirect speech; i.e.

interspersing the sentences with "said he's." "What's bad is that 'epic' cannot be achieved without using the dialectic."

Strehler said he was convinced that nowadays it was impossible to act either Shakespeare or the Greek tragedies without alienation if their performance was to be useful and entertaining.

Brecht once again suggested acting tragic scenes for their comic effect. What is most epic, he maintained, is always the run-throughs, and they should certainly be scheduled for the end of the rehearsals or better still conducted at regular intervals throughout the whole rehearsal period. "The nearer the performance gets to being a run-through, the more epic it will be." Strehler asked if his way of explaining epic portrayal to his actors was the right one, by which he would cite the example of a director acting a scene, showing the actors in outline how to do something and all the time having his explanations ready even if he never voices them.

Brecht approved of this and thought that the actors too could be put in the director's situation if one instituted run-throughs with minimal use of gesture, so that everyone barely indicated how things should go.

Strehler feared that his *Threepenny Opera* production might turn out "neither fish nor fowl." His sense of responsibility had held him back from doing *Mother Courage*, since he was unable to find an epic actress to play the title part. This production of *The Threepenny Opera* too was something that he had been planning for years and always had to put off because of a shortage of suitable actors.

["Über eine Neuinszenierung der Dreigroschenoper," from *Bertolt Brechts Dreigroschenbuch*, Frankfurt, Suhrkamp, 1960, pp. 130 ff. Strehler's production for the Piccolo Teatro, Milan, in 1956 eventually transposed the play to an American setting around the time of the First World War, with the police as Keystone Cops and an early motor car on stage. Brecht and Elisabeth Hauptmann thought it excellent.

At the Geneva Conference of summer 1954 the Western powers, China and the Soviet Union agreed to create two Vietnams, North and South. John Foster Dulles was then U.S. Secretary of State. King Umberto I's reign in Italy was from 1878 to 1900.]

Editorial Notes

1. General

Though there is little in the way of manuscript material or notes to show just how it evolved, *The Threepenny Opera* was clearly one of Brecht's more rapidly written works. Its producer Aufricht only took over the Theater am Schiffbauerdamm at the end of 1927, and it must have been in March or April 1928 that he and his dramaturg Heinrich Fischer went to Brecht in search of a play. What Brecht then offered them—apparently as his own work and under the title *Gesindel* or *Scum*—was a translation of *The Beggar's Opera* which Elisabeth Hauptmann had almost completed; he is said to have shown them the first two scenes. Nothing of this first script has come down to us, and there is no real evidence that Brecht himself had as yet taken any hand in it. The process of "adaptation" credited to him by the original program probably only started once the play itself and the principle of a collaboration with Weill had been accepted. Erich Engel, with whom the two men had been working on the Berlin *Mann ist Mann*, was already earmarked as the play's director.

The next event seems to have been the production of a stage script which was duplicated by Brecht's and Hauptmann's agents Felix Bloch Erben and presumably represented the work done by the collaborators in the south of France that summer. Its title is given as "The Beggar's Opera/Die Luden-Oper [The Ragamuffins' Opera]/By John Gray [*sic*]/translated by Elisabeth Hauptmann/German adaptation: Bert Brecht. Music: Kurt Weill." Though its text is still a good way from the final version it already represents a considerable transformation of the original. Several subsequently discarded characters from Gay's original still remain (notably Mrs. Coaxer and her girls), but Lockit has already been purged, together with all that part of the plot involving him, and replaced by the rather more up-to-date figure of Brown.

Peachum's manipulation of the beggars is also new, as are the first stable and second jail scenes. The main items retained from Gay in this script are, in our present numbering, scenes 1, 3, 4, 5 (which is not yet a brothel but a room in the hotel), 6, 8 and the principle of the artificial happy ending. There are no scene titles. However, Macheath's final speech before his execution is already there, much as in our version, as are several of the songs: "Peachum's Morning Hymn" (whose melody is in fact a survivor from the original, being that of Gay's opening song), "Pirate Jenny," the "Cannon Song," the "Barbara Song," the "Tango-Ballade," the "Jealousy Duet," Lucy's subsequently cut aria (in scene 8), the "Call from the Grave" and the "Ballad in which Macheath Begs All Men for Forgiveness"; also the final chorus. Most of these are not given in full, but only by their titles, and some may not yet have been completed. There are also two of Gay's original songs, as well as two translations from Kipling: "The Ladies" and "Mary, Pity Women." Neither the Gay nor the Kipling songs were, so far as anybody knows, set by Weill, but the latter may explain why the original program spoke of "interpolated songs . . . by Rudyard Kipling."

This script was altered and added to in the course of the rehearsals, when texts of several of the songs were stuck in and the rest added. The piano score, which includes all the present songs apart from the Ballade of Sexual Obsession, was published not long after the première, the text in Brecht's *Versuche 3* only in 1931. This 1931 text has remained virtually unaltered, though Brecht appended a certain amount of alternative material later, and is to all intents and purposes that used for our translation.

2. The 1928 Stage Script

First Act

Scene 1

The dramatis personae originally included Gay's Mrs. Coaxer and Suky Tawdry; Jenny was Jenny Diver, as in Gay, which Brecht later rendered "Spelunken-Jenny" or literally "Low Dive Jenny," perhaps on the assumption that "Diver" meant a habituée of dives. The script starts the play without any scene title and with the following stage directions:

> *Mr. Peachum's house. It is 7 a.m. Peachum is standing at a desk on which lie a ledger and a Bible. Round the walls are notices with such sayings as "Give and it shall be given unto you," "Close not thine ear to misery," "You will benefit from the interests of a powerful organization" and "If you are satisfied tell the others, if you are dissatisfied tell me."*

Peachum sings his "Morning Hymn," then:

> So. Now, one glance at the Bible and then to work. Matthew 5. I'm always combing Matthew for something I can use. No good. I'll have to cut it out once and for all. Salt without an egg. Matthew 6: feeble, feeble. No personality there. Wait. Verse 25: Give and it shall be given unto you. Flat, but it's been used already. Proverbs is still the best, particularly chapter 6. All kinds of useful lessons, if a bit old-fashioned. Yes, a businessman like me, Robert Jeremiah Peachum and Co., who's forced to live among thieves, whores and lawyers, cannot do without God. Or let's say, without God and accountancy. We must add to that application, seriousness, circumspection, genius and economy. Not to mention early rising and kindness and loyalty . . .

This leads to Filch's entrance, after which the dialogue continues much as now up to the production of Outfit C (middle of p. 152). There is then no showcase with wax dummies; instead Mrs. Peachum "*drags out a box full of indescribably ragged clothes.*" Instead of Peachum's speech exhibiting the various outfits, Filch is simply told to "Take off your clothes" etc. (p. 152), and these then become outfit A, the young man who has seen better days.

Filch removes his socks under protest (p. 153), and then as Mrs. Peachum brings in the screen Peachum asks, much as in Gay's scene 4:

> Did that fellow Macheath come round yesterday? The one who's always coming when I'm out?
>
> MRS. PEACHUM   Certainly, Bobby dear. There's no finer gentleman. If he comes from the Cuttlefish Bar at any reasonable hour we're going to a little hop with him—the Captain, Polly, Bob the Saw and me. Bobby, my Dear, is the Captain rich?

The dialogue remains close to Gay's (which we will make identifiable by its use of capital letters for nouns, as in German) down to Mrs. Peachum's statement of her concern about Polly (which comes just before her first song in the *Beggar's Opera*). Then Filch appears in his new begging outfit and asks for a few tips (p. 154).

> PEACHUM *inspects him, then to Mrs. Peachum* Half-wit? Yes, that'll be the best thing. *To Filch*: Nobody stupid can play the half-wit, you know. Come back this evening . . .

etc. (which is not in Gay). But after his "Fifty percent!" Peachum says "To come back to Polly . . . ," and returns to a cross between Gay's text and ours. Thus:

> A handsome Wench in our way of Business is as profitable as at the Bar of a *Temple* Coffee-House. You should try to influence the girl in the right direction. In any thing but Marriage! After that, my Dear, how shall we be safe? You must imagine we can live on air. The way you chuck your daughter around anyone would think I'm a millionaire. The fellow would have us in his clutches in three shakes. In his clutches! Do you think your daughter can hold her tongue in bed any better than you? *Polly* is Tinder, and a Spark will at once set her on a Flame.

> Married! All she can think about is her own Pleasure, not her own Profit. Do you suppose we nurtured her at our breast . . .?
>
> MRS. PEACHUM Our?
>
> PEACHUM All right, you nurtured her; but did you nurture her so we should have no crust to eat in our old age? Married! I expect my daughter to be to me as bread to the hungry—*he leafs through the Book*—it even says so in the Bible somewhere. Anyway marriage is disgusting. I'll teach her to get married.
>
> MRS. PEACHUM Dear Bobby, you're just a barbarian. You're being unfair to her. She is doing exactly what any decent girl would do: a few Liberties for the Captain in the interest of the business.
>
> PEACHUM But 'tis your Duty, my Dear, as her mother, to explain to the girl what she owes to herself, or to us, which amounts to the same thing. I'll go to her this moment and sift her.

At this point, corresponding to the end of Gay's scene 4, Peachum moves on to what became part of his long speech on p. 152, the complaints of client no. 136, then exits telling Mrs. Peachum to get on with ironing in the wax. Left alone, as in Gay's scene 5, she says:

> God, was Bobby worked up! I can't say I blame him, though; I can't say I blame him.

Peachum returns, and the final exchanges are as in our text, less the song.

Scene 2

Again there is no title (this applies throughout the stage script), but the stage direction says "*Empty stable. 5 p.m. the next day. It is fairly dark. Enter Macheath with Matt of the Mint and Polly.*" There is nothing in Gay corresponding to this scene.

The dialogue starts as in our text, roughly as far as Ned's "Dear Polly" (p. 158), though without the lines in which Macheath shows his ignorance of Peachum. After Ned says this Mac, having knocked his hat off, "*shoves him against the wall, pushing his face with the flat of his hand—a favorite maneuver.*" Thence it continues as now down to Polly's inquiry "Was the whole lot stolen?" (p.159).

> MACHEATH   Stolen? Selected! Anybody can steal, and everybody does. But selecting the right items . . . That's where art comes in. What incompetence! [etc. as now, bottom of p. 159].

Thereafter the dialogue is much as now down to Jimmy's "Hey, Captain. The cops!" (p. 163), except that there is no mention of Jenny Diver by Jake (p. 161). Jimmy's exclamation this time heralds Brown's entrance, not that of the Reverend Kimball (who does not appear at all), and it turns out it is Brown's prospective son-in-law the Duke of Devonshire who is the stable's owner: "Did it have to be Teddy's stable?" says Brown. "At this of all times?" Mac welcomes him with "Sit down, ya old blighter and pitch into the egg mayonnaise" (cf. p. 167). He observes the origins of the plates and the eggs, then listens to the gang sing "Bill Lawgen" (which is not from the original) and comments on the salmon:

> Clark's, the fishmongers. Breaking and entering reported this morning. Tastes delicious.

This is where Polly performs "Pirate Jenny," which provokes the same reactions as in our text, apart from its references to Reverend Kimball. After "let's not have any more of it" (p. 166) Mac goes straight on with "You have today in your midst . . ." (p. 167), the speech leading into the "Cannon Song." Only the title of this is given, but its first version had already been written some years earlier and published in the *Devotions for the Home* under the title "Song of the Three Soldiers"; it is sometimes, on no clear grounds, described as "after Kipling."

After the song the text is much as now down to Brown's "There's nothing whatsoever on record against you at Scotland Yard" (p. 169), apart from the interpolation at the end of Macheath's long speech (p. 167) of "Cheers, Brown! And now for some music!"—at which *"Everything is cleared to one side. Three of the guests take it in turns to form a little jazz band.*" This prepares the way for the dance which concludes the scene. During it Macheath stands in the center and says:

> My dear friends. Let us bring this day to a worthy con-
> clusion by conducting ourselves as gentlemen.
> WALTER *dancing with Polly*   Oh, stuff this day.

After which "*The party continues in full swing. Once again we hear the chorus 'Bill Lawgen and Mary Syer'*"—i.e. not the present Love Duet.

Scene 3

This starts close to Gay's scene 6, with indications of some intimacy between Mrs. Peachum and Filch:

> *Mr. Peachum's office. Morning. Mrs. Peachum. Filch.*
> MRS. PEACHUM   Come hither, *Filch.* I am as fond of this
> Child, as though my Mind misgave me he were my own.
> Why are you so sad? Can your mama not help?
> FILCH *tonelessly*   Oh dear, I can't regard you as my mama,
> Mrs. Peachum, even though I shouldn't say it.

He says how hard it is to beg, and regrets his choice of profession. She wants him to find out about Macheath and Polly, who has now been away from home for three days. Filch knows, but as in Gay has promised not to tell:

> MRS. PEACHUM   Right, Filch, you shall go with me into my
> own Room, Filch. You shall tell me the whole Story in
> comfort, Filchy, and I'll give thee a Glass of Cordial
> Médoc that I keep locked up in my bedside table for my
> own drinking. *Exeunt.*

Peachum enters with Polly, and Gay's scene 7 follows, including Polly's song "Virgins are like the fair Flowers," whose text is translated in toto. Mrs. Peachum then appears, but without her song from the original, and goes straight into her opening speech of the scene in our version. A shortened version of Gay's scene 8 dialogue follows, down to where Peachum pinches Polly, asking "Are you really bound Wife to him, or are you only upon liking?"; he forbids Macheath the house,

and Polly (in lieu of "Can Love be control'd by Advice?")
goes into the "Barbara Song" (which expands and updates the
same theme, and whose text is given in full). Mrs. Peachum's
faint (p. 173) then follows much as in Gay, though now she
asks for the Cordial and doubts Polly's "Readiness and
Concern."

Only one beggar then enters, who proves to be the dis-
gruntled no. 136. "First-class stains, Mr. Twantry," says Polly,
handing over the criticized outfit. The problem now, as in
Gay's scene 10, is: how is Polly to live. Peachum answers
"It's all perfectly simple" etc. as now (p. 175), and Polly's
refusal to consider divorce follows. Then back, more or less,
to Gay:

PEACHUM   Yes, yes, yes. You're a silly little goose. But it's
all so simple. You secure what he's got; I get him hanged at
the next Sessions, and then at once you are made a charming Widow.

POLLY   What, murder the Man I love! The Blood runs cold
at my Heart with the very thought of it. But it would be
murder!

PEACHUM   Murder? Rubbish. Self-defense. It's all self-
defense. My position in the world is one of self-defense.

—this last, crucial idea being new. Mrs. Peachum then reminds
Polly of her filial duties, as in Gay, and refers to "Those
cursed Play-Books she reads" before threatening to "tan her
behind" (p. 175). Peachum's last word is "Polly, you will get a
divorce!"

The rest of the scene is not in Gay. It strikes eleven, and
a crowd of beggars streams in—"The second shift," says
Peachum. They arrive decently dressed, but change into their
begging outfits, stumps, bandages etc. This introduces the
present dialogue from the speech of complaint in the middle
of p. 174 down to "This one will do," with the addition of a
tirade by Peachum against his daughter. Mrs. Peachum's speech
"Anyway, he's got several women" (p. 175) follows, after
which the dialogue continues much as ours down to Polly's
"There's nothing on record against Mac at Scotland Yard"
(p. 176):

PEACHUM   Right. Then put on your hat, and we will go to Mr. Brown. *To his wife*: And you'll go to Turnbridge. For the villainy of the world is great, and a man needs to run his legs off to keep them from being stolen from under him.

POLLY   I, Papa, shall be delighted to shake hands with Mr. Brown again.

But in lieu of the first act finale, Polly then sings a translation of Gay's song against lawyers, "A Fox may steal your Hens, Sir."

Second Act

Scene 4 [1 in script]

This is set as "*Stable. Morning. Macheath. Enter Walter.*" The two men start with a version of the Peachum-Filch dialogue from Gay's Act 1, scene 2. Black Moll becomes "Blattern-Molly" ("Pockmarked Molly"), who can be "back on the beat tomorrow," says Macheath. Betty Sly is "Betriebs-Betty" ("Busy Betty"). Tom Gagg is unchanged. After Gay's line "There is nothing to be got by the Death of Women, except our Wives," Walter (not Filch) is sent with a message to Newgate, having first been told to look through the storeroom to see if there are any decent clothes. Mrs. Trapes needs them "to clothe five young pigeons to work Kensington Street." On his exit Polly enters as at the start of our scene, whose opening dialogue approximately follows, as far as the entry of the gang (p. 182). Once again, the listing of the gang members (p. 181) derives from Peachum's speech in Act 1, scene 3 of the original, and includes such figures as Harry Paddington, Slippery Sam ("Schleicher-Samuel") and Tom Tipple ("Tippel-Tom"). The poetic naming of "Bob the Pickpocket alias Gorgon alias Bluff-Robert alias Carbuncle alias Robert the Saw" is mainly from Gay, but Brecht makes him the gang member Polly likes best. The speech about Jack Poole and banking is not in the script; the list simply ends, and Polly says her "Why, Mac!" etc. as on p. 182, to introduce the gang's entry.

Their first exchanges are somewhat different, to where Mac tells them of his "little trip" (p. 182). He and they then go into the storeroom, while Polly delivers a monologue; there is no demonstration of her authority over the gang. They re-enter, and Mac resumes "The rotten part of it is" etc. (p. 183) down to "toffs are all drunk." Robert follows with "Ma'am, while your husband is away" etc.; Polly says "good-bye, Mr. Robert" and shakes hands; then they leave as on p. 184. Her dialogue with Macheath follows as now, as far as "Highgate Heath" (p. 184):

> POLLY   Then everything is all right. Good-bye, Mac.
> MAC   Good-bye, Polly. *He shuts the door behind her. Lighting a pipe*: Polly is most confoundedly bit. Now I must have Women. There is nothing unbends the Mind like them. Cocktails are not nearly such a help.

—the last sentence being Brecht's gloss on Gay's lines. He then opens the storeroom door and tells Walter to assemble the Drury Lane ladies for him at 8 p.m. in Room 5 of the Cuttlefish Hotel (equivalent to the Tavern near Newgate of Gay's Act 2).

> MAC Hurry! *Exit Walter.* This London owes me something for having fixed it up with a capital lot of women.

He speaks the final rhymed couplet, which our text gives to Polly, and there is no Interlude.

Scene 5 [2 in script]

Cuttlefish Hotel. 8 p.m. Room 5. Mac and Walter.
MACHEATH   *rings.*
WALTER   Captain?
MAC   How long am I to wait for the ladies?
WALTER   They're bound to be here soon.

Macheath then sings "The Ballad of the Ladies," translated from Kipling (and now included in GW *Gedichte*, p. 1052). The bell rings again, and they troop in, the complete party from Gay's Act 2, scene 4: Mrs. Coaxer, Dolly Trull, Mrs. Vixen, Betty Doxy, Jenny Diver, Mrs. Slammekin, Suky

Tawdry and Molly Brazen, with Walter bringing up the rear. Macheath makes approximately the same speech of welcome as there, down to where the music strikes up "the *French* tune," i.e. the Cotillon. Molly: "Ach, cash makes you randy" (a phrase of Brecht's which comes in others of his plays); then in lieu of the Cotillon the ladies "*dance a little 'Step,'*" and Gay's dialogue follows, down to Mrs. Vixen's "to think too well of your friends." Mac interrupts it with his "Nice underwear you've got there, Vixen," introducing our present dialogue down to Second Whore's "I just don't wear any" (p. 188). Gay takes over again with the exchange between Mac and Jenny, which leads however not to her "Before the Barn-Door crowing" song but to "the brothel-ballade by Francois Villon," as yet without its text. The hand-reading episode follows as in our text from Dolly's first line down to Mac's "Go on!" (p. 187), after which Jenny says she cannot do so, and then disarms him, aided as in Gay by Suky Tawdry. It is however Mrs., not Mr. Peachum who enters with the constables, and she then makes very much the Peachum speech from Act 2, scene 5 of the original. Walter, who has been sitting reading, runs out like Jake in our text, and all exeunt "*most cere-moniously.*"

Scene 6 [3 in script]

This is described as "*Prison in Newgate. Brown sitting im-patiently in a cell.*" The scene begins as in our text, down to Brown's exit (p. 191). Gay's Act 2, scene 7 then follows, with Smith filling Lockit's rôle. Left alone, Macheath makes his speech "That miserable Brown . . ." as in our text (p. 191), but instead of the exchange with Smith he then continues "But the worst of it . . ." (p. 192) as far as "into a tiger," after which he goes on much as in Gay's scene 8:

> I shall have a fine time on't betwixt this and my Execution. Here must I (all Day long) be confin'd to hear the Re-proaches of a Wench who lays her Ruin at my Door—just when a prisoner has some right at least to peace and soli-tude. But here she comes: Lucy, and I cannot get from her. Wou'd I were deaf!

Lucy enters and upbraids Macheath as in Gay's scene 9, whose dialogue is then approximately followed, omitting the three songs, down to the end of that scene: Lucy's cry "O Mac, I only want to become an honest woman," as in our text (p. 194). After that she *sings the song 'Maria, Fürsprecherin der Frauen,'* i.e. Kipling's "Mary, Pity Women," whose translation follows in full, and is also given in GW *Gedichte*, p. 1055.

The next section is not in Gay: Lucy continues "Oh, Macheath, I do hope you will lift my troubles from my shoulders."

> MAC   Of course. As I said: as soon as I'm master of my own decisions.
>
> LUCY   But how are you going to get free? My father truly was your best friend, and even if you played a dirty trick on him over me he can't realize it. So what is he after you for?
>
> MAC   Don't talk to me about your father.
>
> LUCY   But I just don't understand what could have led him to put you in irons. There's some secret involving Peachum and his making such an awful threat that Daddy fainted on hearing it.
>
> MAC   If that's so it's all up with me.
>
> LUCY   No, no, you must become master of your decisions. My whole life depends on it. You must do all right, Mac. You'll end up all right, Mac.

Polly then appears as in Gay's Act 2, scene 13 (our p. 194), his dialogue being followed approximately as far as the song "How happy could I be with either?" Instead of this song however "*Polly and Lucy sing 'Come on out, you Rose of Old Soho!'*" (whose title only is given, and which could well relate also to the next song "I am bubbled, I'm bubbled, O how I am troubled"). Then Gay's dialogue is resumed as far as Peachum's entrance at the end of the scene, but prolonging the Polly-Lucy dialogue as in our text from Lucy's "What's that? What's that?" (p. 197) to before Peachum's entrance (p. 199). This is then replaced by that of Mrs. Peachum, who drags Polly off much as he did in Gay's scene 14, after which scene 15 is followed for much of the exchanges between Macheath and Lucy, down to her "It's wonderful the way you say that, Say it again" (p. 199). On his saying that she must help him she embroiders Gay's original thus:

> If only I knew what was the matter with my father. Anyway the constables are all drunk and it's the coronation tomorrow and my father sent someone out for fifteen bottles of gin and when he didn't come back at once his worries overcame him and he upped and drank a whole bottle of the housekeeper's scent. Now he's lying drunk as a lord beside his desk muttering "Mackie!" If I can find the key shall I escape with you, darling?

They leave together as at the end of Gay's act. Then a new concluding episode follows, starting with a *"gentle knock"* and Brown's voice calling "Mac!" (p. 199). Peachum appears much as in our text, though without his opening remarks to Smith, and our dialogue follows as far as his "People are sure to say . . . that the police shouldn't have let him escape" (p. 200). He rounds off this speech with "A pity: the coronation might have passed off without a single ugly incident.

BROWN   What is that supposed to mean?

PEACHUM   That as it is the poorest of the poor won't let themselves be done out of attending the coronation tomorrow morning.

BROWN   What do you mean by the poorest of the poor?

PEACHUM   It is reasonable to assume that I mean beggars. You see, it is like this. These poorest of the poor—give and it shall be given unto you, and so on—have nothing in the world apart from celebrations. Well, there are various possibilities. Of course there has to be a criminal. What happens to him is less important. Either they want to see a murderer hanged or they want to see one crowned. All the rest is immaterial.

BROWN   Look here, Mr Peachum, what do you mean by a murderer being crowned?

PEACHUM   Same as you do, Mr. Brown.

BROWN   That's outrageous.

PEACHUM   Quite right, that's outrageous.

BROWN   You have given yourself away, Peachum. Hey, Smith!

PEACHUM   **Don't** bring him into this. Or I'll be **awkward**. There'll be a lot happening tomorrow morning. **The papers** will report how in the morning fog an unusual number of poor people of all kinds could be observed in the twisting alleys, patriots all of them with joyous faces and little signs round their necks: "I gave my leg for the king," or "My arm lies on Clondermell Field," or "Three cheers for the king; the Royal Artillery made me deaf." And all these patriots with just one objective, the streets the coronation procession will take. *Drily*: Of course any of these people would much prefer, just supposing there could be an execution of a really well-known and reasonably popular murderer around the same hour, to attend that, as it is always more agreeable to see murderers hanged than crowned. Your servant, Brown. *Exit*.

BROWN Now only the mailed fist can help. Sergeants! Report to me at the double!

There is no second act finale in the script.

Third Act

Scene 7 [1 in script]

The setting is *"Peachum's Beggars' Outfitting Shop. 5 a.m.,"* and a Salvation Army hymn is being played *off*. Beggars are dressing. Great activity. Peachum is not on, so his opening remark (of our text) occurs later. Otherwise the dialogue is close to ours as far as Brown's entrance (p. 206), except that the Ballad of Sexual Obsession is not included, nor the dialogue following it down to Mrs. Peachum's appearance with the tray (p. 205). Instead there is an exchange between a phony cripple and an authentic one. When Brown enters he *"appears to have been transformed into a tiger,"* and goes round *"spreading alarm like a great beast of prey."* His big opening speech starting "Here we are. And now, Mr. Beggar's Friend" (p. 206) goes on:

In the very earliest times—listen, let this be a lesson to you—humanity understood the idea of friendship. Even the most bestial examples—look carefully—felt the urge to acquire a friend. And whatever they may have done in that gray prehistoric age they stood by their comrades.

Thigh to thigh they sat in danger, arm in arm they went
through this vale of tears, and whatever they grabbed they
shared, man to man: let that be a lesson to you. And that
is what I feel too, just as I've described it. I too, despite all
weakness and temptation, place a value on friendship, and
I too . . .

PEACHUM   Good morning, Brown, good morning.

The speech echoes Brecht's early "Ballad of Friendship"
(*Poems 1913–1956*, p. 52), and after it the dialogue remains
close to ours from Peachum's "Good morning" (p. 206) to
his "You see, Brown" (p. 207) immediately before the music,
though omitting the ten lines before the second drum roll.
Then he goes on to tell Brown that the beggars are fakes, just
a few young people dressing up to celebrate having a king
once more, and concludes "I've nothing against it; it was quite
harmless." When no sound follows he repeats this remark.
Then "*a kind of band is heard playing an excruciating 'Step.'*"

BROWN   What's that?
PEACHUM   Dance music.
  Beggars and whores 'steppen' [dance a "step"].
PEACHUM   Take off those chains, Smith. Yes, this is how the
poor enjoy themselves . . .

He goes up to Brown and says:

As for you, Brown, your situation is no laughing matter.
This is a little dance, but in Drury Lane it is bloody serious.
You see, there are so many poor people. Thousands of
them. When you see them standing outside the Abbey . . .

and so on, roughly as in our text from the bottom of p. 208 to
Brown's exit a page later. Then the *Step* breaks off, the beggars gather round Peachum, and he makes them a long speech
saying how much he has done for them. Pointing out how the
rich cannot bear seeing people collapse from hunger because
they are frightened that it might happen to them too—their
one vulnerable point—he concludes "Tomorrow will show
whether poverty can overcome the crimes of those on top."
And "*the beggars feverishly start getting ready.*" End of
scene.

Scene 8 [2 in script]

This corresponds to our optional scene, and it derives from Gay's Act 3, scenes 7 to 10. It starts thus, with the "Lucy's Aria" whose setting by Weill is given as an appendix to the miniature score of 1972:

> *Newgate. Lucy's bedroom above the cells. Lucy is drinking non-stop.*
>
> LUCY   Jealousy, Rage, Passion and likewise Fear are tearing me to pieces, a prey to the raging tempest, tormented by worry! I have the Rats-bane ready. For the past day she has come here every hour wanting to speak with me. Oh, what a two-faced bitch! No doubt she wants to come and gloat at my desperation. O world! How evil the human race! But that lady doesn't know who she is dealing with. Drinking my gin is not going to help her have a high old time with her Mackie afterward. She'll die thanks to my gin! It's here that I'd like to see her writhing! I rescue him from hanging, and is this creature to skim off the cream? Once that slut has drunk the poison, then let the world breathe freely!

Thereafter the dialogue generally follows Gay's (omitting his songs) down to Polly's "I hear, my dear *Lucy*, our Husband is one of these." Brecht then interpolates:

> LUCY   I'll never be anything but a common trollop of the lowest sort. And why? Because I fail to put everything on a business footing.
>
> POLLY   But my dear, that's a misfortune could occur to any woman.

They continue with the original dialogue, past Lucy's offer of the drink, as far as her "unless 'tis in private" in Gay's scene 10. Then Polly excuses herself, saying she is hungry. The next passage is close to our text from "Polly *gaily*" (p. 214) to Lucy's "They've caught him once more" just before the end of our scene, but with some small changes and one or two additions, of which the most notable is after "Really, I don't deserve it" (p. 214):

LUCY   It's so unfair that one must use such means to keep a
man; but it's one's heart, Polly. But enough of that. *She
takes the gin bottle and empties it, off.*

POLLY   What are you doing?

LUCY *with a peculiar manner*   Emptying it.

POLLY   You really are a hypocritical strumpet. But I spotted
that right away.

LUCY   Yes, Polly. On the edge of the precipice, that's where
you were.

POLLY   Anyway it was very considerate of you. Here, have
a sip of water. You must feel terrible. Why don't you
come and see me. I truly am your friend.

LUCY   Polly, men aren't worth it . . .

There is then no change of scene, since the set is a split one,
with the bedroom above and Macheath's cell below. A change
of lighting introduces our

Scene 9 [still 2 in script]

The bells ring, Smith leads in Macheath, and the dialogue is
much as in our text as far as Smith's exit shrugging his
shoulders (p. 218). Macheath then "*sings the 'Epistle to his
Friends' by François Villon*," in other words our "Call from
the Grave," whose text is given. After its second stanza Mrs.
Coaxer appears, and Macheath tries to borrow £600 from her.
"What! At five in the morning?" she asks. Mac: "Five? *He
bellows*: Five twenty-four!" Smith then puts his question
about the meal. Macheath says there isn't going to be a
mounted messenger arriving like in a play to shout "Halt in the
King's Name!" then tells Smith: "Asparagus!" Mrs. Coaxer
grumbles about her overheads, but eventually agrees that she
might be able to manage £400.

Then the lights go up briefly in the bedroom again, showing
Lucy prostrate, with Polly giving her cold compresses. Enter
Mrs. Peachum, with Filch in attendance carrying a cardboard
box. "Go outside, Filch; this is not for your eyes," she says,
and tells Polly to get changed. "You must do like all widows.
Buy mourning and cheer up." The bedroom darkens and the
light returns to the cell, where Smith makes his inquiry about

the soap (shifted from p. 218). After saying "This place is a
shambles," he brings in the table as on p. 219, followed by
Brown's entrance. The dialogue is then close to ours up to the
end of Macheath's verse (p. 221). More persons in mourning
enter, including Peachum and five beggars on crutches, while
Brown and Macheath prolong their haggling over the former's
percentages. Then Macheath looks at his watch and says
"5:48, I'm lost."

> MAC   Jack, lend me £200. I'm finished. I must have those
> £200—for Polly, you know. 5.50. Here am I, talking . . .
> BROWN *has come up to him*   But Mackie, you have only
> to . . . You have only to ask, you can right away . . . 500
> right away—I owe you so much . . . Do you imagine I've
> forgotten Peshawar?
> MAC *weakly*   200, but right away. Right away, right away.
> BROWN   And Saipong and Azerbaijan and Sire, how we stood
> in the jungle together, shoulder to shoulder, and the Shiks
> mutinied, and you said . . .
> *The bells of Westminster interrupt him. Macheath gets up.*
> MAC   Time is up. Jack, you're too emotional to rescue your
> friend. And you don't even know it.

Smith then opens the door, and a group including eight whores
enters the cell.

> *Walter, with a little money bag, stands near Macheath.
> Mrs. Coaxer too has the money.*
> SMITH   Got it?
> MAC *shakes his head.*

Peachum then asks which is Macheath, as in our text (p. 221),
which thereafter is approximately followed down to (in-
clusive) Jenny's "We Drury Lane girls . . ." (p. 222), but
missing out the second half of Peachum's long speech (from
"Mr. Macheath, you once . . ." to "no place at all") and Matt's
ensuing remarks ("You see, Captain" etc.). Brown too makes
no more reference to Azerbaijan but simply says farewell and
leaves for the Coronation, gulping as he goes. Macheath's
farewell speech follows, starting "Farewell, Jackie. It was all
right in the end" and going on with his "Ladies and gentlemen . . ." as now, down to "So be it—I fall" (p. 223). As in

Gay, however, it is Jemmy Twitcher who has betrayed him, not Jenny.

The speech over, Macheath asks for the doors and windows all to be opened, and *"Through the windows we see treetops crowded with spectators."* He then sings *"Ballad to his Friends by François Villon,"* whose text however is not given. After the ensuing farewells to Polly and Lucy, Macheath is led to the door, the whores sob, and the procession forms behind him. Then:

> *The actor playing Macheath hesitates, turns round suddenly and doubtfully addresses the wings, right.*
>
> ACTOR PLAYING MACHEATH   Well, what happens now? Do I go off or not? That's something I'll need to know by the opening night.
>
> ACTOR PLAYING PEACHUM   I was telling the author only yesterday that it's a lot of nonsense, it's a heavy tragedy, not a decent musical.
>
> ACTRESS PLAYING MRS PEACHUM   I can't stand this hanging at the end.
>
> WINGS RIGHT, THE AUTHOR'S VOICE   That's how the play was written, and that's how it stays.
>
> MACHEATH   It stays that way, does it? Then act the lead yourself. Impertinence!
>
> AUTHOR   It's the plain truth: the man's hanged, of course he has to be hanged. I'm not making any compromises. If that's how it is in real life, then that's how it is on the stage. Right?
>
> MRS PEACHUM   Right.
>
> PEACHUM   Doesn't understand the first thing about the theater. Plain truth, indeed.
>
> MACHEATH   Plain truth. That's a load of rubbish in the theater. Plain truth is what happens when people run out of ideas. Do you suppose the audience here have paid eight marks to see plain truth? They paid their money *not* to see plain truth.
>
> PEACHUM   Well then, the ending had better be changed. You can't have the play end like that. I'm speaking in the name of the whole company when I say the play can't be performed as it is.
>
> AUTHOR   All right, then you gentlemen can clean up your own mess.

MACHEATH   So we shall.

PEACHUM   It'd be absurd if we couldn't find a first-rate
dramatic ending to please all tastes.

MRS PEACHUM   Right, then let's go back ten [sic] speeches.

—and they go back to Macheath's "So be it—I fall" once
more. Then after the farewells to Polly and Lucy:

POLLY   *weeping on his neck*: I didn't get a proper wedding
with bridesmaids, but I've got this.

LUCY   Even if I'm not your wife, Mac . . .

MAC   My dear Lucy, my dear Polly, however things may
have been between us it's all over now. Come on, Smith.
*At this juncture Brown arrives in a panting hurry and his
gala uniform.*

BROWN *breathlessly*   Stop! A message from the Queen! Stop!
*Murmurs of "Rhubarb" among the actors, with an occa-
sional amazed* "From the Queen?"

Then Brown calls into the wings for "Bells!" and makes his
speech as now (p. 225), adding at the end "Where are the
happy couples?"

MRS. PEACHUM *nudges the others*:   Happy couples!
*Whores, bandits and beggars pair off with some hesitation,
choosing their partners with care.*

Peachum thumps Macheath on the back and says "It's all right,
old man!" Mrs. Peachum speaks the last speech as now given
to Peachum, and the final chorale is given in full. After it
Mrs. Peachum has the concluding line: "And now. To Westminster!"

3. From the Stage Script to the Present Text

The prompt-book for the original production, which established the greater part of the final text, is essentially a copy of
the stage script just discussed with new typescript passages
interleaved, texts of songs, and many cuts. It is now in the
East German Academy of Arts in Berlin. At the beginning

there is a full text of the Ballad of Mac the Knife only lacking its stage directions, while interleaved in the first act are the "No, they can't Song," the "Love Duet," the finale, and two verses of the "Ballad of Sexual Obsession." The version of Peachum's opening speech cited above is deleted and replaced by ours; the speech presenting the Types of Human Misery also seems to have been added; and there is a fresh version of the ending of the scene, starting from Filch's protest at washing his feet (p. 153), virtually as now. In the stable scene the start is retyped and the "Bill Lawgen and Mary Syer" song penciled in; the rest emerges more or less in its final form, aside from the presentation of the nuptial bed, which is still missing. Scene 3 seems to have been completely revised twice, the first time remaining close to the stage script, the second resulting almost in the text as now, apart from the section on p. 176 where Peachum apostrophizes Macheath (which is also lacking where recapitulated in scene 9).

In the second act an amendment to the end of scene 4 made the gang go out shouting "Three cheers for Polly!," who then went on to sing "Nice while it lasted" and from that to her monologue as in the stage script. This was then changed to give the complete text as now spoken over the music, from "It's been such a short time" on. The song, of course, is all that remains of the second of the Kipling ballads, whose refrain it is; it was omitted from the song texts as published by Universal-Edition in 1928. The "Ballad of Sexual Obsession," which follows in our text, is inserted before the beginning of the scene, but was omitted from the production and from the piano score of 1928. Scene 5, the brothel, was revised as far as the Villon song (or "Tango Ballade"), but the setting remained the Cuttlefish Hotel; thereafter there were cuts. In scene 6 the only important additions were the text of the "Jealousy Duet" and Peachum's Egyptian police chief speech (p. 200), which replaced the speech cited above in answer to Brown's "What do you mean?" The text of the second act finale, too, was inserted just before the end of the scene.

In the third act scene 7 was redesignated "*Peachum's Count-ing-House*" and entirely revised; the additions included the "Ballad of Insufficiency" (described as "sung before the

Sheriff of London") and the remaining verse of the "Ballad of Sexual Obsession." Brown's long speech about friendship was cut, also virtually everything following his exit. Though Lucy's aria at the beginning of scene 8 was now cut out for good, the cut was not actually marked, perhaps because the whole of that scene was omitted from the production. Thereafter in the equivalent of our scene 9 Mrs. Coaxer's appearance was cut, likewise most of the passage where Macheath tries to borrow money from Brown, down to Smith's opening of the door. What follows was retyped, again however omitting Peachum's apostrophizing of Macheath (p. 176). Peachum's verse speech was interpolated and the third finale revised. The scene titles were separately listed, with instructions for their projection.

A later version of the Bloch stage script bore the title "The Threepenny Opera (The 'Beggar's Opera'). A play with music in a prologue and eight scenes from the English of John Gay," then gave the credits as before. The first published edition was number 3 of Brecht's *Versuche* series, which appeared in 1931 and described it as "an experiment in epic theater." This contained the text as we now have it, as also did the collected Malik edition of 1938. After the Second World War, however, Brecht made certain revisions, notably for a production at the Munich Kammerspiele by Hans Schweikart in April 1949. For this he devised the amended song texts now given as an appendix to the play, and made some small changes in the first act, eliminating for instance the entry of the five beggars in scene 3. He discarded these improvements in the 1950s when it was decided to include the play in volume 3 of the new collected edition, for which he went back to the *Versuche* text. The new songs, for instance, were not used in Strehler's Milan production of 1956, though this included a version of the final chorale which Brecht wrote for the occasion and whose German text has been lost. A rough rendering would be:

> Since poverty won't haunt this earth for ever
> Don't blame the poor man too much for his sins
> But fight instead against perverted justice
> And may it be the human race that wins.

10—Vintage Ad Lists—198—Nick
7 on 8 Helvetica w bold 25 ems.

J—Ads—

VINTAGE FICTION, POETRY, AND PLAYS

V-814   **ABE, KOBO** / The Woman in the Dunes
V-2014   **AUDEN, W. H.** / Collected Longer Poems
V-2015   **AUDEN, W. H.** / Collected Shorter Poems 1927-1957
V-102   **AUDEN, W. H.** / Selected Poetry of W. H. Auden
V-601   **AUDEN, W. H. AND PAUL B. TAYLOR (trans.)** / The Elder Edda
V-20   **BABIN, MARIA-THERESA AND STAN STEINER (eds.)** / Borinquen: An Anthology of Puerto-Rican Literature
V-271   **BEDIER, JOSEPH** / Tristan and Iseult
V-523   **BELLAMY, JOE DAVID (ed.)** / Superfiction or The American Story Transformed: An Anthology
V-72   **BERNIKOW, LOUISE (ed.)** / The World Split Open: Four Centuries of Women Poets in England and America 1552-1950
V-321   **BOLT, ROBERT** / A Man for All Seasons
V-21   **BOWEN, ELIZABETH** / The Death of the Heart
V-294   **BRADBURY, RAY** / The Vintage Bradbury
V-670   **BRECHT, BERTOLT (ed. by Ralph Manheim and John Willett)** / Collected Plays, Vol. 1
V-759   **BRECHT, BERTOLT (ed. by Ralph Manheim and John Willett)** / Collected Plays, Vol. 5
V-216   **BRECHT, BERTOLT (ed. by Ralph Manheim and John Willett)** / Collected Plays, Vol. 7
V-819   **BRECHT, BERTOLT (ed. by Ralph Manheim and John Willett)** / Collected Plays, Vol. 9
V-841   **BYNNER, WITTER AND KIANG KANG-HU (eds.)** / The Jade Mountain: A Chinese Anthology
V-207   **CAMUS, ALBERT** / Caligula & Three Other Plays
V-281   **CAMUS, ALBERT** / Exile and the Kingdom
V-223   **CAMUS, ALBERT** / The Fall
V-865   **CAMUS, ALBERT** / A Happy Death: A Novel
V-626   **CAMUS, ALBERT** / Lyrical and Critical Essays
V-75   **CAMUS, ALBERT** / The Myth of Sisyphus and Other Essays
V-258   **CAMUS, ALBERT** / The Plague
V-245   **CAMUS, ALBERT** / The Possessed
V-30   **CAMUS, ALBERT** / The Rebel
V-2   **CAMUS, ALBERT** / The Stranger
V-28   **CATHER, WILLA** / Five Stories
V-705   **CATHER, WILLA** / A Lost Lady
V-200   **CATHER, WILLA** / My Mortal Enemy
V-179   **CATHER, WILLA** / Obscure Destinies
V-252   **CATHER, WILLA** / One of Ours
V-913   **CATHER, WILLA** / The Professor's House
V-434   **CATHER, WILLA** / Sapphira and the Slave Girl
V-680   **CATHER, WILLA** / Shadows on the Rock
V-684   **CATHER, WILLA** / Youth and the Bright Medusa
V-140   **CERF, BENNETT (ed.)** / Famous Ghost Stories
V-203   **CERF, BENNETT (ed.)** / Four Contemporary American Plays
V-127   **CERF, BENNETT (ed.)** / Great Modern Short Stories
V-326   **CERF, CHRISTOPHER (ed.)** / The Vintage Anthology of Science Fantasy
V-293   **CHAUCER, GEOFFREY** / The Canterbury Tales (a prose version in Modern English)
V-142   **CHAUCER, GEOFFREY** / Troilus and Cressida
V-723   **CHERNYSHEVSKY, N. G.** / What Is to Be Done?
V-173   **CONFUCIUS (trans. by Arthur Waley)** / Analects
V-155   **CONRAD, JOSEPH** / Three Great Tales: The Nigger of the Narcissus, Heart of Darkness, Youth
V-10   **CRANE, STEPHEN** / Stories and Tales
V-126   **DANTE, ALIGHIERI** / The Divine Comedy
V-177   **DINESEN, ISAK** / Anecdotes of Destiny

V-80   **REDDY, T. J.** / Less Than a Score, But A Point: Poems by T. J. Reddy
V-504   **RENAULT, MARY** / The Bull From the Sea
V-653   **RENAULT, MARY** / The Last of the Wine
V-24   **RHYS, JEAN** / After Leaving Mr. Mackenzie
V-42   **RHYS, JEAN** / Good Morning Midnight
V-319   **RHYS, JEAN** / Quartet
V-2016 **ROSEN, KENNETH (ed.)** / The Man to Send Rain Clouds: Contemporary Stories by American Indians
V-976   **ROTHENBERG, JEROME AND GEORGE QUASHA (eds.)** / America a Prophecy: A New Reading of American Poetry from Pre-Columbian Times to the Present
V-366   **SARGENT, PAMELA (ed.)** / Bio-Futures: Science Fiction Stories about Biological Metamorphosis
V-876   **SARGENT, PAMELA (ed.)** / More Women of Wonder: Science Fiction Novelettes by Women about Women
V-41   **SARGENT, PAMELA (ed.)** / Women of Wonder: Science Fiction Stories by Women About Women
V-838   **SARTRE, JEAN-PAUL** / The Age of Reason
V-238   **SARTRE, JEAN-PAUL** / The Condemned of Altona
V-65   **SARTRE, JEAN-PAUL** / The Devil & The Good Lord & Two Other Plays
V-16   **SARTRE, JEAN-PAUL** / No Exit and Three Other Plays
V-839   **SARTRE, JEAN-PAUL** / The Reprieve
V-74   **SARTRE, JEAN-PAUL** / The Trojan Women: Euripides
V-840   **SARTRE, JEAN-PAUL** / Troubled Sleep
V-443   **SCHULTE, RAINER AND QUINCY TROUPE (eds.)** / Giant Talk: An Anthology of Third World Writings
V-607   **SCORTIA, THOMAS N. AND GEORGE ZEBROWSKI (eds.)** / Human-Machines: An Anthology of Stories About Cyborgs
V-330   **SHOLOKHOV, MIKHAIL** / And Quiet Flows the Don
V-331   **SHOLOKHOV, MIKHAIL** / The Don Flows Home to the Sea
V-447   **SILVERBERG, ROBERT** / Born With the Dead: Three Novellas About the Spirit of Man
V-945   **SNOW, LOIS WHEELER** / China On Stage
V-133   **STEIN, GERTRUDE** / Autobiography of Alice B. Toklas
V-826   **STEIN, GERTRUDE** / Everybody's Autobiography
V-941   **STEIN, GERTRUDE** / The Geographical History of America
V-797   **STEIN, GERTRUDE** / Ida
V-695   **STEIN, GERTRUDE** / Last Operas and Plays
V-477   **STEIN, GERTRUDE** / Lectures in America
V-153   **STEIN, GERTRUDE** / Three Lives
V-710   **STEIN, GERTRUDE & CARL VAN VECHTEN (ed.)** / Selected Writings of Gertrude Stein
V-20   **STEINER, STAN AND MARIA-THERESA BABIN (eds.)** / Borinquen: An Anthology of Puerto-Rican Literature
V-770   **STEINER, STAN AND LUIS VALDEZ (eds.)** / Aztlan: An Anthology of Mexican-American Literature
V-769   **STEINER, STAN AND SHIRLEY HILL WITT (eds.)** / The Way: An Anthology of American Indian Literature
V-768   **STEVENS, HOLLY (ed.)** / The Palm at the End of the Mind: Selected Poems & A Play by Wallace Stevens
V-278   **STEVENS, WALLACE** / The Necessary Angel
V-896   **SULLIVAN, VICTORIA AND JAMES HATCH (eds.)** / Plays By and About Women
V-63   **SVEVO, ITALO** / Confessions of Zeno
V-178   **SYNGE, J. M.** / Complete Plays
V-601   **TAYLOR, PAUL B. AND W. H. AUDEN (trans.)** / The Elder Edda
V-443   **TROUPE. QUINCY AND RAINER SCHULTE (eds.)** / Giant Talk: An Anthology of Third World Writings
V-770   **VALDEZ, LUIS AND STAN STEINER (eds.)** / Aztlan: An Anthology of Mexican-American Literature

11—Vintage Ad Lists—198—Nick
7 on 8 Helvetica w bold   25 ems.

K—Ads—

VINTAGE POLITICAL SCIENCE AND SOCIAL CRITICISM

V-568 **ALINSKY, SAUL D.** / Reveille for Radicals
V-736 **ALINSKY, SAUL D.** / Rules for Radicals
V-726 **ALLENDE, PRESIDENT SALVADOR AND REGIS DEBRAY** / The Chilean Revolution
V-286 **ARIES, PHILIPPE** / Centuries of Childhood
V-604 **BAILYN, BERNARD** / Origins of American Politics
V-334 **BALTZELL, E. DIGBY** / The Protestant Establishment
V-571 **BARTH, ALAN** / Prophets With Honor: Great Dissents & Great Dissenters in the Supreme Court
V-791 **BAXANDALL, LEE (ed.) AND WILHELM REICH** / Sex-Pol.: Essays 1929-1934
V-60 **BECKER, CARL L.** / The Declaration of Independence
V-563 **BEER, SAMUEL H.** / British Politics in the Collectivist Age
V-994 **BERGER, PETER & BRIGITTE AND HANSFRIED KELLNER** / The Homeless Mind: Modernization and Consciousness
V-77 **BINZEN, PETER** / Whitetown, USA
V-513 **BOORSTIN, DANIEL J.** / The Americans: The Colonial Experience
V-11 **BOORSTIN, DANIEL J.** / The Americans: The Democratic Experience
V-358 **BOORSTIN, DANIEL J.** / The Americans: The National Experience
V-501 **BOORSTIN, DANIEL J.** / Democracy and Its Discontents: Reflections on Everyday America
V-414 **BOTTOMORE, T. B.** / Classes in Modern Society
V-742 **BOTTOMORE, T. B.** / Sociology: A Guide to Problems & Literature
V-305 **BREINES, SIMON AND WILLIAM J. DEAN** / The Pedestrian Revolution: Streets Without Cars
V-44 **BRINTON, CRANE** / The Anatomy of Revolution
V-30 **CAMUS, ALBERT** / The Rebel
V-966 **CAMUS, ALBERT** / Resistance, Rebellion & Death
V-33 **CARMICHAEL, STOKELY AND CHARLES HAMILTON** / Black Power
V-2024 **CARO, ROBERT A.** / The Power Broker: Robert Moses and The Fall of New York
V-862 **CASE, JOHN AND GERRY HUNNIUS AND DAVID G. CARSON** / Workers Control: A Reader on Labor and Social Change
V-98 **CASH, W. J.** / The Mind of the South
V-555 **CHOMSKY, NOAM** / American Power and the New Mandarins
V-248 **CHOMSKY, NOAM** / Peace in the Middle East? Reflections on Justice and Nationhood
V-815 **CHOMSKY, NOAM** / Problems of Knowledge and Freedom
V-788 **CIRINO, ROBERT** / Don't Blame the People
V-17 **CLARKE, TED AND DENNIS JAFFE (eds.)** / Worlds Apart: Young People and The Drug Problems
V-383 **CLOWARD, RICHARD AND FRANCES FOX PIVEN** / The Politics of Turmoil: Essays on Poverty, Race and The Urban Crisis
V-743 **CLOWARD, RICHARD AND FRANCES FOX PIVEN** / Regulating the Poor: The Functions of Public Welfare
V-940 **COBB, JONATHAN AND RICHARD SENNETT** / Hidden Injuries of Class
V-311 **CREMIN, LAWRENCE A.** / The Genius of American Education
V-519 **CREMIN, LAWRENCE A.** / The Transformation of the School
V-808 **CUMMING, ROBERT D. (ed.)** / The Philosophy of Jean-Paul Sartre
V-2019 **CUOMO, MARIO** / Forest Hills Diary: The Crisis of Low-Income Housing
V-305 **DEAN, WILLIAM J. AND SIMON BREINES** / The Pedestrian Revolution: Streets Without Cars
V-726 **DEBRAY, REGIS AND PRESIDENT SALVADOR ALLENDE** / The Chilean Revolution
V-638 **DENNISON, GEORGE** / The Lives of Children
V-746 **DEUTSCHER, ISAAC** / The Prophet Armed
V-748 **DEUTSCHER, ISAAC** / The Prophet Outcast
V-617 **DEVLIN, BERNADETTE** / The Price of My Soul

V-634 **LEWIS, OSCAR** / A Death in the Sanchez Family

V-421 **LEWIS, OSCAR** / La Vida

V-370 **LEWIS, OSCAR** / Pedro Martinez

V-533 **LOCKWOOD, LEE** / Castro's Cuba, Cuba's Fidel

V-787 **MALDONADO-DENIS, DR. MANUEL** / Puerto-Rico: A Socio-Historic Interpretation

V-406 **MARCUS, STEVEN** / Engels, Manchester and The Working Class

V-480 **MARCUSE, HERBERT** / Soviet Marxism

V-2002 **MARX, KARL AND DAVID FERNBACH (ed.)** / Political Writings, Vol. I: The Revolutions of 1848

V-2003 **MARX, KARL AND DAVID FERNBACH (ed.)** / Political Writings, Vol. II: Surveys from Exile

V-2004 **MARX, KARL AND DAVID FERNBACH (ed.)** / Political Writings, Vol. III: The First International and After

V-2005 **MARX, KARL AND QUINTIN HOARE (trans.)** / Early Writings

V-2001 **MARX, KARL AND MARTIN NICOLOUS (trans.)** / The Grundrisse: Foundations of the Critique of Political Economy

V-619 **McCONNELL, GRANT** / Private Power and American Democracy

V-386 **McPHERSON, JAMES** / The Negro's Civil War

V-928 **MEDVEDEV, ROY A.** / Let History Judge: The Origins & Consequences of Stalinism

V-112 **MEDVEDEV, ZHORES A.** / Ten Years After Ivan Denisovitch

V-427 **MENDELSON, MARY ADELAIDE** / Tender Loving Greed

V-614 **MERMELSTEIN, DAVID (ed.)** / The Economic Crisis Reader

V-307 **MIDDLETON, NEIL (ed.) AND I. F. STONE** / The I. F. Stone's Weekly Reader

V-971 **MILTON, DAVID & NANCY AND FRANZ SCHURMANN (eds.)** / The China Reader IV: People's China

V-905 **MITCHELL, JULIET** / Woman's Estate

V-93 **MITFORD, JESSICA** / Kind and Usual Punishment

V-539 **MORGAN, ROBIN (ed.)** / Sisterhood is Powerful

V-389 **MOYNIHAN, DANIEL P.** / Coping: On the Practice of Government

V-107 **MYRDAL, GUNNAR** / Against the Stream: Critical Essays on Economics

V-730 **MYRDAL, GUNNAR** / Asian Drama: An Inquiry into the Poverty of Nations

V-170 **MYRDAL, GUNNAR** / The Challenge of World Poverty

V-793 **MYRDAL, JAN** / Report from a Chinese Village

V-708 **MYRDAL, JAN AND GUN KESSLE** / China: The Revolution Continued

V-834 **NEWTON, HUEY P.** / To Die for the People

V-2001 **NICOLOUS, MARTIN (trans.) AND KARL MARX** / The Grundrisse: Foundations of the Critique of Political Economy

V-377 **NIETZSCHE, FRIEDRICH AND WALTER KAUFMANN (trans.)** / Beyond Good and Evil

V-369 **NIETZSCHE, FRIEDRICH AND WALTER KAUFMANN (trans.)** / The Birth of Tragedy and The Case of Wagner

V-985 **NIETZSCHE, FRIEDRICH AND WALTER KAUFMANN (trans.)** / The Gay Science

V-401 **NIETZSCHE, FRIEDRICH AND WALTER KAUFMANN (trans.)** / On the Genealogy of Morals and Ecce Homo

V-437 **NIETZSCHE, FRIEDRICH AND WALTER KAUFMANN (trans.)** / The Will to Power

V-803 **NOVAK, ROBERT D. AND ROWLAND EVANS, JR.** / Nixon in the White House: The Frustration of Power

V-689 **AN OBSERVER** / Message from Moscow

V-383 **PIVEN, FRANCES FOX AND RICHARD CLOWARD** / The Politics of Turmoil: Essays on Poverty, Race & The Urban Crisis

V-743 **PIVEN, FRANCES FOX AND RICHARD CLOWARD** / Regulating the Poor: The Functions of Public Welfare

V-128 **PLATO** / The Republic

V-719 **REED, JOHN** / Ten Days That Shook the World

VINTAGE CRITICISM: LITERATURE, MUSIC, AND ART

V-570	**ANDREWS, WAYNE** / American Gothic
V-418	**AUDEN, W. H.** / The Dyer's Hand
V-887	**AUDEN, W. H.** / Forewords and Afterwords
V-161	**BROWN, NORMAN O.** / Closing Time
V-75	**CAMUS, ALBERT** / The Myth of Sisyphus and Other Essays
V-626	**CAMUS, ALBERT** / Lyrical and Critical Essays
V-535	**EISEN, JONATHAN** / The Age of Rock: Sounds of the American Cultural Revolution
V-4	**EINSTEIN, ALFRED** / A Short History of Music
V-13	**GILBERT, STUART** / James Joyce's Ulysses
V-407	**HARDWICK, ELIZABETH** / Seduction and Betrayal: Women and Literature
V-114	**HAUSER, ARNOLD** / Social History of Art, Vol. I
V-115	**HAUSER, ARNOLD** / Social History of Art, Vol. II
V-116	**HAUSER, ARNOLD** / Social History of Art, Vol. III
V-117	**HAUSER, ARNOLD** / Social History of Art, Vol. IV
V-610	**HSU, KAI-YU** / The Chinese Literary Scene
V-201	**HUGHES, H. STUART** / Consciousness and Society
V-88	**KERMAN, JOSEPH** / Opera as Drama
V-995	**KOTT, JAN** / The Eating of the Gods: An Interpretation of Greek Tragedy
V-685	**LESSING, DORIS** / A Small Personal Voice: Essays, Reviews, Interviews
V-677	**LESTER, JULIUS** / The Seventh Son, Vol. I
V-678	**LESTER, JULIUS** / The Seventh Son, Vol. II
V-720	**MIRSKY, D. S.** / A History of Russian Literature
V-118	**NEWMAN, ERNEST** / Great Operas, Vol. I
V-119	**NEWMAN, ERNEST** / Great Operas, Vol. II
V-976	**QUASHA, GEORGE AND JEROME ROTHENBERG (eds.)** / America A Prophecy: A New Reading of American Poetry from Pre-Columbian Times to the Present
V-976	**ROTHENBERG, JEROME AND GEORGE QUASHA (eds.)** / America A Prophecy: A New Reading of American Poetry from Pre-Columbian Times to the Present
V-415	**SHATTUCK, ROGER** / The Banquet Years, Revised
V-435	**SPENDER, STEPHEN** / Love-Hate Relations: English and American Sensibilities
V-278	**STEVENS, WALLACE** / The Necessary Angel
V-100	**SULLIVAN, J. W. N.** / Beethoven: His Spiritual Development
V-166	**SZE, MAI-MAI** / The Way of Chinese Painting
V-162	**TILLYARD, E. M. W.** / The Elizabethan World Picture